New International

A MAGAZINE OF MARXIST POLITICS AND THEORY

NUMBER 9   1994

Contents

D1611935

EDITOR Mary-Alice Waters

MANAGING EDITOR Steve Clark

CONTRIBUTING EDITORS Jack Barnes, Sigurlaug Gunnlaugsdóttir, Carl-Erik Isacsson, Nat London, Steve Penner, Ron Poulsen, Russell Johnson, Samad Sharif, Jonathan Silberman, James Mac Warren

New International is edited in collaboration with *Nouvelle Internationale*, Michel Prairie, editor, *Nueva Internacional*, Martín Koppel, editor, and *Ny International*, Carl-Erik Isacsson, editor. Many of the articles that appear here in English are also available in French, Spanish, and Swedish. All four publications are available from New International, 410 West St., New York, NY 10014

Cover photograph: July 19, 1979:
Sandinista fighters, entering Managua, celebrate triumph of revolution.
Cover design by Toni Gorton

New International is distributed internationally by Pathfinder Press:
Australia (and Asia and the Pacific):
    Pathfinder, 19 Terry St., Surry Hills, Sydney, N.S.W. 2010
    Postal address: P.O. Box K879, Haymarket, N.S.W. 2000
Britain (and Europe, Africa except South Africa, and Middle East):
    Pathfinder, 47 The Cut, London, SE1 8LL
Canada:
    Pathfinder, 4581 rue St-Denis, Montreal, Quebec, H2J 2L4
Iceland:
    Pathfinder, Klapparstíg 26, 2d floor, 101 Reykjavík
    Postal address: P. Box 233, 121 Reykjavík
New Zealand:
    Pathfinder, La Gonda Arcade, 203 Karangahape Road, Auckland
    Postal address: P.O. Box 8730, Auckland
Sweden:
    Pathfinder, Vikingagatan 10, S-113 42, Stockholm
United States (and Caribbean, Latin America, and South Africa):
    Pathfinder, 410 West Street, New York, NY 10014

IN THIS ISSUE

O N JULY 19, 1980, Cuban president Fidel Castro spoke in Managua to the half million participants swelling the celebration of the first anniversary of the Nicaraguan revolution. "I'm sure you all realize what it means, the impression, the happiness, the enthusiasm, the optimism, the emotion involved in arriving at the second Latin American country to free itself from imperialism," he said.

One week later in Cuba, Castro spoke to the participants, including enthusiastic delegations of international guests, gathered at the annual rally marking the anniversary of the 1953 assault on the Moncada garrison that opened the Cuban revolution. "In this hemisphere there are now not two but three of us, because Grenada also has to be included. . . . [The] three of us have shaken the yoke of imperialism in the last twenty years in a radical way, once and for all."[1]

"One must have a sense of history to know . . . what revolution means here, next to the imperialist monster," Castro had told delegates to the Third Congress of the Federation of Cuban Women a few months earlier in March 1980. "Yes, what the Cuban revolution and its firm, unwavering line has meant. One needs a sense of history and of realities to understand the merit of the Sandinista revolution, the merit of the Grenadian revolution.

"Grenada, Nicaragua, and Cuba are three giants rising up to defend their right to independence, sovereignty, and justice, on the very threshold of imperialism."[2]

ENDNOTES FOR THIS ARTICLE BEGIN ON PAGE 297.

What had "shaken the yoke of imperialism in a radical way" was the extension of the socialist revolution in the Americas, a socialist revolution opened two decades earlier with the triumph of the workers and farmers of Cuba. That victory electrified revolutionary-minded workers, farmers, and youth throughout the Americas. In marked contrast, the world's wealthiest and most powerful capitalist class, speaking with a single bipartisan voice from Washington and Wall Street, reacted to the victory of the Cuban toilers and to their government's expropriation of the U.S. and domestic exploiters in 1960 with an uncompromising hostility that has never ceased being the touchstone of U.S. government policy toward Cuba.

In 1979 workers and farmers in both Nicaragua and Grenada did even more than oust corrupt and brutal tyrants who had sold these nations' patrimony to Washington. They displaced from political power the entire class of exploiting landowners and big businessmen, ushering in popular revolutionary governments that began to encroach on capitalist economic prerogatives and social relations that deprive the toiling majority of the social wealth they create and that reproduce the horrors of capitalism generation after generation. The toilers of Grenada, led by the New Jewel Movement, and of Nicaragua, led by the Sandinista National Liberation Front (FSLN), reignited the revolutionary enthusiasm and commitment born of the Cuban revolution, as they confirmed in life that "only the workers and peasants will go all the way"—the battle cry of Augusto César Sandino, who led the fight for Nicaragua's national sovereignty against Yankee domination in the 1920s and early 1930s.

The U.S. rulers, for their part, were determined to act to prevent the ultimate threat to the power and prerogatives of the propertied in the Americas—the development of two "new Cubas" in the Western Hemisphere.

D∪RING THE INITIAL YEARS of the Nicaraguan revolution, the FSLN leadership, despite errors and political hesitations, pursued a course that promoted the organization and mobilization of the workers and peasants of Nicaragua. The new government increasingly used its power to advance the toilers' class interests against the exploiters both at home and abroad. These actions gave a boost to popular struggles against the U.S.-backed landlord-capitalist tyrannies in El Salvador and Guatemala, linked up with the revolution in Grenada, and gave a powerful new impetus to political leaps forward by the workers in Cuba.

"Today it is the heroic workers and peasants of Nicaragua who are on the front lines of the advancing world socialist revolution," the Socialist Workers Party (SWP) of the United States affirmed in a resolution on the Nicaraguan revolution adopted soon after the July 1979 triumph and printed in this issue of *New International.* "We will be tested by our capacity to respond with courage and decisiveness, to throw our forces into this struggle without hesitation or delay, to mobilize and lead all those we influence."

SWP National Secretary Jack Barnes reiterated in a November 1979 report, also printed here, that the party counted itself among those in the international working-class movement "who embraced the revolution, saw its worker and peasant character, recognized the revolutionary qualities of its leadership, sought to learn from it, and reflected this approach in our press and political activity."

The *Militant* newsweekly and the Spanish-language magazine *Perspectiva Mundial* opened a Managua reporting bureau just weeks after the July 1979 triumph. Over the next ten years articles, interviews, and documents—written or prepared by fellow workers from inside the revolution—were featured regularly in these two socialist publications, helping readers follow, understand, learn from, and, most important, act in response to developments in Nicaragua.

New International, this magazine of Marxist politics and theory, was relaunched in large part in response to these post-1979 revolutionary advances in the Americas. Our inaugural issue in 1983 explained that the magazine "will give particular attention to the revolutionary struggles in Central America and the Caribbean today. These struggles have already led in Nicaragua and Grenada to the extension of the American socialist revolution opened in Cuba a quarter century ago, as well as to an escalating war by Washington and counterrevolutionary forces in the region to crush the insurgent workers and peasants and roll back their conquests."

Pathfinder Press—which publishes works of revolutionary and communist leaders, and distributes *New International* and its French-, Spanish-, and Swedish-language sister magazines, *Nouvelle Internationale, Nueva Internacional,* and *Ny International*—has produced and kept in print two collections of speeches and writings by Sandinista leaders from the early years of the revolution: *Sandinistas Speak* and *Nicaragua: The Sandinista People's Revolution.* This year, in conjunction with the publication of this issue of *New International,* Pathfinder will also publish *Carlos Fonseca Speaks: Building Nicaragua's Sandinista National Liberation Front, 1960-1976*—a collection of writings and speeches by the communist leader and founder of the FSLN who was killed in combat three years prior to the triumph of the revolution.

Young people, trade unionists, working farmers, and others from the United States and other countries rallied to defend the Nicaraguan revolution against the U.S.-organized counterrevolution. Tens of thousands followed the "Managua trail," visiting Nicaragua on their own or as part of work brigades or trips organized to help them participate in the revolution and learn from it. During the opening years of the revolution in particular, such experiences led the most determined and farsighted of these individuals to join the communist movement.

Revolutionary-minded workers and youth the world over sought to draw lessons from the political and social transformations under way in Nicaragua and Grenada and from the new boost they gave to the Cuban revolution. At an international socialist conference in Ohio hosted by the Socialist Workers Party and Young Socialist Alliance in August 1980, SWP leader Mary-Alice Waters, currently the editor of *New International,* gave a talk entitled "Proletarian Leadership in Power: What We Can Learn from Lenin, Castro, and the FSLN," which was subsequently published by Pathfinder. "We go to the Nicaraguan revolution, to the Cuban revolution, to the Grenadian revolution to learn—not to teach," Waters said, "to absorb everything we can to better prepare ourselves for the struggles that are coming.

"This is not because we think we have nothing to offer. But every revolution," she said, "is a complex living organism with its own concrete set of class relationships. . . . To apply the science of Marxism, we can't just read a book, or study the last revolution, and mechanically transfer its tactics. We have to understand the revolution as an organic, living whole."[3]

Spanning the decade of the revolution's rise and decline, the reports and resolutions published in this issue were discussed and adopted by the leadership of the U.S. Socialist Workers Party and communist leagues in Australia, Britain, Canada, France, Iceland, New Zealand, and Sweden. At the heart of the documents published here is the impact of the Nicaraguan revolution in opening new possibilities for the reinforcement of international communist leadership, and for the building of revolutionary workers parties and socialist youth organizations in the United States and around the world.

Defeats in 1980s

Less than a decade after workers and farmers governments came to power in Nicaragua and in Grenada, both had been defeated. By the close of the 1980s Cuba once again stood alone as the only workers and farmers government in the world.

Among many who had once rallied to support these revolutions, it is still considered in bad taste to assess the political causes of these defeats, or frequently even to acknowledge the fact that defeats have occurred.

In the case of Grenada, the strangling of the revolution is largely written off by former partisans as the product of the U.S.-organized invasion and occupation of the island in late October 1983. What is left unspoken—or conveniently erased from memory—is that the workers and farmers government headed by Maurice Bishop had already been destroyed in a murderous, Stalinist-led counterrevolutionary coup two weeks prior to the U.S. onslaught. For the more than four years that the popular revolutionary government existed, Washington had been compelled to limit its actions against this anticapitalist revolution to a barrage of lies and hostile propaganda, economic and political pressure, brutal but isolated terrorist operations, and military threats and provocations. The U.S. rulers knew that Grenadian working people were ready to defend their conquests arms in hand against imperialist aggression.

By the time the U.S. marines and army rangers landed at Grenada's Point Salines on October 25, however, the island no longer had "a government worth defending, one supported by the people," Fidel Castro pointed out in a 1985 interview. The door had been opened to the defeat and demoralization that the U.S. invasion and occupation represented. The accomplishments of the workers and farmers government in Grenada and the truth about its overthrow are discussed in detail in the article "The Second Assassination of Maurice Bishop" by Steve Clark in *New International*, no. 6.[4]

WITH REGARD TO NICARAGUA, leaders of the Sandinista National Liberation Front (FSLN), as well as many of those in the United States and around the world who apologize for their current political perspectives, deny that the foundations of the revolutionary government had totally eroded before the February 1990 electoral defeat of the FSLN. Much less do they trace that erosion to the political degeneration of the FSLN itself— from the uncompromising revolutionary organization that set out on an anti-imperialist and anticapitalist course in 1961 and eventually led the workers and peasants in the victorious 1979 insurrection, to the radical bourgeois electoral party the FSLN had been transformed into by the close of the 1980s. Ignored completely are the Stalinist, social democratic, and other petty-bourgeois pressures that had an increasing impact on the Sandinista leadership.

Instead, the blow to the Nicaraguan revolution is largely reduced by the FSLN leadership and its backers to an electoral defeat orchestrated by Washington. Meanwhile, the Sandinista revolution—today presented as having established a classless "democracy," shorn of any anticapitalist dynamic or popular revolutionary character—is somehow in suspended animation awaiting the 1996 presidential elections, when it is hoped the FSLN will sweep back into office.

A few months after the 1990 election, Víctor Tirado, a member of the FSLN National Directorate, sought to rationalize this defeat and generalize this rationalization to all of Latin America and the rest of the semicolonial world. "The cycle of anti-imperialist revolutions conceived of in the 1950s is finished," Tirado said. "[T]he best we can aspire to is coexistence with imperialism, even though it hurts to say so. To have good relations with them and that they let us develop." (Tirado uses "we" and "us" as pronouns for a Nicaragua with no class distinctions.)

Noam Chomsky, a professor at MIT and prominent opponent of U.S. military intervention in the Third World, has presented a more systematic version of this view on the university lecture circuit and in a spate of books and pamphlets. To Chomsky—an anarchist, or as he sometimes calls it, a proponent of "libertarian socialism"—the outcome in Nicaragua confirms a conclusion he had already drawn from the Vietnam War: that successful popular revolutions are impossible until the United States government has been qualitatively weakened at home. "Contrary to what virtually everyone—left or right—says, the United States achieved its major objectives in Indochina," Chomsky insists in a 1992 booklet entitled *What Uncle Sam Really Wants.* "Vietnam was demolished. There's no danger that successful development there will provide a model for other nations in the region. . . . Vietnam is a basket case. . . . The Third World must learn that no one dare raise their head. The global enforcer will persecute them relentlessly if they commit this unspeakable crime."

So it was in Nicaragua too, Chomsky says. "Back in 1981," Chomsky writes, "a State Department insider boasted that we would 'turn Nicaragua into the Albania of Central America'—

that is, poor, isolated and politically radical—so that the Sandinista dream of creating a new, more exemplary political model for Latin America would be in ruins. . . .

"US achievements in Central America," Chomsky says, are "a major tragedy, not just because of the appalling human cost, but because a decade ago there were prospects for progress toward meaningful democracy and meeting human needs. . . . These efforts might have worked and might have taught useful lessons to others plagued with similar problems—which, of course, was exactly what US planners feared. The threat has been successfully aborted, perhaps forever."

Forever! In short, it is futile for the toilers to organize and work toward carrying out a truly radical social revolution in today's world.

This issue of *New International* presents a sharply different view, a working-class view, of the Nicaraguan revolution's historic accomplishments and of the lessons that can be drawn by working people not only from its rise and development but also from its degeneration and decline. The defeats that occurred were not inevitable. At the cost of tens of thousands of lives and devastating economic dislocation, Nicaragua's toilers had courageously defended their revolution against the U.S. imperialist–organized counterrevolution. By the end of 1987, steeled by their victory over the "contras," hundreds of thousands of Nicaraguan workers and toiling farmers—including the best of the youth of the nation—were hungry for the leadership necessary to deepen the struggle to consolidate a workers state, a state that would act consistently to advance the class interests of working people against the capitalist landlords and factory owners. The defeat of that anticapitalist perspective, and of the revolutionary government that could have made it a reality, was the product of the course taken by the FSLN leadership in face of the class pressures and internal divisions that came to a head in the closing years of the 1980s.

July 1979: an anticapitalist revolution
The July 1979 revolution in Nicaragua was born out of a pop-

ular insurrection in the cities and uprisings in the countryside organized to bring down Anastasio Somoza, the last representative of a despotic landlord-capitalist dynasty installed by the U.S. marines in the 1930s. A nucleus of Nicaraguan youth inspired by and determined to emulate the Cuban revolution had formed the FSLN in the early 1960s and initiated guerrilla actions against Somoza's National Guard. By the time of the final battles in 1979, tens of thousands of toilers had participated—far more than the organized combatants of the FSLN.

The new government brought to power by the July 1979 insurrection encouraged the formation of unions, peasant organizations, women's groups, and youth groups. It nationalized the domestic banks and insurance companies, established controls on export trade, and expropriated several factories. It replaced the Somozaist National Guard with the Sandinista People's Army and Sandinista Police, and began forming popular militias in rural communities and urban neighborhoods and workplaces.

Through an accumulation of measures during its opening weeks and months that encroached on capitalist property and prerogatives, the new FSLN-led power rapidly emerged as a workers and farmers government. The stages and key turning points in the unfolding of this anticapitalist revolution, propelled by the FSLN leadership in response to large-scale mobilizations and expanding organization of the toilers, are concretely detailed in the documents in this issue.

Poor peasants and farm laborers, armed with a government that allied their interests to those of the urban workers, began to press their way into political life through fighting to advance land reform, the rights of rural workers, and electrification; through mass participation in a literacy drive; and through the building of their own organizations of struggle. In the cities, unorganized workers rapidly established trade unions. They set up neighborhood defense committees to defend the revolution and enforce the measures of the new government. They demanded that the government take over factories where the owner, even if not an open Somozaist, was slashing capital spending and production or carrying out other forms of economic sabotage; a number of such firms were nationalized.

Women organized to advance their fight for equality in both the countryside and cities. On the Atlantic Coast, home to most Nicaraguans who are Indian or Black, hundreds of tiny fishing and farming settlements came alive following Somoza's overturn. *Costeños* opened a struggle against racial discrimination and for the political, economic, and cultural autonomy of the region, long a victim of isolation, plunder by U.S. and Canadian companies, benign neglect by Managua, and consequent extreme underdevelopment.

The revolutionary government took steps to make education and health care available to all. It organized efforts to deal with the housing crisis faced by the overwhelming majority of working people in Nicaragua, including initial steps limiting rents, supplying sanitation and water facilities, and launching programs to construct new, low-cost homes, especially in the countryside.

But the FSLN leadership did not respond in a revolutionary way to all of the popular demands and aspirations unshackled by the overthrow of the hated Somoza tyranny. As described in the documents that follow, the new government's land policy during the opening years of the revolution, in response to mobilizations and land occupations by poor peasants and counterpressures from "patriotic" large landowners, sometimes advanced and then, more and more, hesitated and stalled.

The Sandinista leadership was at first also blind—and on the part of some leaders outright opposed—to the aspirations of Indians and Blacks on the Atlantic Coast for an end to racial and national inequality, including the region's long-standing political subservience and economic subordination to the Pacific Coast. The counterrevolution made hay of the Sandinistas' initial default. Organizations based among Indians and other Atlantic Coast residents took up arms against the revolutionary government, forming alliances with the contra bands. The FSLN government finally acceded to demands for an autonomy process in the region in the mid-1980s, qualitatively strengthening the unity of the revolution.

As the war against the U.S.-organized contra army intensified, the Sandinista government abandoned its course of relying on a politically motivated volunteer army to defeat the counterrevolution. The military conscription introduced in 1983—to whose support the large majority of workers and peasants had not been totally won—became another political issue on which the contra forces played with some success.

Cuba's internationalist aid

From the origins of the FSLN-led struggle in the 1960s, revolutionary Cuba provided irreplaceable internationalist aid. Following the 1979 victory, this assistance was extended to meet any help requested of the Cuban people by the Nicaraguan government.

A thousand Cuban teachers participated in the 1980 literacy crusade, bringing experience from their own 1961 campaign and Cuba's ongoing efforts to raise the educational and cultural level of working people. By 1982 some two thousand Cuban teachers had crossed the Caribbean to Central America, most of them serving in the most poverty-stricken and militarily dangerous locations in the countryside to train Nicaraguan teachers who gradually replaced them over the next couple of years. Cuba built a 150-bed hospital in Managua; provided nearly a thousand doctors, nurses, and other medical personnel to work throughout the country; and organized training of Nicaraguan medical personnel in public health and preventive medicine.

Some five hundred Cuban construction workers helped build a modern sugar mill for the Nicaraguan government to process one of the country's main export products; not only the labor but all the machinery, building materials, and other inputs were donated by the Cuban government. Cuban workers, engineers, and technicians helped with the construction of other factories, roads, bridges, and agricultural and fishing installations as well. During the latter 1980s, Cuba annually sent four shipments of food, clothing, and other basic items to Nicaragua's economically backward north Atlantic Coast; this solidarity was of such a scope as to be sufficient to meet the needs of fifty thousand people, a third of the region's population. When a hurricane devastated the Atlantic Coast town of Bluefields in 1989, the Cuban government sent 300 volunteers to help build 1,000 new houses to replace some of the 6,000 destroyed in the storm.

In line with its proletarian internationalist policies, the Cuban government also offered every kind of military assistance to its compañeros in Nicaragua, who faced the challenge of arming and training a revolutionary workers and peasants army and militias in the very process of defending the new government against counterrevolutionary terror and U.S.-organized sabotage. The Cuban government provided badly needed light and heavy weaponry, as well as military trainers and advisers. The Sandinistas, Fidel Castro told a Spanish reporter in 1985, "had to build a new army, training hundreds of thousands of citizens in defense, so they needed teachers, instructors, and advisers, and we have provided them."

Workers and farmers government

Recognizing the anticapitalist dynamic of a workers and farmers government such as the one that emerged from the 1979 revolution in Nicaragua is "not to express certainty that it is foreordained under all circumstances to expropriate the bourgeoisie and become a workers state," SWP leader Jack Barnes explained in his 1979 report. "It's to recognize a tendency and a fact, in order better to learn from it and throw our weight in the scales to help the revolutionary leadership move it forward."

"Such a situation is inherently unstable," the SWP leader pointed out. "Class confrontations will arise that will be decisive in determining which way the process will develop. As each one arises, the government throws its weight to resolving it in a proletarian direction—toward socialism—or in a bourgeois direction toward reversing the toilers' gains. So far the direction in Nicaragua has been unambiguous.

"Making this characterization involves a recognition that further decisive challenges for the FSLN are down the road," Barnes said. "The process in Nicaragua will either go forward to the establishment of a workers state or backward to the overthrow of the workers and farmers government and the consolidation of a bourgeois government and the capitalist state. This government will support and lead the masses to establish a workers state or it will be eroded, weakened, and overthrown."

The Sandinista leadership's initial course was in continuity with nearly two decades of revolutionary political work by the FSLN, codified in the Historic Program of the FSLN, drafted by Carlos Fonseca and first published in 1969.

Prior to the 1959 triumph in Cuba, Fonseca and other young fighters had joined the Moscow-oriented Nicaraguan Socialist Party (PSN) hoping to find an organization through which to advance the fight for national liberation and socialism. But these Nicaraguan revolutionists were deeply affected by the political accomplishments of the Cuban leadership, which had to bypass the pro-Moscow Popular Socialist Party in order to carry out a course of action capable of bringing down the Batista dictatorship. Drawing the lessons of the Cuban revolution, Fonseca became convinced of the need to break with the Stalinists and their self-serving dogma that a worker and peasant revolution with an anticapitalist thrust was not on the historical agenda in Latin America and the Caribbean.

The PSN leadership, Fonseca wrote in 1969, "could not distinguish between the justice of the anti-Somozaist opposition and the maneuvers" of its bourgeois leadership, who "carried out all kinds of compromises with the Somoza regime." Following the founding of the FSLN in 1961, Fonseca said, some of those attracted to the new organization retained illusions in the Socialist Party for several years, while others recoiled from Marxism due to its association in their minds with the PSN's sectarian factionalism and class collaborationism. But "it was only a question of time before the youth and people of Nicaragua would begin to distinguish between the false Marxists and the true Marxists," he wrote.[5]

FSLN's Historic Program

The FSLN's Historic Program, reprinted in these pages, pledged to destroy the Somoza dictatorship's "military and bureaucratic apparatus" and "establish a revolutionary government based on an alliance of the workers and peasants and a convergence of all patriotic forces opposed to imperialism and the oligarchy." The new government, said the program, would establish broad democratic rights and initiate social, political, and economic measures to "create a Nicaragua that is free of exploitation, oppression, and backwardness." The program called for "an immediate and massive distribution of land, taking what was stolen by the big landlords and giving it back to the toilers (small producers) who labor on it." It pledged "a massive campaign to immediately wipe out illiteracy" and measures to uproot the "odious discrimination" suffered by women, as well as by Blacks and Indians living on the Atlantic Coast and elsewhere.

On international perspectives, the program declared that a workers and peasants government would "put an end to the foreign policy of subservience to U.S. imperialism" and "actively support the struggle of the peoples of Asia, Africa, and Latin America against both traditional and modern forms of colonialism, and against the common enemy: U.S. imperialism." It extended support to "the struggle of the Black people and all the people of the United States for genuine democracy and equal rights."

The FSLN's Historic Program pledged to "expropriate the landed estates, factories, companies, buildings, means of transportation, and other enterprises fraudulently acquired by the Somoza family [and] their accomplices"; to "nationalize the holdings of all foreign companies that exploit mineral, forest, maritime, and other natural resources"; to "establish workers control over the management of factories"; and to "plan the national economy, putting an end to the anarchy characteristic of the capitalist system of production."

Washington organizes counterrevolution

The revolutionary government's steps to organize workers and farmers to carry out this program were electrifying to workers, peasants, and youth throughout the region and even worldwide. The U.S. imperialist rulers, having stood behind Somoza to the last ditch, sought to pressure the new government, economically and politically, to back off its course. Failing in this effort too, Washington by late 1981 had begun training and financing a counterrevolutionary army headed by former members of Somoza's officer corps.

Over the next six years, the U.S.-organized contras mounted armed assaults and waged a murderous war to destroy the revolution. Washington orchestrated this mercenary force from the U.S. Southern Command in the Panama Canal Zone and from a string of rapidly established U.S. military bases in Honduras, just north of Nicaragua. The CIA and Pentagon organized covert operations such as the mining of Nicaragua's harbors (damaging at least seven foreign ships), the bombing and shelling of fuel depots and oil pipelines, and the destruction of crops and agricultural machinery and installations.

These terrorist actions were carried out not just by U.S.-organized ex–National Guardsmen and other Nicaraguans, but also by U.S. personnel and counterrevolutionary Cubans on the CIA payroll. Supply flights of food and ammunition for contra bands operating inside Nicaragua, for example, were flown out of El Salvador's Ilopango airport under the direction of Luis Posada, who is widely known to have organized (along with Orlando Bosch) the 1976 bombing of a Cubana Airlines commercial flight after its takeoff from Barbados, killing all seventy-three passengers aboard. The Nicaraguan army's downing and capture of U.S. pilot Eugene Hasenfus in October 1986 lifted part of the veil off Washington's direct involvement in the contra war and forced them to shift their logistics operation from Ilopango.

Coming showdown in Caribbean

Washington's launching of the contra war was accompanied by intensified preparations for military aggression against Grenada and Cuba, as well as increased military aid to the beleaguered Salvadoran dictatorship. To this end, U.S. military bases were refurbished and expanded—from the U.S. armed forces Caribbean Task Force in Key West, Florida (established by the Carter administration in reaction to the Nicaragua and Grenada revolutions), to installations in Puerto Rico, the Panama Canal Zone, and elsewhere in the region. The U.S.-organized contras in Honduras also collaborated with the rightist regime in that country to assassinate its opponents in the unions and on campuses.

"The imperialists have no alternative but to fight to reverse this altered relationship of class forces brought about by the revolutionary advances in the region," warned the Socialist Workers Party in a resolution adopted in 1985 that is printed in this issue of *New International.* "With the support of both political parties of U.S. imperialism, the Pentagon is steadily deepening its military intervention in El Salvador. . . . The U.S. government is fielding a Somocista mercenary army to weaken and if possible overthrow the workers and peasants government in Nicaragua. . . . Washington is trying to convert Honduras into a virtual U.S. military base. It is pushing to transform the entire region, including the U.S. colony of Puerto Rico, into a military staging ground for its counterrevolutionary war."

The intensified U.S. military pressures in the wake of the Nicaraguan and Grenada revolutions led to renewed threats and provocations against Cuba, including a practice invasion of the island staged by the marines on the beaches of the U.S.-occupied Guantánamo naval base on the eastern end of the island.

"Washington's stubborn refusal to allow the peoples of the Caribbean and Central America to run their own governments, control their own resources, and chart their own destinies carries a grave threat of war" in the entire region, said the Socialist Workers Party's National Committee in a May 1980 statement entitled "The Coming Showdown in the Caribbean," printed in this issue of *New International.* Confronted with this mounting imperialist threat, the Cuban government responded by mobilizing the workers and farmers to defend their revolutionary conquests and national sovereignty. In April and May 1980 there were three enormous popular mobilizations in Cuba, including a March of the Fighting People in Havana and other cities of some five million people, half the island's population.

"Carter cannot get five million Americans—or even a fraction of that number—to demonstrate for his policy toward Latin America," said the 1980 SWP National Committee statement. "And it's no wonder. Why should U.S. workers fight our brothers and sisters in Latin America? . . . The plunder of imperialist exploitation serves only to strengthen the same giant U.S. corporations that attack our wages, jobs, and union rights here at home."

In January 1981 the Cuban government launched the Territorial Troop Militia; over the next few years, some 1.5 million workers, farmers, students, and other volunteers were armed and trained in military skills. Weapons and uniforms for the militia have been paid for through voluntary contributions by the Cuban people.

To SUPPLEMENT THESE MEASURES of revolutionary self-defense, Cuba's communist leadership also sought a commitment of military assistance from the government of the Soviet Union. But they learned once again—as they had during the so-called missile crisis in October 1962—that the privileged bureaucratic caste in Moscow was anything but a steadfast internationalist ally.[6] In a 1993 interview Cuba's minister of the armed forces, Raúl Castro, described an official visit to Moscow in the early 1980s "to communicate to the Soviet leadership our own government's opinion on the urgent need to take extraordinary political and diplomatic actions in order to check renewed U.S.

intentions to attack Cuba militarily." The Cuban delegation met with a top-ranking official of the Soviet government and Communist Party.

"The Soviet leader's reply was categorical," Raúl Castro said. "In the event of U.S. aggression toward Cuba, 'We cannot fight in Cuba because you are 11,000 kilometers away from us. Do you think we're going to go all that way to stick our necks out for you?' Those were his very words. . . .

"Although for many years we had been working on the assumption that the USSR would not go to war over Cuba and we would have to rely solely on our own forces," Raúl Castro said, "it was at that moment of greatest danger that the Soviet leadership clearly and officially informed us . . . that in the event of military aggression by the Pentagon, Cuba would find herself dramatically alone."

The central leadership of the revolution "suffered silently the bitter burden," he said. "We learned from the experience and drew greater strength to prepare ourselves for taking on our historic mission alone."

"Since the USSR has disappeared and its most confidential files are no longer confidential," he told the interviewer, "there's no longer any reason to keep it a secret."[7]

Setbacks and defeats in 1980s

By the mid-1980s revolutionary struggles in the Central American and Caribbean region had suffered a number of setbacks and defeats.

In Guatemala the U.S.-backed regime had dealt severe blows to guerrillas leading a struggle against the dictatorship there.

In El Salvador a 1981 "final offensive" by the Farabundo Martí National Liberation Front (FMLN) had failed. Unions and other political organizations were driven underground, with opponents of the regime tortured and dumped in alleys on a daily basis by death squads run by the officer corps. In the countryside, U.S.-trained battalions engaged in massacres of peasants, hoping to wipe out support for the FMLN. The ferocious repression failed to end popular resistance, but the civil war entered a stalemate, with neither side able to defeat the other. In addition, in 1983 a Stalinist faction led by Salvador Cayetano Carpio, founder of one of the FMLN's component organizations, organized the assassination in Nicaragua of Mélida Anaya Montes (Commander Ana María), who had broken with Carpio's efforts to block unification of these groups. When the truth about this crime was uncovered by the Sandinista police, Carpio committed suicide and his supporters split from the FMLN, forming their own, Stalinist grouping.

The most serious setback was the 1983 murder of Grenadian prime minister Maurice Bishop by a Stalinist faction in the leadership of the ruling New Jewel Movement, overthrowing the workers and farmers government, and the subsequent U.S. invasion of that island. With Bishop's assassination and the subsequent U.S. invasion and occupation, one of the "three giants" was defeated, and the loss was felt deeply in Cuba, in Nicaragua, throughout the Caribbean, and among revolutionists in the United States and elsewhere who had been inspired by the Grenada revolution.

'Iran-contra,' covert operations, and imperial presidency

Despite bipartisan determination in Washington to reverse the revolution in Nicaragua, by 1984 tactical divisions had opened among the U.S. rulers over the political price they were beginning to pay at home and in Latin America for publicly financing and directly involving themselves with mercenary bands carrying out terrorist activities against a popular government. Antiwar protests were growing in the United States, and unlike during the early anti–Vietnam War movement, as the 1985 SWP resolution notes, sections of the union movement were "involved from the beginning in opposing Washington's war moves."

In 1984 Congress adopted the so-called Boland Amendment cutting off military aid to the mercenaries. The bipartisan war party in Washington responded by setting up a covert operation run by Lt. Col. Oliver North from the White House basement in close coordination with then–CIA director William

Casey. Over the next couple of years, they poured millions of dollars into the contras' coffers. Funds were raised from a variety of sources—from contributions by individual U.S. capitalists such as the notorious union-buster Joseph Coors, to large contributions by the royal family in Saudi Arabia, to clandestine arms sales to Iran. The exposure in November 1986 of the so-called "Iran-contra," or "Contragate," operation put a spotlight on the reality that such covert military operations had become one of the necessary and institutionalized bipartisan methods of carrying out U.S. foreign policy.

I N JANUARY 1994, just weeks before this issue of *New International* came off the press, the Reagan-appointed special prosecutor, Lawrence Walsh, publicly issued his final report on Contragate. While the investigation had begun with the bang of a government crisis in late 1986, it ended with a whimper seven years later. Of the fourteen Reagan administration figures Walsh had brought charges against for their involvement in the Iran-contra operation or its cover-up, he had won eleven guilty pleas or convictions. But the convictions of Oliver North and White House national security adviser John Poindexter were subsequently overturned by a higher court. And during his last weeks in office, President George Bush—himself unambiguously implicated in Walsh's final report for participating in the cover-up while Reagan's vice-president—gave a Christmas Eve pardon to former defense secretary Caspar Weinberger and five others. In Weinberger's case, this was the first time in U.S. history that a president had pardoned someone under indictment before a trial had even begun.

Walsh's report finds that "senior Reagan administration officials engaged in a concerted effort to deceive Congress and the public about their knowledge of and support for" North's operation and that Reagan "participated or at least acquiesced" in the cover-up. The report also says that the White House made North and two former national security advisers, Poindexter and Robert McFarlane, into "scapegoats whose sacrifice would protect the Reagan administration in its final two years."

This is all true enough. But the stakes in the Iran-contra scandal have nothing to do with the pecking order of guilt and accountability in the executive branch, nor even with a supposed conflict between the White House and Congress, as insisted upon by liberals, social democrats, and Stalinists alike.

In fact, both Democratic and Republican members of Congress had openly backed funding for the contras from 1981 to 1984. Afterwards, during the congressional "ban" on U.S. funding, prominent members from both parties winked at ongoing aid to the contras, whose scale of operations could have been sustained in no other way. In his 1991 book *Under Fire: An American Story*, Oliver North—who says "President Reagan knew everything"—also explains that after Congress cut off funds to the contras, he still gave "numerous briefings about the resistance" to members of the Democrat-dominated House Intelligence Committee "and to dozens of their congressional colleagues."

"Many of them had been to the region," North wrote, "visited the camps, met with resistance leaders, and seen the close quarters at Ilopango Air Force Base, where the resistance planes were stationed. For years they had been asking CIA briefers about the sources of contra support and they had all seemingly accepted the Agency's claims of ignorance."

As the *New Yorker* magazine lamented in commenting on North's book when it appeared in late 1991, the lieutenant colonel's activities, "although they violated the Boland Amendment, were an open secret in Washington. (As is often the case, making a policy covert served as a way of removing it from public debate.)"

That, of course, is the purpose of the covert character of these operations.

What's more, just months before Contragate became public and Eugene Hasenfus's plane was shot down over Nicaragua, the bipartisan Congress had voted to resume open military and so-called humanitarian aid to the contras, ultimately providing them with some $200 million extending right up to the eve of the February 1990 Nicaraguan elections.

No wonder Theodore Draper—a prominent liberal historian who has been the main chronicler of the multitudinous accounts of the Iran-contra affair—pens the following epitaph on the Walsh investigation: "Can something on the order of the Iran-contra affairs happen again in the United States? I am not sanguine that we have been inoculated against some sort of repetition." As Draper concludes, the "Iran-contra events may be more important as a warning of what can go wrong in the American system than as a bar to its going wrong again."[8]

The pervasive secrecy of government and the strengthening of the executive branch reflect the reality of the evolution of the U.S. imperialist state and bipartisan foreign policy in the closing decades of this century. The Walsh report is the chronicle of "covert" actions foretold, not forestalled.

Among members of Congress and the ruling capitalist families they represent, covert military operations have become such an institutionalized and necessary mode of functioning that the rulers muddled through the government crisis sparked by the Iran-contra revelations with only minor scrapes and bruises. Two decades earlier, Watergate had banged them up much more badly. That scandal had been a product of deep divisions within the ruling class over the appropriate response to big changes in U.S. politics registered by mass opposition in the streets to the Vietnam War and the still-reverberating effects of mass struggles for Black rights over the prior fifteen years. In addition, the White House–instigated burglary of the Democratic Party's election campaign offices, which triggered the scandal, was such a flagrant factional abuse within the ruling class and their institutions that, given the temper of the times, the resulting fissure widened beyond their initial intent.

For the working class and its allies, the Iran-contra affair underlines the growing threat to democratic rights in the United States, as the capitalist rulers in both parties increasingly find it necessary to cloak in secrecy the actions they must take to protect their class interests in face of the growing new world disorder.[9]

More recently, for example, the U.S. rulers resorted to sweeping lies and half-truths to justify their war preparations against Iraq in late 1990; they then fabricated "news" on an hourly basis in early 1991 throughout their six-week bombardment and one-hundred-hour invasion of Iraq in order to cover up the massive scale and heinous character of the slaughter. Two years later, with the complicity of the big-business-owned press, Washington is still suppressing the truth about the U.S. army's "turkey shoot" against retreating Iraqi troops and fleeing civilians on the road from Kuwait to Basra; the burying alive in the desert sands of Iraqi soldiers who were unequipped to fight and were trying to surrender; and other horrors that have been covered up altogether. (Washington also wishes the Israeli Defense Ministry would shut up about the fact that the Pentagon's headline-hyped Patriot antiaircraft missiles, far from deflecting and destroying incoming Iraqi Scud missiles, actually increased damage and casualties on the ground.)[10]

Defeat of the contras
The U.S. government crisis in the wake of the Iran-contra revelations did, however, weaken the imperialist-organized efforts to crush the Nicaraguan revolution.

The workers, peasants, and youth in the Sandinista army fought courageously and gained confidence and experience in combat against the contras. Some 30,000 lives, out of a population of 3.5 million, were lost in the fighting—the proportional equivalent of more than 2 million deaths in the United States, more than five times the number of U.S. soldiers killed in action in World War II, the Korean War, and the Vietnam War combined. Tens of thousands of Nicaraguans were maimed and hundreds of thousands left homeless.

By the latter half of 1987, however, the Nicaraguan government had broken the momentum of the contra army and defeated it. Over the next few years, the contra bands never mounted an order of battle beyond terrorist acts. The place of the Cuban government in aiding this triumph by Nicaragua's workers and peasants was substantial. For concrete political and military reasons, units of Cuban volunteers were never fielded in the same way against the contra army as they were in Angola against apartheid's invading troops and CIA-funded Angolan rightists. But Cuba's practical, internationalist commitment to a victory in Nicaragua's revolutionary war was its Cuito Cuanavale in the Americas.[11]

The victory over the contras was codified in the agreement signed by the presidents of Nicaragua, Honduras, Costa Rica, El Salvador, and Guatemala on August 7, 1987, in Guatemala City. The accords stipulated that by November 7, 1987, each of the five governments would establish a cease-fire with "irregular" military forces fighting in their country, extend full amnesty to those who had taken up arms, and lift all restrictions on civil liberties. The Nicaraguan government moved immediately to implement the accords.

A resolution adopted by the SWP Political Committee at the time, printed in these pages, hailed the revolutionary victory over the contras, pointing to the prospects that triumph opened for Nicaraguan working people to deepen the revolution in their class interests. Further advances along the anticapitalist course the workers and farmers government had charted at its outset, the resolution said, would be facilitated by the FSLN leadership's decision following the signing of the Guatemala accords to lift emergency war measures, such as censorship and suspension of the right of habeas corpus. Some such steps had been necessary to meet the challenge of the war. But maintaining restrictions under these new conditions, the resolution pointed out, would be "an obstacle to advancing the political education, orientation, and organization of the working people in the city and countryside as the class struggle deepens in Nicaragua."

In face of the imperialist-backed assault and Washington's unrelenting propaganda campaign against the Sandinista government, most class-conscious workers in Nicaragua had supported the FSLN's efforts to maintain a united front with the dwindling number of capitalists and landowners willing to back the war against the contras. The anticapitalist measures that marked the revolution's opening years were not extended during the mid-1980s. Some important democratic advances were made, however, such as the intermittent granting of more land to peasants and farm laborers and the initiation of the autonomy process on the Atlantic Coast.

Now, with the defeat of the contras, the September 1987 resolution said, "we will see more clearly, with fewer disguises, what it means to be a workers and farmers government—not a workers state, and not a capitalist regime. The essential fact that the class struggle between the working classes and the exploiting classes is the spring, the dynamic, of change in Nicaraguan society will be more visible both inside and outside Nicaragua."

The resolution pointed out that until the contras were defeated "the Reagan administration had been able to maintain the initiative, pushing hard on the right flank of the rightward-shifting bipartisan consensus around the need to overthrow the Nicaraguan government. That initiative has now shattered following the Iran-contra exposures and the Guatemala accords." But the U.S. rulers, it said, "cannot and will not come to an 'accommodation' with the Nicaraguan revolution as long as it remains a revolution. Nicaragua cannot 'buy peace' through measures relating to maintaining the mixed economy, restoring civil liberties, or other similar moves." This was to prove bitterly true.

Revolutionary war forged working-class cadres
The revolutionary war the Sandinistas fought and won had forged the cadres who could now be redeployed to help lead the class struggle forward in the postwar situation. Thousands of workers, peasants, and youth had gained leadership experience and confidence in the war effort. As the army demobilized, these cadres began returning to the factories, fields, working-class neighborhoods, and rural villages.

If consciously led by the FSLN to deepen an anticapitalist political course, these cadres could have put their energies to work and rapidly gained further revolutionary class-struggle experience in efforts to extend union rights and workers control in the factories; to deepen the fight for land and the wherewithal to till it by poor and landless peasants; to organize rural wage laborers to defend their class interests; to draw more women into the labor force and advance their fight for equality, including abortion rights and other demands; and to mobilize the toilers on the Atlantic Coast to use the autonomy process— which had been decisive in winning the majority there to the fight against the contras—to improve the social and cultural conditions in the most economically backward region of the country.

Coming on top of Nicaragua's legacy of imperialist-caused underdevelopment, economic production in the 1980s had been devastated by war-caused disruption of plantings and harvests, the destruction of agricultural machinery and buildings, Washington's suspension of aid and 1985 cutoff of trade, U.S.-organized sabotage of port facilities and other infrastructure, and the death and maiming of tens of thousands of peasants and workers. By the latter half of 1987, the Sandinista government estimated that Nicaragua had suffered nearly $700 million in direct costs of destroyed productive capacity and an overall economic toll of $3.7 billion, including lost aid and trade. These are devastating figures for an economy and a population the size of Nicaragua's.

In the mid-1980s the Soviet government had been providing economic aid to Nicaragua, largely in the form of bilateral trading credits, freeing the FSLN government from having to exhaust its hard-to-come-by reserves of dollars and other convertible currencies. While this assistance was well below Nicaragua's needs, it nonetheless met most of the country's petroleum requirements and was among its main sources of international financial assistance and trade relations. In 1987, however, as the Stalinist regime plunged into deepening crisis and ever more desperately sought acceptance into the world capitalist order, Moscow began cutting oil supplies to the Sandinista government and drastically reduced its purchase of Nicaraguan exports. The energy crisis in Nicaragua that year was met in part through Cuba's internationalist donation of extra fuel.

The growing economic pressures created obstacles to moving forward in Nicaragua. These hurdles could not be overcome, the SWP's 1987 resolution pointed out, by continuing to pursue "a kind of 'war communism' without the economic foundations of a workers state." The revolutionary government would undoubtedly have had to tack, maneuver, and sometimes retreat in face of the strength of imperialism and the remaining class enemies of the toilers inside Nicaragua.

But any necessary maneuvers and retreats had to be explained frankly and clearly to the toilers, including the reasons for these measures, their goals, and the dangers they posed for the exploited classes. The workers and peasants had to be organized to press for solutions that would protect their basic living standards to the degree possible and that would strengthen their alliance and their social position vis-à-vis the exploiters.

Over the course of 1988 and 1989, workers and peasants came into increasing conflict with the owners of the factories, giant farms, and commercial enterprises. As the class interests of the exploited and the exploiters clashed ever more sharply, however, it became clear from the FSLN leadership's decisions at each turning point that they had rejected an anticapitalist course.

As explained in the August 1989 report by Larry Seigle to the SWP National Committee that closes this issue of *New International,* "The problems the toilers face today do not stem from the fact that the FSLN government did not go faster than it did toward expropriating capitalist property in 1979 or in 1980 or in 1981. The problem is that the FSLN government is no longer traveling on the road it was traveling in 1979, 1980, and 1981. It is no longer preparing the Nicaraguan toilers to move toward a socialist revolution. It is going in the opposite direction."

The FSLN turned away from drawing the vanguard of Nicaragua's working class and rural toilers into the leadership of the

Sandinista movement and organizing a revolutionary organization, a communist party, that could lead them in using the workers and farmers government to defend their class interests. Such a line of march would have inevitably resulted—at whatever pace and through whatever concrete stages, but also with whatever explosive and irrepressible class confrontations—in new and more far-reaching assaults on the prerogatives and property of the capitalists.

FSLN leadership rejects working-class course
The political degeneration of the FSLN leadership in face of these new challenges is described in the 1989 SWP resolution, "Defend Revolutionary Nicaragua: The Eroding Foundations of the Workers and Farmers Government," and in the two reports on that resolution by SWP leader Larry Seigle, who headed the *Militant*'s Managua bureau at the time. These documents round out this issue of *New International.*

Land reform came to a virtual standstill, as the FSLN turned over leadership of the Sandinista peasants organizations to capitalist farmers and guaranteed them that no further land would be taken to meet the needs of landless tillers; in January 1989 the FSLN government declared an end to any further land expropriations. The burden of the capitalist economic crisis in the cities was placed on the backs of the working class, as wage controls and severe austerity measures were imposed. By the opening of 1990 the *New York Times* could write that the FSLN leadership had decided "to revive their battered economy with an austerity program so conventional and market-oriented that it has been compared to the methods of the International Monetary Fund."

The Sandinista union leadership largely retreated to the role of justifying government policies before the working class. The neighborhood, women's, and youth organizations, already weakened in the mid-1980s, degenerated into staff organizations, while the popular militias had already ceased functioning except in rural areas under direct contra threat. The FSLN leadership pulled back from the fight for women's equality and from the struggle against racial discrimination and national oppression on the Atlantic Coast. As a result of these policies, the worker-peasant alliance that had formed the social foundation of the revolutionary government was undermined.

The Sandinista leadership now presented the fight for national unity to defeat the contras as a political justification for class collaboration, which they implemented through the call for *concertación*—a "social pact"—with the landlords and capitalists. Reliance on capitalist market relations and deepening integration into the world capitalist system was more and more openly defended by the entire top FSLN leadership as a way out of Nicaragua's economic crisis and as the way forward for economic and social development. It became common for FSLN leaders to reject Marxism and communism as outmoded at best and to present the Nicaraguan revolution as charting some supposed "third road" between capitalism and socialism.

As this political evolution accelerated, the Nicaraguan government in December 1989 signed an accord, along with other Central American governments, demanding that the FMLN in El Salvador "immediately and effectively cease its hostilities" and take steps toward "demobilization." The accord also pledged "decisive support of Salvadoran president Alfredo Cristiani and his government."

Impact of Stalinism
In all of these cases, the Sandinista leaders turned away from reliance on the organization, mobilization, and political consciousness of the workers and peasants—the course that three decades earlier, under the impact of the Cuban revolution, had determined the break of the FSLN's founding leaders from Stalinism. It was that revolutionary orientation that had laid the political basis for the successful insurrection by the workers and peasants that brought down the Somoza tyranny and initially set the new government on a revolutionary proletarian course.

By the end of the 1980s, however, at the very time the anti-working-class regimes and apparatuses in Eastern Europe and the Soviet Union were beginning to crumble, the FSLN leadership returned politically to the Stalinist rationalizations that the most conscious fighters in both Nicaragua and Cuba had rejected in order to make possible a revolution. Under various names, Stalinist parties in those countries and throughout Latin America and elsewhere had insisted for decades that anticapitalist revolutions were precluded in the colonial and semicolonial world. Only the fight for "democracy" was on the agenda historically in these countries, the Stalinist manuals taught, and to accomplish this the working class and national liberation movements had to pursue a strategic course of collaboration with "progressive" layers of the domestic exploiters and subordination to the procapitalist policies of these exploiters. From the mid-1930s on, this class-collaborationist course disarmed revolutionary-minded workers, peasants, and youth in the Americas and worldwide, leading to numerous missed opportunities and bloody defeats.[12]

The socialist revolution in Cuba gave the lie to this Stalinist justification for class collaboration. "Had we been willing to follow the schemas, we would not be gathered here today," Fidel Castro said in 1988 at the annual July 26 rally marking Cuban revolutionists' assault on the Moncada garrison in 1953. "We would not have had a July 26, we would not have had a socialist revolution in this hemisphere—perhaps there would not have been any yet. Had we been willing to follow the schemas, theory had it that no revolution could be made here; that's . . . what the manuals used to say."

Nearly three decades after the victory in Cuba, Castro said, only one other "true and profound revolution" had been made in the Americas and—unlike Grenada by then—survived. That was the Nicaraguan revolution. "There have been no other ones in the rest of Latin America. . . . Rickets, malnutrition, children without schools, young people unemployed and without universities are everywhere and there's been no revolution."

In Cuba, Castro said, "we drew our own conclusions starting from the principles of socialism," not from the manuals. Cuban freedom fighters said "there are objective conditions in Cuba for a revolution; what's missing are subjective conditions. . . . [S]tarting out from a true appraisal of our people, their characteristics, their history, the objective realities that afflicted them, even if they were not as bad as those that afflicted other countries on our continent," Castro said, "we arrived at the conclusion that the revolution was possible in our country. This is why our country, which was the last one—the last one!—to free itself from Spain, became the first one to free itself from U.S. imperialism in this hemisphere, the first one! And the first one to carry out a socialist revolution."[13]

Revolutionists in many countries of the Americas sought to learn the lessons from the experience of the revolution in Cuba and blaze a different trail. Maurice Bishop and his comrades had done so in Grenada, as had Carlos Fonseca and his compañeros in Nicaragua, creating the political preconditions for the victories in 1979 that opened a new stage in the advance of the socialist revolution in the Americas.

Defeat of workers and farmers government

This was the revolutionary course the FSLN leadership rejected coming out of the victory over the contras in 1987. Its political degeneration accelerated throughout 1988 and 1989, bringing about the defeat of the workers and farmers government that had come to power a decade earlier.

No other workers and farmers regime had ever existed for more than a year or so—three or four years at most—without either going forward to the expropriation of the capitalist class and establishment of a workers state (e.g., Russia in 1918, Yugoslavia in 1947, China by 1952, Cuba in 1960, and southern Vietnam in 1978) or backward to the reconsolidation of a bourgeois government and capitalist state. The documents that close this issue explain why the process in Nicaragua was more protracted before the question was settled.

The form taken by the defeat of the workers and farmers government in Nicaragua was also unique. In Hungary and Bavaria in 1919, short-lived workers and farmers regimes were crushed in bloody landlord-capitalist counterrevolutions. In Algeria in

1965 and Grenada in 1983, workers and farmers governments were overthrown in military coups organized by sections of the leadership of the radical petty-bourgeois organizations that had led these revolutions; but in both cases the central leading figures in those revolutionary governments—Ahmed Ben Bella in Algeria, Maurice Bishop in Grenada—were overthrown. Ben Bella was jailed, and Bishop and dozens of other Grenadian revolutionists were massacred by the Stalinist faction around Bernard Coard.[14]

In Nicaragua, on the other hand, the entire top leadership of the FSLN united around the political course that by the end of 1989 had gutted the workers and farmers government. There was no coup, no jailings or murders, not even a change of personnel.

The FSLN regime that was defeated electorally in February 1990 had already ceased to be a workers and farmers government.

February 1990 elections
The Sandinista leadership transformed the FSLN into a bourgeois electoral machine in 1989 and early 1990. They went into the February 1990 elections anticipating they would win at the polls, but at the same time paving the way for a coalition government in which they would include some bourgeois opposition figures. The final documents in this issue, prepared in late 1989, assumed the FSLN would gain a majority vote in the elections.

The Sandinista leadership's reversal of their anticapitalist course, however, was not sufficient to convince Washington that an FSLN-led government—which would still be looked to by large numbers of working people to use the momentum from an election victory to a return to a revolutionary road—could be a reliable client for imperialism in the region. Washington helped patch together and finance a coalition of bourgeois parties to challenge the FSLN in the elections. Heterogeneous in composition, the National Opposition Union (UNO) included liberal bourgeois forces that had been part of the anti-Somoza

fight in the 1970s (some of whom were aligned with the FSLN
briefly), conservative politicians and businessmen, contra leaders, and two Stalinist organizations in the labor movement that
had long opposed the FSLN.

Workers both in Nicaragua and throughout the world had an
important stake in the outcome of the election. As an editorial
in the *Militant* the week of the voting pointed out, UNO "makes
no bones about its ties to Washington. Far from it. If victorious
it would establish a government subservient to the U.S. rulers'
economic and political interests. . . . The FSLN clearly stands
for the right of the Nicaraguan people to their sovereignty and
self-determination. Its victory over UNO in the elections would
be a further demonstration that working people in that country
refuse to bow to Washington's dictates." A victory by UNO
would narrow the space for workers and peasants to organize
against the rollback of gains they had conquered following the
July 1979 revolution.

But the FSLN leadership's social and political course following the defeat of the contras had led to an accelerating demobilization and disorientation of working people in Nicaragua.
Given the government's record in practice, the FSLN election
slogan—"We are winning. Everything will be better"—rang hol-
low in the ears of growing numbers of toilers. As a result, UNO
won a hearing for its demagogic argument that the only way
forward was to elect a new government able to negotiate aid
and investment from the U.S. and other imperialist powers,
thereby alleviating the spiraling economic crisis devastating
toilers in the city and countryside. The FSLN was unable to attract larger layers of the middle class, and the petty bourgeoisie
in its big majority rallied to the UNO campaign as well. Although the FSLN received the largest number of votes of any
single party, the UNO coalition won the elections, placing Violeta Chamorro, figurehead of the liberal bourgeois opposition,
in the presidency.

The FSLN leadership rapidly pledged to help lead an orderly
transition to the new regime. Outgoing president Daniel Ortega declared the election results a step toward the "consolida-

tion of democracy" and sought to assure his supporters that the revolution was not over—the FSLN would continue to govern "from below," a phrase that was rapidly to become more and more empty of any revolutionary content and sour in the ears of working people in Nicaragua.

"For the time being we are determined to contribute to the maintenance of stability," said FSLN commander Tomás Borge, former head of the interior ministry, in a May 1990 interview, "and to contribute to the maintenance of this government during the six years it is scheduled to govern Nicaragua in accordance with the law."

The FSLN leadership discouraged strikes or other protests, encouraging working people to rely on FSLN deputies in the National Assembly to act for them. Anything that threatened "stability," they argued, would dampen prospects for foreign capitalist investment and could even bring on U.S. aggression.

In April 1990 the Chamorro forces formed a coalition government of the UNO forces, including liberals, conservatives, and some ex-contras. As part of the transition agreement with the FSLN leadership, a few of its leaders remained in the government, most notably Gen. Humberto Ortega, who was kept on as head of the army. Some top police officials who were in the FSLN also stayed on the job. The decision by the new bourgeois government to retain Sandinistas in these positions registered a combination of two factors: first, the existing relationship of forces in Nicaragua, eleven years after a mass, popular revolution that had destroyed the old bourgeois army and put a new army in its place under FSLN command; and second, the political about-face by the FSLN leadership, culminating in its decision to serve as a prop for capitalist rule and defense of the bourgeois state in Nicaragua.

The retention of Humberto Ortega as head of the army, however, displeased both Chamorro's most conservative Nicaraguan allies and Washington. The U.S. rulers have used this as one of the pretexts to dole out aid to the new Nicaraguan government with an eyedropper, with even these droplets being bestowed or withheld as rewards or punishment depending on the regime's degree of servility.

Washington's failure to come through with any substantial package of grants and loans during the four years since the election, as Nicaragua sinks deeper and deeper into poverty, has also accelerated the pace at which rival bourgeois forces in the UNO coalition have fallen out among themselves. In September 1992 UNO's delegation in the National Assembly expelled from the coalition those members closest to President Chamorro and her top cabinet aide, Antonio Lacayo, and then walked out of the legislative body in January 1993, depriving it of a quorum for a full year. Only in January 1994 did further splits in UNO once again make it possible for the National Assembly to function.

Prospects for Cuban revolution

The victories of the Grenada and Nicaraguan revolutions in 1979 had given great new impetus to the socialist revolution in Cuba. The mass mobilizations against Washington's threats and provocations in the opening years of the 1980s, and the formation of the volunteer Territorial Troop Militia in 1981, drew millions of Cuban workers and farmers into revolutionary political activity in ways that had been on the decline over the previous decade. Despite rising productivity and an improving standard of living in the 1970s, Cuba had been marked by growing social stratification and political demobilization and retreat of working people, in large part as a result of the Cuban government's adoption of economic planning and management priorities, and related political policies, modeled on those of the Soviet bureaucratic regime.

Cuban communists had never retreated from their internationalist commitment to aid those fighting imperialist oppression anywhere in the world, as witnessed by the hundreds of thousands of Cubans who volunteered for duty in Angola from 1975 on. But the revolutionary prospects opened in the Americas at the beginning of the 1980s created the conditions to begin reversing the increasingly negative economic, social, and political consequences of the domestic course embarked upon

over the previous decade. A new trail began to be blazed with
political changes in economic priorities in late 1984, leading to
the launching in early 1986 of what was called the rectification
process. The political course that had been argued for by
Ernesto Che Guevara during the early 1960s, and that had been
implemented in limited ways in those years, was once again put
forward by Cuban president Fidel Castro as an example to be
studied and emulated.

Voluntary work brigades were relaunched in the latter 1980s
to meet pressing social needs such as housing and day care.
Steps were taken to begin decreasing the gap between the high-
est- and lowest-paid workers by raising the living standards of
the worst-off layers in the countryside and cities. Policies were
initiated to counter the growth of those profiteering off shortages of housing and food. Action was taken to eliminate privileges and mobilize against abuses, waste, and outright corruption by growing middle-class layers in state enterprises and the
apparatus of the party and state.

Food self-sufficiency was put forward as an urgent priority by
the Cuban leadership, as it had been prior to the decision in the
1970s to accept investment priorities and trading policies
pressed on them by the Moscow-dominated Council for Mutual
Economic Assistance (Comecon). New projects were launched
to develop and diversify industrial production. Special volunteer
labor contingents began to be organized as a political vanguard
within the working class. Taken together, the political dynamic of
these measures was to begin renewing and strengthening the organization and mobilization of expanding layers of the working
class as a conscious communist leadership of the Cuban toilers.
The decisive victory of the Cuban, Angolan, and Namibian
forces at Cuito Cuanavale in early 1988, and the consequent decision of the South African apartheid regime to open negotiations leading to withdrawal from Angola and independence for
Namibia, gave another gigantic boost to the confidence and
combativity of the communist vanguard in Cuba.

The cumulative effects of the defeats of the workers and
farmers governments first in Grenada and then in Nicaragua

over the 1980s, however, and their impact in pushing back revolutionary struggles elsewhere in Central America and the Caribbean, dealt a political blow to the Cuban revolution. There was no longer what Fidel Castro had called another "true and profound revolution" moving toward socialism anywhere in the Americas, or in the world. With the Stalinists' bloody destruction of the Maurice Bishop–led New Jewel Movement in Grenada, and the FSLN's rejection of a proletarian course, there was no longer another revolutionary leadership that held state power and used it to advance the class interests of workers and farmers at home and internationally. In this way, Cuban communists were once again alone.

COMING ON THE HEELS of these political setbacks, Cuba at the opening of the 1990s also confronted the sudden collapse of its long-standing economic aid from the Soviet Union, much of which took the form of import subsidies and higher export prices than could be fetched by hard-currency trade on the world capitalist market. The ensuing shortages and economic dislocation brought to an end many initiatives at the heart of the rectification campaign, such as the volunteer construction minibrigades and vanguard contingents, and cut deeply into the living conditions of working people and the production capacity of Cuban agriculture and industry.

The future of the Cuban revolution—today being forced to retreat under pressure of the most difficult economic conditions it has ever faced—will not be settled in Cuba alone, however. Struggles by workers and farmers in Latin America and the Caribbean, in the United States, and around the world in the years ahead will be decisive to the ability of the Cuban working class to defend its socialist conquests. A new generation of Cuban revolutionists confronts the challenge of strengthening the vanguard social and political role of the working class; their success will determine prospects of reconquering socialist policies that the Cuban revolution is being forced to retreat from today. And those prospects will improve as the conflicts and crises generated by the growing disorder of the world capitalist system create conditions in the Americas and elsewhere for popular struggles and rebellions, for the forging of new working-class leaderships, and for renewed revolutionary victories.

FSLN's evolution since 1990

Today the FSLN functions as a bourgeois opposition party in Nicaragua with the goal of regaining office through the 1996 elections. Within this electoralist framework, the FSLN leadership responds to strikes or other social conflicts by speaking as an instrument for class reconciliation, one that is based among and sympathetic to the popular masses, but that speaks and acts on behalf of the stability of the nation as a whole. This political character of the FSLN was affirmed and deepened at the Sandinistas' July 1991 congress, which officially replaced the Historic Program as the organization's guide with a new "Principles and Program" document explicitly aimed at achieving class peace and "stability."

While strikes by workers are inevitable given the deep economic crisis, former president Daniel Ortega said in his closing speech to the congress, "the causes for the strikes must be found, to then avoid the strikes, to avoid more tension." The aim of the FSLN, Ortega said, must be to "incorporate people from different economic classes and social sectors . . . so that we turn the FSLN in this new phase into a political force that is capable of representing . . . all the social sectors and all the economic sectors in our country."

Also speaking at the FSLN congress, Chamorro cabinet chief Antonio Lacayo pointedly told delegates he was "pleased with the policy of national reconciliation and your pledge to work for a social and economic pact" between contending classes.

A February 1994 statement by the FSLN National Directorate on the sixtieth anniversary of Sandino's death described the current organization this way: "The FSLN is open to all sectors of Nicaraguan society and aspires to represent all of society, whether from a position of opposition or while in power, in order to achieve democracy, economic development, and social justice. Its primary concerns are the poor and unemployed, who constitute the majority of Nicaraguans."

The FSLN sought to ratify its class-collaborationist course in mid-1990 by applying to join, as a full member, the Socialist International—the loose association of bourgeois social democratic parties dominated by imperialist labor parties in Britain, Germany, France, Spain, Sweden, and elsewhere in Western Europe. *La Prensa*, the Managua daily that has long served as a mouthpiece for Nicaragua's capitalist class, hailed the FSLN leadership's action, saying the newspaper "regards it as splendid news."

A class gulf began opening between the top FSLN leadership and the workers and peasants as the momentum of the revolution slowed in the mid-1980s. As in other Third World countries with limited modern class development and low levels of literacy, a disproportionate number of central FSLN leaders were middle class in their origins, with several having been born into the country's leading landowning or other ruling capitalist families. While outstanding individual workers leaders have emerged from such social backgrounds over the past 150 years, alien class pressures and values can and do mount in leaderships with such a composition under conditions where the working class and other toilers are pushed toward the margins of politics and are unable to place their stamp on the organization and its leading committees.

That is what happened in Nicaragua throughout the latter half of the 1980s. The FSLN's course blocked the road to bringing more workers into the leadership. The accelerating class polarization within the Sandinista movement inevitably bred layers that had a material stake in maintaining their relatively privileged positions. The festering corruption came to a head publicly in the weeks prior to Chamorro's inauguration in 1990, as many Sandinista officials shamelessly grabbed government-owned homes, lands, and other resources for their personal use. This wholesale public larceny became widely known in Nicaragua as *la piñata*, after the Latin American holiday custom of breaking open a suspended papier-mâché animal and then scrambling for the falling goodies. Meanwhile, the majority of the demobilized ranks from both the Sandinista and contra armies have been left with little or no means of support.

With occasional mild criticisms, the FSLN leadership has supported the antiworker, antipeasant austerity measures imposed by the Chamorro government. Sandinista leaders have backed the return of expropriated factories to former capitalist owners, so long as they were not open Somozaists. In a November 1993 interview with the Nicaraguan newspaper *El Semanario,* FSLN commander Bayardo Arce said that the privatization of the telephone and postal service, the Nicaraguan Institute of Energy, and the waterworks and sewerage system were "absolutely necessary," while opposing privatization of health care, schooling, and social security. Arce said that Daniel Ortega, "who is sometimes singled out as the [FSLN] spokesman, has been very clear, stating that he does not want us to return to the decade of the '70s and that we clearly cannot return to the '80s."

But all the talk about *concertación* and class peace, and all the efforts to impose them, have not brought economic and social stability to Nicaragua. Some 60 percent of the population is unemployed or underemployed. Real wages, health care, and education are all on the decline. Tens of thousands of peasant families who became refugees during the war, and many in the ranks of both the Sandinista and contra armies, returned to no homes and often no land, while former contra officers and bourgeois opposition figures who went into exile after 1979 returned and had land or other property abundantly bestowed on them.

The already paltry foreign aid the Chamorro government had promised it would attract actually declined further in 1993, as imperialist governments and institutions such as the World Bank and International Monetary Fund demanded ever more severe cuts in social services and food subsidies and more sweeping privatization of state-owned properties. Imperialist trusts have been unwilling to put money into Nicaraguan industry, which is outmoded, noncompetitive, and has a unionized work force forged in a revolution that despite recent setbacks remains more combative and class conscious than in neighboring countries. Some $10 billion is owed to imperialist banks and international financial institutions, which skim tens of millions of dollars in interest payments from the wealth produced by Nicaraguan workers and peasants each year.

Reaction to FSLN leadership's course
From within the popular masses no coherent class-struggle political alternative to the FSLN leadership's course could arise under conditions of retreat and deprivation. There has been, however, continued resistance by layers of workers and peasants to the worsening conditions they face as a result of the capitalist crisis and the government's tightening austerity measures. Trade unionists, for example, have spoken out over the past year against the FSLN leadership's decision to support, with some cosmetic reforms, the heart of the government's privatization policy.

More important, public transportation workers waged a hard-fought strike in September 1993, winning their demand that the government repeal a new vehicle tax and roll back fuel price increases. When the government reneged on the agreement in January 1994, the workers relaunched the strike, suspending it in early February when the government agreed to return to the negotiating table and to release all arrested strikers with no reprisals against them.

In a year-end interview in December 1993, Gen. Humberto Ortega sought to justify the use of what once had been a revolutionary army to defend the interests of the bourgeois government and the class of exploiting landlords and factory owners it represents. "It is important to realize that ours is a national army," Ortega told Managua TV Channel 4. "It is no longer an army responsible to a political party, as it was in the past. In the past, we were a direct expression of the Sandinista National Liberation Front, a party. It is no longer that way. We know it is important to be an institution of the Nicaraguan state that serves all Nicaraguans, regardless of their political, ideological, or religious position."

Ortega failed to point out that under capitalism whenever

one serves "all," those with the greatest wealth get the best service.

Even apologists for the course of the Sandinista leadership have been shaken by their more and more overt actions in defense of capitalist profits, property, and prerogatives. For example, the year-end review in the January 1994 issue of *Barricada International*—produced by cadres of the FSLN and their supporters from abroad—frets that "the tacit support that the FSLN has given the government has cost the party sympathizers and damaged its prestige and that of its leaders in the eyes of many people, given that the deterioration in social services and the resulting misery have reached unbearable levels." And referring to the army's suppression of a rebellion by former FSLN soldiers in Estelí in July 1993, killing up to sixty of them, the *Barricada International* article comments that "Humberto Ortega apparently wanted to prove to society that he could restore order, but he was widely criticized for the brutality of the response. Rank and file Sandinistas were among the most outraged."[15]

Debates over the FSLN leadership's course are surfacing in the press and publications in Nicaragua. An opinion article in the Managua daily *El Nuevo Diario* in December 1993, for example, commented on President Chamorro's announcement two months earlier at an armed forces celebration that Humberto Ortega would retire from his position sometime in 1994.[16] Chamorro's seemingly abrupt announcement of the general's retirement, the writer of the opinion article said, "demonstrated Sandinism's lack of real weight in its relations with the government, so painstakingly and at such great cost worked out by the national [FSLN] leadership, using the argument—contradicted by reality—of preserving to the utmost the gains of the revolution. . . . The national leadership apparently got itself into trouble without any hope of escape when it gave up the Sandinista Front's political program, which has never lost its force. . . ."

No alternative course presented
Despite various degrees of disappointment and disillusionment, there is no organized political voice in the FSLN or in

the working-class movement in Nicaragua, or any broad political current in the world workers movement, that openly faces up to the reality that the FSLN as constituted today is no longer a revolutionary organization. It has been transformed by its central leadership into a radical bourgeois electoral party that is an obstacle to the working class regaining the class independence, organization, and self-confidence needed to wage the necessary battle to build a communist party and once again overturn capitalist rule.

As the documents that round out this issue explain, there is no shortcut to that goal. The FSLN earned its place as the political vanguard of the workers and peasants of Nicaragua through enormous effort and sacrifice; it led them in the victorious popular insurrection of July 1979 and in carrying out the anticapitalist course during the opening years of the revolution that advanced the class interests of the toilers and made it possible for them to defeat the U.S.-backed counterrevolution. All sorts of Stalinist and ultraleftist forces disqualified themselves for leadership, aiming factional barbs at the FSLN while standing aside from the central tasks of the struggle. Some of these forces have ended up in the UNO coalition, while others continue to function as ultraleft sects. None point a path toward building a proletarian communist party in Nicaragua.

Like working people in other countries, however, workers and peasants in Nicaragua today live and work in a world marked by a global economic depression, social crisis, intensifying capitalist trade conflicts, growing pressures toward imperialist military intervention and wars, and the rising class tensions and political polarization that inevitably accompany such instability. Events in the final months of 1993 and opening weeks of 1994 alone give the lie to the myth promoted both by the current bourgeois government in Nicaragua and by the FSLN leadership, each in their own way, that capitalism can somehow bring economic development, social peace, and political democracy to the peoples of Latin America.

In the northern Argentine province of Santiago del Estero in December 1993, thousands of workers rose up in rebellion, tak-

ing over provincial buildings, in protest of the authorities' failure
to pay government workers since August. Argentine president
Carlos Menem sent in federal police in face of the uprising. Another working-class explosion rocked the northern Argentine
city of Tucumán in March 1994.

In January 1994 Mexican troops unleashed bloody repression in the southern state of Chiapas in the wake of widely publicized guerrilla operations in several towns. These events put a
spotlight on the desperate living conditions of, and discrimination against, the majority Indian population of Chiapas, most
of whom are poor peasants and farm laborers, as well as on the
repressive policies of the Mexican regime.

These class conflicts sharpened in the two Latin American
countries most often portrayed today as among the "economic
miracles" of the capitalist market system—two of the countries
into which the most capital is pouring. Nicaragua, on the other
hand, has joined Haiti in recent years as one of the two poorest
countries in the Americas.

Reknitting revolutionary continuity

Out of deepening capitalist crisis and the resistance it will
spur, a new generation of working-class fighters will emerge in
Nicaragua who will retrace their continuity to the Marxist
road charted in the 1960s and 1970s by Carlos Fonseca and
codified in the FSLN's Historic Program. No one can predict
the forms or the pace of such struggles. But like workers elsewhere around the world, fighters in Nicaragua will find their
way back to the lessons of the socialist revolution in Cuba, to
the writings and speeches of communist leaders such as
Ernesto Che Guevara and Fidel Castro. They will learn from
the accumulated class-struggle experience of the working class
in other times and other parts of the world—from the writings
of V.I. Lenin, Leon Trotsky, and other Bolshevik leaders of the
Russian revolution; from the writings of Karl Marx and Frederick Engels, the founders of the modern communist workers
movement.

The experiences from the fight to make the socialist revolution in the Americas are of great importance for revolutionary-minded workers, farmers, and youth the world over. As the lessons of Contragate confirm once again, every deep-going struggle by working people, no matter where it occurs, will confront the implacable hatred of U.S. capitalism's ruling families, who will use their massive economic and military power—covertly and overtly—to defend their class interests.

But defeats are far from inevitable, despite what petty-bourgeois misleaderships preach to working people and rebel youth the world over. Whether in the classical Stalinist variant, in the libertarian anarchist packaging of a Noam Chomsky, or in the apologetics of a Daniel Ortega, the bottom line is always the same: It's unwise to pursue a revolutionary road anywhere in the world today. The odds are against you. The rich and the mighty will punish you. Lasting victories are not possible. The fight for socialism is a utopia. So lower your sights to something you might be capable of doing.

For communists, on the contrary, the prospect of successful anticapitalist revolutions is an eminently practical political question. The objective preconditions for proletarian revolutions already exist, and these conditions have ripened throughout expanding portions of the world since the opening decades of this century. The working class is larger and stronger than it has ever been. It is more international in its scope, spread across every inhabited continent on earth. It is more color-blind, more multilingual and multinational in every major imperialist country. More women than ever before have been drawn into all aspects of economic production and social life, from Managua to Manitoba.

Moreover, the biggest obstacle to working-class victories and advances—the Stalinist counterfeit of Marxism that was accepted for good coin by millions for some six decades—has crumbled. The police-state apparatuses of the privileged castes in the grotesquely deformed workers states of Eastern Europe and the USSR have fallen, along with the international murder machine that did the bidding of the Moscow regime around the world.

For Marxists there is nothing inevitable about most victories or defeats. The outcome depends above all on the courage, capacities, internalized class-struggle experience, and political clarity of a communist vanguard forged by revolutionary workers in the course of deepening battles by the working class, farmers, and youth.

When workers and their oppressed and exploited allies enter into revolutionary struggle, there is never a guarantee of lasting victory, and there never can be. The workers' line of march worldwide is a long and jagged one. In the most fundamental sense, there will never be a lasting victory until the proletarian revolution has triumphed on a world scale, socialism has begun to be built, and the state and other institutions of class society have started to wither away.

In any particular revolution there is never any way to be sure beforehand what social, political, and military forces will bear down on the triumphant workers and their vanguard political organizations. Even the most outstanding leaderships produced by the toilers have been shattered under such pressures, or have been forced into unanticipated retreats.

Was the October 1917 revolution worth it, given the conquest of the Stalinist counterrevolution in little more than a decade? Was the Vietnamese revolution worth it, despite the horrible toll inflicted on the workers and peasants by Washington both during and after the war? Was the Grenada revolution worth it, knowing what we now know of the outcome due to the crimes of Stalinist assassins? Was the Cuban revolution worth it, in face of the grinding economic and social pressures the toilers face today, with no assurances of when or how their current forced retreat will be reversed? Was the Nicaraguan revolution worth it, given the story traced in the pages that follow?

Communist workers unequivocally answer "yes" in each case. Because what *is* the lasting result of every deep-going popular revolution—and what is of decisive importance to the future of the toiling majority of humanity—is the accumulated revolutionary experience of the working-class vanguard, its continuity of struggles, and the lessons from those victories and defeats absorbed over generations.

T HE WORLD CLASS STRUGGLE and prospects for the toilers were changed forever by what the Bolshevik-led workers and peasants accomplished more than seventy-five years ago. Revolutionary-minded youth in the United States and elsewhere were won to the communist movement by what they saw happening in Cuba in the early 1960s, and that socialist revolution has swelled the ranks of fighters for national liberation and socialism through-out the world ever since. Several generations were first impelled into political action by the struggle of the Vietnamese, Grena-dian, and Nicaraguan people, and thousands of them have been attracted to communist organizations as a result of those experi-ences.

The writings of Karl Marx, Frederick Engels, V.I. Lenin, Leon Trotsky, Rosa Luxemburg, Fidel Castro, Ernesto Che Guevara, Maurice Bishop, and many other revolutionists and commu-nists; the programmatic documents of the world workers move-ment, from the International Working Men's Association of Marx and Engels to the Communist International in Lenin's time and those who fought to carry on its work following the Stalinist degeneration—all these are a permanent legacy of the revolutionary struggles of the working class. They are part of the political arsenal of the international workers movement that embraces the works of other outstanding revolutionists such as Malcolm X, Nelson Mandela, and Thomas Sankara, as well as leaders of the communist movement in the United States.

Writing in the aftermath of the defeat of the world's first workers government—the Paris Commune, which was drowned in blood in 1871 by the bourgeoisie of France after just seventy-two days in power—Karl Marx pointed out that the workers "did not expect miracles from the Commune. . . . [They] have no ready-made utopias to introduce *par décret du peuple* [by de-cree of the people]. They know that in order to work out their own emancipation, and along with it that higher form to which present society is irresistibly tending by its own economical agencies, they will have to pass through long struggles, through a series of historic processes, transforming circumstances and men. They have no ideals to realize, but to set free elements of the new society with which old collapsing bourgeois society itself is pregnant."

In that most fundamental sense, Marx said, "The great social measure of the Commune was its own working existence."[17]

A quarter of a century earlier, Marx as a young revolutionist had summed up in the following words the germ of a new world outlook that would soon lead him to be recruited by revolutionary workers and join them in launching the first modern communist organization: "The philosophers have only *interpreted* the world in various ways; the point, however, is to *change* it."[18]

More than a century later, in February 1962, the general assembly of the newly victorious socialist revolution in Cuba put forward the same perspective in a declaration to the oppressed and exploited throughout the Americas and the world: "It is the duty of every revolutionist to make the revolution."[19]

That strategic orientation—phrased in different ways, but arising from the practical experiences of the world working class spanning a century and a half of struggle—remains the starting point for communists to this day. The victory of the dictatorship of the proletariat is inevitable, opening the construction of socialism on a world scale. How and when the working class and its allies will triumph, however, we do not know. But we do know that the road will be longer and bloodier if revolutionists do not orient, above all, toward building a communist organization to make the revolution and dare to seize the chance when it occurs.

For more than a half decade after the 1979 revolutions in Nicaragua and Grenada, the revolutionary government in Cuba was no longer the sole exemplar of a workers and farmers government, as it had been for the previous twenty years. Understanding the lessons from the accomplishments and, then, the defeats of those two workers and farmers governments is part of the necessary preparation to defend the gains of the Cuban revolution in the most effective way—by building communist workers parties throughout the Americas and throughout the world that can do in those countries what the Cuban workers have done.

The documents in this issue of *New International* stand as a record of how a party of industrial workers in the United States, the Socialist Workers Party, and communist leagues in a number of other imperialist countries, responded to the Nicaraguan revolution as communists, participated in it, defended it, and sought to learn from it and share its lessons with other working people. These resolutions and reports are also a powerful vindication of revolutionary journalism. Because all of them draw on a decade of week-by-week reportage from inside the Nicaraguan revolution, and from inside that country's toiling classes, organized by the Managua bureau of the *Militant* and *Perspectiva Mundial.* The practical conclusions and theoretical insights presented in these pages are the fruits of work by not only the more than twenty volunteer members of the bureau's writing staff over that ten-year period, but also by all those whose financial contributions and sales efforts to get working-class literature into the hands of as many readers as possible have made it possible to sustain these publications.

None of the documents have been edited or changed from how they first appeared between 1979 and 1989, except for the addition of subheadings, the correction of typographical and grammatical errors and a few mistaken dates or figures, and the preparation of explanatory notes to aid the reader. Reading these ten years of resolutions and reports is not only one of the best ways to study the Nicaraguan revolution and its turning points. It is also a way for working-class fighters and youth— wherever they live and work—to understand the importance of forging a communist party to prepare for the coming class battles with the employers and their governments.

Steve Clark
March 24, 1994

NICARAGUA

HONDURAS

PUERTO CABEZAS ●

EL SALVADOR

●Ocotal

ESTELÍ ●

●MATAGALPA

●CHINANDEGA

●LEÓN

MANAGUA ✪

Masaya●

GRANADA ●

BLUEFIELDS ●

Pacific Ocean

Atlantic Ocean

COSTA RICA

LIST OF INITIALS

AMNLAE	Association of Nicaraguan Women–Luisa Amanda Espinoza
AMPRONAC	Association of Women Confronting the National Problem
ANDEN	National Association of Nicaraguan Educators
ATC	Rural Workers Association
CDCs	Civil Defense Committees
CDSs	Sandinista Defense Committees
CDTS	Sandinista Workers Defense Committees
CST	Sandinista Workers Federation
ENABAS	Nicaraguan Basic Foods Enterprise
EPS	Sandinista People's Army
FDR	Revolutionary Democratic Front (El Salvador)
FLN	National Liberation Front (Algeria)
FMLN	Farabundo Martí National Liberation Front (El Salvador)
FSLN	Sandinista National Liberation Front
GRN	Government of National Reconstruction
INRA	National Institute of Agrarian Reform (Cuba)
INRA	Nicaraguan Institute of Agrarian Reform
LMR	Revolutionary Marxist League
MAP	People's Action Movement
MILPAS	Anti-Somoza People's Militias
NEP	New Economic Policy (USSR)
NJM	New Jewel Movement (Grenada)
OST	Socialist Workers Organization (Costa Rica)
PCN	Communist Party of Nicaragua
PSN	Nicaraguan Socialist Party
SWP	Socialist Workers Party (U.S.)
UNAG	National Union of Farmers and Ranchers
UNO	National Opposition Union
YSA	Young Socialist Alliance (U.S.)

**Insight into the strategic thinking and
revolutionary activity of one of the outstanding
communist leaders of the 20th century**

The Bolivian Diary *of*
Ernesto Che Guevara

Guevara's account, newly translated, of the 1966-67 guerrilla struggle in Bolivia.

A day-by-day chronicle of the campaign by one of the central leaders of the Cuban revolution to forge a continent-wide revolutionary movement of workers and peasants capable of contending for power.

This new edition also includes Fidel Castro's introduction, accounts by guerrilla leaders who survived, excerpts from diaries of other combatants, and documents written by Guevara in Bolivia. Much of this material appears in English for the first time. 350 pp. $19.95

Bolivian Diary
Ernesto Che Guevara

Guevara (with pipe) and other combatants in Bolivia.

1. THE TRIUMPH
OF THE NICARAGUAN
REVOLUTION

The triumph of the FSLN-led government gave an impulse to workers and farmers struggles. Above, a February 1980 demonstration in Managua organized by the Association of Rural Workers (ATC); 30,000 peasants and agricultural workers called for a radical land reform and improved conditions for rural toilers.

1979:

THE REVOLUTIONARY CHARACTER OF THE

SANDINISTA NATIONAL LIBERATION FRONT

by Jack Barnes

R EVOLUTIONS ARE ACID TESTS. Weaknesses that are underneath the surface are suddenly exposed in the heat of the struggle of great class forces that are outside the control of anyone.

The Nicaraguan revolution precipitated a major split on a world scale among those who call themselves Trotskyists.[1] Some currents reacted to this revolution in a completely sectarian way, placing their own organizational concerns and formal schemas ahead of the interests of the Nicaraguan toilers and the world revolution. These forces included Nahuel Moreno's Bolshevik Faction, which engineered the criminal Simón Bolívar Brigade adventure in Nicaragua; the so-called Organizing Committee for the Reconstruction of the Fourth International; and other sectarian groupings.[2]

Since the leaders of these groups who were also elected leaders of the Fourth International persisted in their maneuvers against the Nicaraguan revolution, its Sandinista leadership,

---

This report by the national secretary of the Socialist Workers Party of the United States is based on the resolution "Nicaragua: How the Workers and Farmers Government Came to Power," which was adopted by the SWP National Committee in January 1980 and is reprinted on pages 77-116. The report was presented to the November 1979 World Congress of the Fourth International.

ENDNOTES FOR THIS ARTICLE BEGIN ON PAGE 301.

and the Fourth International, we correctly threw them out a few days ago. Now they are giving aid and comfort to the imperialist campaign against Nicaragua by holding rallies against alleged political repression in Nicaragua.

But the Nicaraguan revolution has also precipitated important divisions within the United Secretariat of the Fourth International. When the revolution first occurred last summer, we hoped this would not be the case. In early August [1979], a majority of the Secretariat Bureau reached agreement on a statement on the revolution, and a large delegation traveled together to Nicaragua. There, further agreement seemed to be reached, including a common approach toward condemning the Simón Bolívar Brigade adventure and a common political stance toward the necessary measures taken by the FSLN (Sandinista National Liberation Front) to deal with this problem.[3]

Not long after the Nicaraguan trip, however, differences began to appear. And they center not on the label of workers and farmers government. They are over the political approach to this revolution and to its leadership.

On the one hand were those who embraced the revolution, saw its worker and peasant character, recognized the revolutionary qualities of its leadership, sought to learn from it, and reflected this approach in their press and political activity. On the other hand were those who, because of preconceived schemas or parochial concerns, adapted to sectarianism and, to one degree or another, recoiled from identifying with the Sandinista leadership.

At the heart of this discussion today is this political approach to the Nicaraguan leadership. And this is intimately connected to the different approaches in the world movement to the revolutionary Cuban leadership and the current in the Caribbean and Central America that looks to the Cuban socialist revolution and its leadership team.

How our movement approaches this current is decisively important. Because a wrong approach is an obstacle to our very reason for existence—constructing a mass revolutionary proletarian international.

That's the debate that's being opened here today.

The Nicaraguan revolution sent shock waves throughout the imperialist ruling classes, and they have begun to respond. Just in the few days since we've been here at the World Congress, the imperialists and sections of the Nicaraguan bourgeoisie have made a number of probes. And we can expect many more as the revolution continues to advance and deepen.

At the same time, something totally unplanned and unanticipated is occurring in the United States, precipitated by what happened in an embassy thousands of miles away in Iran.[4] A chauvinist, warmongering propaganda campaign has been launched by the Carter administration. This will bring to a new stage the battle in the United States for the minds of the American workers, a battle over the *political* capacity of imperialism to use its military power as the ruling class probes to see what possibilities are open to it. And this will have a great deal to do with the coming showdowns in Central America and the Caribbean.

These are the kinds of things we can't predict. We can't predict all the moves of the bourgeoisie or their reaction to sharpening struggles. We can't predict or control the actions of the masses. And we can't predict all the tactical moves a pragmatic imperialism will make.

THERE IS NO SINGLE imperialist tactic being used against free Nicaragua. When Washington was surprised by the manner in which the Somoza regime was overthrown and the Sandinistas took power, they backed off tactically from seeking to block the FSLN from wielding governmental power. But economic aid was withheld and reactionary imperialist-backed probes, and eventual military action, remain constant threats.

I will concentrate on four basic aspects of what the position of the Fourth International should be on (1) the nature of the post–July 1979 government, (2) the FSLN leadership and our attitude toward it, (3) the contradictions that the toilers of Nicaragua inherit and how they are being resolved to move the revolution forward, and (4) our responsibilities from the point of view of the new opportunities opening for building a world party of socialist revolution.

❖

To understand the character of the government in Nicaragua today, we have to begin with the fact that no one, including the FSLN, anticipated what was going to happen in July [1979]. A mass upsurge and insurrection occurred in face of the last-minute attempts of imperialism and a sector of the non-Somozaist bourgeois opposition to block this powerful intervention of the masses, including attempts to get the FSLN to lay down their arms and last-ditch attempts by the Somozaists to hold on when Somoza fled. The scope and power of this mass uprising led to the final shattering and demoralization of the National Guard. In this process, not only was the Somozaist state apparatus smashed, but much of the bourgeois opposition became discredited. Thus, an unanticipated situation faced the FSLN— the leadership of the insurrection—after July 19.

Before July 19 the FSLN leadership thought that the relationship of forces would make it necessary to incorporate a certain number of National Guard units into the new army and police. They were convinced that the provisional revolutionary government that they would participate in would initially be a coalition regime with a substantial bourgeois majority. Such a regime had already been outlined in formal agreements with bourgeois opposition forces.

The first big test
But something else happened. The FSLN had another option, thanks to the intervention of the masses. And this was the first big, postinsurrection test facing the FSLN.

They did not set up a bourgeois coalition regime. They took the power and used it to begin the national reconstruction of devastated Nicaragua.

What was this bourgeois regime that they thought would

come into being, and that they had agreed to in San José, Costa Rica, only ten days before the insurrectional victory?

It did not center around the proposed five-person junta alone, but this junta combined with a Council of State. The Council of State was not only to share all legislative powers with the junta but was also to have veto power over any junta decision, to be able to pass any laws of its own with a two-thirds majority, to draft a constitution, to draft electoral laws, to set up the entire judicial structure, and to set up the interior ministry and all the police forces of the country.

This Council of State was to have an overwhelming majority of bourgeois forces. Of the thirty-three seats agreed to in the Council of State, between six and nine at maximum were partisans of the FSLN. The bourgeoisie, through their own parties, through the Chamber of Commerce, through organizations of industrialists, through the Catholic hierarchy, would have dominated the government. All were to receive representation with full vote.

But this bourgeois-dominated institution did not come into existence.

In the month to six weeks following July 19, the opportunity appeared for the FSLN to follow another course. And they took it.

There was a bourgeois coalition regime in Nicaragua—on paper. It had been set up in Costa Rica. But it was violently aborted before it came to life.

Instead the FSLN-led junta alone named the ministers. The convocation of the Council of State was repeatedly postponed. Finally it was announced in October that it would be set up in a number of months, probably in May 1980, but that its original composition was now totally invalid because of the revolution. Its composition would now reflect the preponderant weight of the new mass organizations in Nicaragua.

In the light of this evolution, a debate among partisans of the Nicaraguan revolution opened up over whether the junta rules by a majority vote or unanimous vote. The truth is that it rules by neither. It rules by the relationship of class forces. Three junta members are partisans of the FSLN, two are bourgeois figures.[5] The FSLN controls the interior ministry, the army, the police, the agrarian reform. It leads the mass organizations.

Unlike Cuba in early 1959, the ministers do not form a legislative cabinet; there is no bourgeois president with veto power.

The FSLN-led revolutionary army is not an element of an alternative power outside the governmental framework. Each and every move of the Sandinista army, each and every decision, has been ratified by the government, as have been such moves as setting up INRA (Nicaraguan Institute of Agrarian Reform), which was done immediately following the insurrection, in the same weeks as the decision to abort the bourgeois coalition regime.

So to understand what happened, it is necessary to realize that before July 19 the FSLN had agreed there was going to have to be a coalition government, to a large degree dominated by the bourgeoisie. This government was going to find itself in a series of contradictions with the rebel army, which the Sandinistas had every intention of holding on to and building. In many ways this would have been similar to what occurred in Cuba for a number of months after January 1959.

But the masses themselves, in the weeks of fury in July, created an entirely unanticipated relationship of class forces and smashed the maneuvers of the imperialists. In the face of the new opportunities this created, the FSLN did something different from what they had planned on doing. And a different governing power came into being.

Revolutionary measures

The character of this new power, though, could only be determined by what it did. And what it did is outlined in our resolution before you.[6]

To date, the steps taken by the new government include the nationalization of all the assets of Somoza and his associates; nationalization of domestic banking, and controls on all foreign banking; beginning the agrarian reform under the control of INRA; concentration within the agrarian reform on cooperativism; beginning the organization of the agricultural workers; state control over the export of all cash crops in the countryside;[7] nationalization of land, sea, and air transport; taking over the necessary equipment to give the FSLN one of the two major daily papers in the country and radio and television outlets; the launching of large-scale programs, under conditions of harsh austerity, for education, health, and social security. A bill of rights making the interests of the workers and peasants dominant was proclaimed. And the new government has adopted a firm anti-imperialist and internationalist stance concerning Indochina, the Mideast, and Carter's war moves in the Caribbean.[8] It responded to the [October 1979] coup in El Salvador by immediately and unconditionally supporting the revolutionists and the masses against the new regime.[9]

The FSLN has led the mobilization of the masses, including in large demonstrations, like the one to greet Premier Pham Van Dong and the Vietnamese delegation. On November 7, 100,000 Nicaraguans were mobilized in Managua to honor the FSLN's founding leader Carlos Fonseca, who fell in the struggle, and, de facto, to answer the rightist involvement in the demonstration of 8,000-10,000 to greet the archbishop of Managua that had occurred a few days earlier.

The FSLN-led government set up a centralized Sandinista army. The leadership had taken the most dependable of the fighters in the militias and the guerrilla units and integrated them as the political-military cadres to carry out the necessary job of building up an effective revolutionary army.

At the same time, it has publicly pledged to build broad-based militias. These volunteer forces will be based in the workplaces and will receive professional training.

The organization of the CDSs (Sandinista Defense Committees) and the unions has continued. The nationalization of the banks was followed by the nationalization of the insurance companies. A couple of weeks ago the first imperialist property was hit, with the nationalization of the American- and Canadian-dominated gold and other mines. Housing reconstruction has begun.

The list of accomplishments of the new Nicaraguan government is contained in the resolution, so I won't attempt to repeat everything. But the nationwide literacy drive is especially important, not only as a way of eliminating illiteracy—a precondition to expanded workers' control—but as a means of carrying the revolution to the countryside and forging a link between the peasantry and the government and urban masses. And as a way of educating revolutionary youth about the real life of the rural toilers. It also plays a role in the organization of the defense of the country against counterrevolutionary forces along the Honduran border.

These are not the type of actions that a Council of State dominated by the Chamber of Commerce, the industrialists' organizations, the Catholic hierarchy, and all the bourgeois parties would carry out.

These are not the initial moves of a bourgeois coalition government in a poverty-stricken, devastated country.

These are the moves of a workers and farmers government.

One thing must be very clear. Recognizing that a regime is a workers and farmers government is not a matter of praising it or pinning a medal on it. It's not to give it moral credit, if anyone is so arrogant as to believe that can be given from outside. It's not to express certainty that it is foreordained under all circumstances to expropriate the bourgeoisie and become a workers state. It's to recognize a tendency and a fact, in order better to learn from it and throw our weight in the scales to help the revolutionary leadership move it forward.

There can be a workers and farmers government where an objective analysis of the facts would lead to pessimistic conclusions about its capacity to move forward to mobilize the masses to expropriate the exploiters and more and more directly govern. But in any case, it's important to recognize the fact of the existence of a workers and farmers government.

The workers and farmers government in Nicaragua had its origin in a movement with a radical antidictatorial and anti-imperialist political program. The new government has not yet proclaimed the revolution to be socialist but it has spoken more clearly in class terms than the Cuban leadership did for the first nine months of the Cuban revolution.

The FSLN-led government came to power as a result of popular mass struggle, culminating in a civil war. The FSLN was resolute in combating bourgeois armed power, in disarming it, in calling for the masses to arm themselves, and in organizing a revolutionary army to defend the conquests of the masses. It has organized and mobilized the CDSs, the unions, the youth and women's organizations, the agricultural workers, and opened a war on illiteracy in a determined drive to crush counterrevolution and to educate the toilers to govern.

The tendency of the new government is not to attack the masses. Its tendency is to respond to the masses and their initiatives to move forward.

Capacity and tendency

The determination that the new government is a workers and farmers government is not made by measuring the extent of the nationalizations, or the scope of the remaining problems and difficulties, which are very real. As Joe Hansen put it in reference to Cuba nineteen years ago, such a determination is made by the government's "tendency to respond to popular pressures for action against the bourgeoisie and their agents, and its capacity, for whatever immediate reasons and with whatever hesitancy, to undertake measures against bourgeois political power and against bourgeois property relations.

"The extent of these measures," Joe said, "is not decisive in determining the nature of the regime. What is decisive is the capacity and tendency"—as shown by its *deeds*.[10]

Beginning the week of the insurrection, up to the actions it took last week, this new government has acted in just this way. There is no bourgeois coalition government that has acted like this, or *could* act like this.

Confrontations down the road

This is neither a bourgeois government nor yet a proletarian government. It's a workers and farmers government in a country in which bourgeois property and social relations weigh heavily.

Such a situation is inherently unstable. Class confrontations will arise that will be decisive in determining which way the process will develop. As each one arises, the government throws its weight to resolving it in a proletarian direction—toward socialism—or in a bourgeois direction toward reversing the toilers' gains. So far the direction in Nicaragua has been unambiguous.

Making this characterization involves a recognition that further decisive challenges for the FSLN are down the road. The same was true in Algeria—our recognition that the Ben Bella regime became a workers and farmers government did not imply a guarantee that the FLN (National Liberation Front) would lead the socialist revolution to victory. The same characterization of the Cuban government after the summer of 1959 also did not mean placing confidence in the July 26 Movement, at that stage, to lead the process to culmination in socialist revolution. The Fidelistas at that point did not even claim to be socialist. They denied they were Marxists at the time the government became a workers and farmers government.[11]

The process in Nicaragua will either go forward to the establishment of a workers state or backward to the overthrow of the workers and farmers government and the consolidation of a bourgeois government and the capitalist state. This government will support and lead the masses to establish a workers state or it will be eroded, weakened, and overthrown.

But this fact—that the key conflicts will be between the masses and the remaining bastions of capitalist power—does not obviate the fact that the class character of the government is crucial. Its weight in the coming struggles will be decisive. The government is a government that is supported by the masses—and correctly so. It is seen by them as a government that acts in their interests, that can help them move forward. This is a correct perception, not a wrong perception.

Cuba 1959–Nicaragua 1979

It's instructive to compare the new Nicaraguan government to the provisional revolutionary government that was formed in Cuba in January 1959, before the establishment of a workers and peasants government. Even those of us who went through the early Cuban experience tend to telescope in our memory the different stages.

The situation in Cuba in the first part of 1959 was, in certain ways, a situation of dual power.[12] But not primarily dual power on a military level. In fact, if we were just referring to two opposed military powers, there wasn't much dual power, because the Rebel Army was controlled by the July 26 Movement.

The duality was not on the military level, but between two genuine conflicting *political* powers. The government, in which sovereignty and legitimacy on that level resided, acted as a political power, whose course was not in the same direction as the course that began to be charted by the July 26 Movement. The two courses more and more diverged from each other. More and more, the government majority—President Manuel Urrutia, many ministers, the judiciary—became an *antagonist* of the leadership of the revolution, both within the government and without, not one of the *components* of the revolution.

To a large degree, then, you had what could genuinely be called dual power, which was solved by the action of the masses and reflected on the governmental level. You don't resolve dual power like this simply by removal of some ministers. The removal of the bourgeois ministers was the reflection of a change in the class character of the government and the class relationship of forces in the country.

What was the real situation in Cuba? At first, the police were virtually unpurged. The first purge of the police didn't happen until the summer and fall of 1959.

The judiciary was relatively unpurged too. It was *used* by the bourgeoisie to block agrarian reform measures and other changes. While a dual judicial system existed for the few weeks necessary to try the Batista torturers and murderers, the first purge of the judiciary didn't come until November 1959, and then a second one came later. In Nicaragua the FSLN has prevented the emergence of an independent judiciary that can block revolutionary decisions in spite of the fact that this was called for in the pre–July 19 agreements. Many judicial matters are handled by the FSLN-controlled Ministry of the Interior.

The militia in Cuba was not even proposed until late October 1959. It was set up in the next three months with no effective military training, as Fidel Castro later pointed out, and that was changed only after the Bay of Pigs.[13]

G-2, the secret police, was not in the hands of the July 26 Movement until June 1959, when Ramiro Valdés took over command from a bourgeois army officer. INRA (National Institute of Agrarian Reform) was not even set up until the end of May or beginning of June. There were no July 26–led union organizing efforts until the end of May, when the Humanist Workers Front was set up. There was no union organizing in the countryside until after that, with the setting up of the union structures by INRA.

There was no equivalent of the CDSs, because the victory over Batista did not result from a mass urban insurrection. There was no equivalent to the organization of the CST (Sandinista Workers Federation) and the ATC (Rural Workers Association). There was no equivalent to the immediate launching of a mass women's organization, or of the organization of a revolutionary youth organization. And the last major bourgeois minister, Rufo López-Fresquet, was not even purged until February 1960—many months after a workers and farmers government had come into existence in Cuba.

These differences between the early period of the Cuban revolution and the new Nicaraguan revolution do not mean the FSLN is "better" than the Castro team. No. What these differences mean is that in Cuba there was a real conflict, with a real bourgeois coalition government, facing another power center—the revolutionary armed forces, increasingly backed by mass mobilizations. This contradiction and conflict was resolved between June and October 1959.

This is the opposite of the reality in Nicaragua today.

Character of the FSLN leadership
On the question of the character of the FSLN and our attitude toward it.

They have one great advantage over the Cubans of 1959—they stand on the shoulders of the Cubans.

Their heritage is not just Sandinista, not just anti-imperialist. They were trained, molded, and even carried out faction fights in a framework of looking to the Cubans as the leadership of a Marxist current the Sandinistas were part of.

One cannot read the speeches of FSLN leaders like Carlos Fonseca[14]—speeches in the late 1960s and early 1970s, which have been published and are now circulated in Nicaragua—without seeing the difference in how the FSLN posed class questions, as compared to the positions of the early July 26 Movement.

The FSLN leaders have proven themselves to be revolutionists. They not only responded to pressure from the masses but they seized the opportunity created by the masses, took power, and have led the way forward.

The coming task will *not* be establishing a workers and farmers government. It will be to use this governmental power in dealing definitively with the economic and political power of the bourgeoisie when it is used to obstruct the revolution. In the countryside, this power is symbolized by ownership of cotton and coffee, and in the cities, by bourgeois ownership and control in industry and commerce.

There will be no way of avoiding this confrontation because the bourgeoisie will begin to react to incursions on its prerogatives. *This* is what the confrontation will be about.

Of course, the difficulties facing the revolution are great. The extent of bourgeois ownership, its strength in the countryside, its positions of influence not only in these areas but through its connections, especially international monetary connections, with its imperialist allies are real. The bourgeoisie also wields a certain amount of de facto, day-to-day, decision-making power through technocrats and in the economic ministries.

At the same time, terrible austerity has been forced upon the FSLN-led toilers by the devastation they inherited from Somozaism and imperialism. It would be false, however, to deduce from these objective difficulties facing the revolution that it will be halted or fail. Not at all. It will be the mobilization and organization of the masses, and the capacities of the leadership, that will determine which way the coming conflicts will be resolved.

Neither the imperialists nor the Nicaraguan bourgeoisie are orchestrated by Alfonso Robelo or anyone else. The current tactics that imperialism and the "anti-Somoza" national bourgeoisie are using are not permanent. The tactics they try at any one time are one thing. The coming conflicts, in which there will be uncontrolled elements, are another.

The masses will have a decisive say in these confrontations as well. They will respond. They have joined and are building their mass organizations to respond to challenges from the capitalists. They've been taught by their leaders that this is the purpose of their mass organizations, and they will attempt to use them to further their own class interests. Their actions can even go beyond what the FSLN thinks is possible. The last time this happened, in the insurrection, the FSLN itself responded to the masses.

It is important not to misjudge the stage of the revolution, and therefore misjudge the tasks before it. The government is not the center of bourgeois power, opposed to a center of power of the toilers. To the contrary, the government, as shown by its actions, is *in harmony with*, not *in opposition to*, the proletarian direction and tendency of the leadership of what Lenin called a real peoples' revolution.

It is this very fact that poses the following alternative: Either the bourgeoisie must change the government or its economic power will progressively be crushed and a workers state established.

If you have the wrong position on the government, if you think the new Nicaraguan government is more or less the kind of government that existed in Cuba the first six months of 1959, if you think that kind of conflict is the central contradiction, then you will be wrong on the timing, pace, and ultimately the tasks of the Nicaraguan revolution. You misjudge the leadership; you misorient our members. An increasingly sectarian stance is bred.

Revolutionary Cuba and the coming confrontation
A factor that will be decisive to the future of this government is how Cuba will respond to conflicts and confrontations down

the road. Those who, unlike me, are pessimistic on this score should feel even more obligated to throw everything into mobilizing defense of the Nicaraguan revolution, because what Nicaragua will face will be awesome if this pessimistic view is correct.

We are being tested in these events like everyone else.

We believe the stakes in Nicaragua are enormous. What is being fought out now is whether or not the socialist revolution in the hemisphere that opened with the Cuban victory will be extended and the second workers state in the Americas will be consolidated.

A positive outcome of this struggle will have a gigantic impact on Central America, on the Caribbean, on Latin America, on North America. It is inconceivable that this could happen without attempts by Yankee imperialism to stop it from occurring. Regardless of what tactics they use, they will not simply sit back and allow that to occur. Although they are not in good shape given the world relationship of class forces today, the exact political shape they will be in when this showdown happens will be decided in struggle.

We must assume, as the Nicaraguans assume, as the Cubans assume, that the showdown stage of the revolution, which could coincide with the struggle for power in other parts of Central America, will be met by the power of Washington. And in this conflict, Cuban aid will be extremely important.

I'm convinced that the Cubans will come to the defense of Nicaragua when it comes to a confrontation, even war, with American imperialism. I'm absolutely convinced that not only are the masses of Cuba ready to die for Nicaragua, but that the Castro leadership will respond decisively to any U.S. use of military force. I believe they will do this no matter what Moscow's position is.

The fates of the Cuban and Nicaraguan revolutions are now intertwined. It's too late to separate them. And their intertwining extends toward Grenada, and could encompass El Salvador and Guatemala in the future.

It's important—as the Cubans insist—to recognize that this

relation is not a one-way street.

If Nicaragua moves toward greater workers democracy, and forms of workers participating in governing, toward further development of mass organizations, this will have a powerful impact on Cuba.

If the socialist revolution is extended, it will deepen the revolutionary spirit and atmosphere in Cuba. And if the Cubans have to come to the aid of the Nicaraguans in such an international showdown, it will affect the relationship of class forces on a world scale. It will deeply affect the class struggle in the United States. Because any showdown like this will pose the question of war or peace to the American working class. It will test whether we are correct in what we say about the depth of the antiwar attitudes among American workers.

It will also mean a total new shake-up favorable to building a world movement of socialist revolution.

If a defeat takes place, the consequences will also be enormous.

We're convinced that the stakes are high in Central America. We're convinced that regardless of the exact timing, a showdown cannot be avoided. It must be assumed that imperialism will intervene, and it must be assumed that Cuba will respond. And we must act on that assumption.

This helps explain the deep-going internationalism of the Nicaraguan leadership.

Building a world revolutionary party

How can we use this opening, meet this responsibility, which the emergence of a new levy of revolutionists onto the world scene offers, to build the world party of socialist revolution?

This is not a new question for us. It's one we've been grappling with and acting on since the emergence of the Castro leadership, an anti-Stalinist revolutionary leadership, two decades ago. But the victory of the Sandinistas marks a major extension of what Joe Hansen—in his 1967 preface to *Che Guevara Speaks*—pointed to as "the rise of a generation of revolutionary fighters . . . effective leader[s], committed to the socialist goal, whose outlook converged more and more with the classical revolutionary Marxist tradition that stood behind the October 1917 Russian Revolution."[15]

What does this mean for our movement? How must we respond to this opportunity?

We place ourselves with the FSLN leaders, with the militants, with the workers, on the road to reconstructing Nicaragua, to the expropriation of the bourgeoisie and the defeat of imperialism and to the extension of the revolution. That's our common road with them—the elimination of bourgeois power and the defeat of imperialism. Within that common framework we learn, we present our ideas, we apply our program.

Here there is a big difference between the majority resolution and the one I am reporting for. The differences are not mainly about the objective contradictions the revolution faces, on which the two resolutions agree. It's recognizing where the government and where the masses are in the revolutionary process, the character of the leadership, what that means about the coming confrontations, and how we act as part and parcel of that process.

The Fourth International must turn outward toward the Nicaraguan revolution and its revolutionary leadership, away from responding to sectarian pressures, away from narrow preoccupations. If we write a single word in a single resolution because some sectarian accuses us of "liquidating" or not wanting to build a party, that's a betrayal, a dereliction of our duty as revolutionists. We say what we have to say about the Nicaraguan revolution not to answer sectarians, not to cover ourselves in case the FSLN doesn't measure up to its historic responsibilities—and they have measured up just fine so far—but in order to train the cadres of the International as part of the vanguard of the workers of the world on how to move in a situation like this to join with other revolutionists in building an international current capable of moving toward a real mass world party of socialist revolution.

This means approaching this leadership as fellow revolutionists, as fellow revolutionary leaders, who are proving themselves in action and correctly expect us to do the same where we have forces. It means reversing the dangerously sectarian, and ignorant, underestimation of the Castro leadership. It means gladly accepting, rather than resisting, when a chance presents itself not to swim against the stream.

We have to see the Nicaraguan revolution as *our* revolution. *Our* future is deeply involved in the outcome in Nicaragua. It's not just in the United States and Canada, or in Colombia and Mexico, where Nicaragua will have a great amount to do with building the Fourth International, but throughout the entire world.

It was not the Fidelistas or Sandinistas who were riven with sectarian responses to the revolutionary events in Nicaragua—it was the Fourth International. It is not only the Fidelistas and Sandinista leadership who will be tested by the coming events—it is us. They have passed mighty tests; we must recognize this to do so ourselves. If we can do this, if we can *learn* from living revolutions, if we can *act* as revolutionists when the opportunity arises, we can play an indispensable role in taking another step toward a mass world party of socialist revolution. This is our challenge and this is our opportunity—the greatest since the founding of the Fourth International.

- Educating for communism
- Fighting U.S. embargo against Cuba
- Uprooting apartheid in South Africa
- Defending abortion rights
- Protesting police brutality
- Origins and impact of world economic crisis
- Supporting trade union struggles

From defending the socialist revolution in Cuba to opposing imperialist war, from struggles for union rights to the "culture war," the *Militant* takes the side of workers and working farmers around the world. News and analysis each week of major developments in world politics, economics, and workers conflicts in the U.S.A.

The Changing Face of U.S. Politics

Working-Class Politics and the Trade Unions
BY JACK BARNES

A book for the new generation of workers entering the mines, mills, and factories throughout the world, and for all young fighters against war, racial discrimination, cop brutality, and assaults on women's rights.

It explains how workers can build the kind of party needed to lead struggles that can transform trade unions into a revolutionary social movement against all forms of capitalist oppression and exploitation.

Reports by Jack Barnes and resolutions of the Socialist Workers Party examine the process of building such a revolutionary workers party in today's world of economic depression, deepening trade conflicts, antiunion assaults, and increasing pressure on workers' rights and individual liberties. Now in new, expanded edition. $19.95

MINERS ON STRIKE AT BUCK CREEK COAL, SULLIVAN, INDIANA, MAY 1993

FROM PATHFINDER. SEE ADDRESSES ON PAGE 2

NICARAGUA:

HOW THE WORKERS AND FARMERS

GOVERNMENT CAME TO POWER

T HE PRIMARY PURPOSE of the following theses is to clarify (1) the class character of the Nicaraguan government today, and (2) why the Nicaraguan revolution and the evolution of the Sandinista National Liberation Front are central to our strategic task of building the world party of socialist revolution necessary to lead the toilers in the overthrow of world capitalism.

1. Between late May and July 19, 1979, deep-going popular insurrections in the main cities of Nicaragua—prepared by the Sandinista National Liberation Front and coordinated with an FSLN military offensive—toppled the U.S.-backed dictatorship of Anastasio Somoza. The victory was the culmination of two months of general strikes and armed uprisings in the cities by the workers, semiproletarian masses, youth, and sectors of the petty bourgeoisie; land occupations and other mobilizations by the poor peasants and agricultural laborers in the rural districts; and stepped-up guerrilla operations and a concerted military drive by the FSLN.

These were the motor forces of the climactic stage in the struggle against the dictatorship and U.S. imperialism. They gave the revolution a powerful anticapitalist impulse.

This resolution was adopted by the National Committee of the Socialist Workers Party on January 5, 1980.

The final year of the revolutionary struggle was marked by widespread organization of the masses in neighborhood committees and self-defense units, as well as by increased organization in workplaces and the countryside. This occurred both on the initiative of the FSLN and spontaneously in response to the worsening living conditions and brutal repression under Somoza. In addition, as the final struggle gathered momentum the ranks of the FSLN's military units were swelled by thousands of young workers, poor peasants, students, the unemployed, and radicalized petty-bourgeois forces. This included many Latin Americans from other countries who joined the fight against Somozaism and Yankee imperialism.

As one city after another was liberated from Somoza's National Guard under the combined blows of FSLN units and popular insurrections, Civil Defense Committees (CDCs) and militias organized military defense and took over such vital tasks in the neighborhoods as food distribution, health care, sanitation, and the dispensation of justice to Somozaist torturers. Sandinista Workers Defense Committees (CDTS) arose in some factories and workplaces, the nuclei of what was to become the Sandinista Workers Federation (CST). Other mass organizations—the women's group AMPRONAC (later to become the Association of Nicaraguan Women), the Rural Workers Association (ATC), the July 19 Sandinista Youth, the teachers union (ANDEN)—also got their start in the period before and during the insurrection.

Alongside this intervention of the toiling masses and development of proletarian forms of organization, the bourgeois forces opposed to Somoza underwent a process of disintegration. Most desperately sought a compromise with the dictatorship while some belatedly threw in their lot with the insurrection. This sharp shift in the relationship of class forces is a key factor in explaining the dynamics of the socialist revolution now unfolding in Nicaragua.

Triumph over Somoza

2. Following Somoza's flight on July 17, the disintegration of

the National Guard accelerated. His stand-in, Francisco Urcu-yo, had promised to transfer power to a five-person junta of the Government of National Reconstruction (GRN). This was supposed to pave the way for the integration of some National Guard units into the new army and the appointment of a bourgeois-dominated Council of State. The formation of this junta and its responsibilities had been announced July 9 in Costa Rica as part of the post-Somoza governmental program agreed to by the FSLN and some of the bourgeois opposition forces.

With U.S. support, however, Urcuyo attempted to hold on to state power and demanded the FSLN lay down its arms. This provoked the final FSLN push on Managua and a popular mass uprising there in which Somoza's "bunker" was captured and tens of thousands of weapons were seized and distributed. The GRN program had stated that the new army would incorporate "soldiers and officers who demonstrated honest and patriotic conduct" and were not guilty of "corruption, repression, [and] crimes against the people." But the section of Somoza's National Guard that did not escape to Honduras scattered under the impact of the mass insurrection.

The revolutionary triumph over Somozaism was thus a sweeping one, in which large sections of the previous state apparatus—in particular, the entire repressive apparatus—were dismantled and replaced, resolving the situation of dual power that had developed in Nicaragua in the final weeks prior to Somoza's fall. As a result, a well-trained professional Sandinista army is beginning to be built entirely around a cadre of FSLN guerrillas and militia fighters.

The triumph in Managua, following that in other main cities, achieved with organized mass participation and by revolutionary means, established both the FSLN's leadership authority among the masses and its decisive political decision-making power. The contrast during the drive to victory between the courage and dedication of the Sandinistas and the hesitations and maneuvers of the bourgeois opposition did not go unnoticed in the working-class neighborhoods or in the countryside. It had a profound impact on the consciousness of FSLN militants and leaders and on the political course they have followed.

3. It soon became obvious that the new governing power—the way in which important decisions of state were actually being made and implemented—was qualitatively different from the bourgeois coalition government projected in the July 9 GRN program and the Fundamental Statute decreed July 20.

The five-person junta that replaced Somoza took the form of a coalition of three FSLN leaders with two figures from the bourgeois opposition.[1] This was similar to the form taken by the junta's cabinet of ministers: several of the initial appointees were FSLN leaders (e.g., interior, agrarian reform, and social welfare), while others—including the head of the Central Bank—were bourgeois figures, usually serving alongside FSLN vice-ministers.

But this is not the totality of the actual government. In fact, the key elements of the new state structure fall outside the framework promised in the July 9 program of the GRN.

The government itself includes the FSLN leadership, the Sandinista armed forces, as well as the Nicaraguan Institute of Agrarian Reform and to some extent the mass organizations led by the FSLN.

The GRN program stipulated the appointment of a Council of State. This body was to "share legislative powers" with the junta, draw up drafts of a new constitution and electoral law, appoint the judiciary, and have the power to veto, with a two-thirds vote, decisions taken by the junta.

By agreement prior to the Managua insurrection, the Council of State was to be composed of thirty-three representatives from the bourgeois opposition parties, the chambers of commerce and industry and other capitalist organs, the Catholic Church hierarchy, the FSLN, trade unions, and other groups. Its proposed composition guaranteed bourgeois domination. For its part the FSLN was to have had somewhere in the range of six members. The Nicaraguan capitalists and imperialism counted on the

ENDNOTES FOR THIS ARTICLE BEGIN ON PAGE 306.

council to serve as a brake on the social and economic measures instituted following Somoza's downfall and to be the institution that exercises sovereignty. It was to draft a bourgeois constitution according to which a bourgeois judicial system, headed by a Supreme Court, would block "unconstitutional" inroads on property and other "normal" bourgeois prerogatives.

IN THE FIRST WEEKS following July 19 it was widely assumed that the Council of State would be rapidly installed. A tentative convocation date of September 15 was even announced. But that date came and went, and amid growing agitation by bourgeois forces for the convocation of the Council of State, the junta announced October 22 that convocation of the council was being postponed until May 4, 1980. In the intervening months it was to be "restructured" to provide representation above all to the new mass organizations—the CDSs, CST, ATC, women's association, Sandinista youth, etc. These organizations, with FSLN backing, have launched a campaign demanding the Council of State be a council of toilers dominated by CDS representation and that of other mass organizations.

The postponement and proposed restructuring of the Council of State represents one of the major results on the governmental level so far of the dramatic shift in the relationship of class forces as the revolutionary process has deepened in Nicaragua.

Nothing has been done to begin drafting a bourgeois constitution to provide legitimacy to capitalist rule. Instead, in late August the junta decreed a Statute on the Rights of Nicaraguans that not only guarantees basic political freedoms such as speech, press, and assembly, but also women's equality and the priority of the social and economic rights of the toilers over the property and prerogatives of the capitalists.[2]

Furthermore, the entire judicial system was purged, and while a Supreme Court has been appointed, as described in the GRN program, its functions are limited to matters such as divorce cases.

In addition, some ministries initially headed by bourgeois figures had no fundamental decision-making authority. The most striking example of this was the Ministry of Defense, nominally headed by ex–National Guard colonel Bernardino Larios (who led a coup attempt against Somoza in 1978 and later fled to Panama). Larios had no authority whatsoever over the Sandinista People's Army (EPS), which since its formation has been firmly under the command of the Sandinista Front. The commander in chief of the EPS, FSLN leader Humberto Ortega, was named not by Larios or even by the GRN junta but rather by the FSLN Joint National Directorate. (The decision was later ratified by the junta.)

In late December Larios was replaced by Humberto Ortega as part of a broad governmental reorganization. (Ortega remains commander in chief.) Not once during his brief term in office did Larios issue a statement, hold a news conference, or appear at a public event.

The reorganized Ministry of Defense will oversee all the Sandinista armed forces. The Sandinista People's Militias are to be greatly expanded, under the direction of newly named Vice-Minister of Defense Edén Pastora ("Commander Zero").[3] The Sandinista National Police, constructed from the bottom up out of young Sandinista fighters, falls under the Ministry of the Interior, headed by FSLN commander Tomás Borge.

The Ministry of Planning was initially headed by bourgeois technocrat Roberto Mayorga. He has now been displaced by FSLN commander Henry Ruiz, who explained upon taking the post that the planning ministry "is the key to the present situation, and the FSLN National Directorate has thought it necessary to assign a member of the Directorate to this post." Ruiz will oversee implementation of the 1980 Plan for Economic Reactivation, which represents the new government's initial steps toward economic planning.

In the field of agriculture all major decisions and policy statements have been made and implemented by the Nicaraguan Institute of Agrarian Reform (INRA), headed by FSLN commander Jaime Wheelock. Modeled after Cuba's INRA, this agency was not mentioned in the GRN's July 9 program or the Fundamental Statute.

INRA, which has branches in every province of the country, was consolidated at the end of December under the revamped Ministry of Agricultural Development, which Wheelock was appointed to head (retaining the post of INRA director). The first minister of agricultural development, a landowner appointed in July, had been in a similar position to that of defense minister Larios.

The FSLN's National Directorate functions as a source and wielder of governing power outside the terms of the GRN accord. This was politically codified on September 1, 1979, when, during a military parade and rally to spur construction of the EPS, the nine members of the National Directorate were proclaimed Commanders of the Revolution, that is, of the entire process and not simply of the army or the formal government. During this initial stage of the revolution, it is the Commanders of the Revolution—not the bourgeoisie operating through the Council of State as they had planned—who have played the decisive role governing together with the Sandinista-dominated junta.

THE RISING IMPORTANCE of new mass organizations and especially of the CDSs (none of which were contemplated in the GRN program) is among the most outstanding of the post-liberation developments. It is on the expansion and consolidation of the CDSs, the unions of workers and peasants, the other mass organizations, and the Sandinista army, that the authority of the FSLN is largely based. To varying degrees, all of these are already taking on decision-making and administrative functions at the workplace, farm, neighborhood, and municipal levels. By the end of 1979, provincewide coordination of the CDSs was under way and one national gathering of CDS representatives had already been held. Sandinista leaders have announced that a delegated CDS congress will be held early in 1980.

So the government that was consolidated soon after Somoza's fall is not that projected by the GRN program.

Social and economic steps

4. The accumulation of progressive social and economic measures in the first months of the revolution demonstrates that the Nicaraguan toilers, under FSLN leadership, have set off down a promising road oriented toward expropriation of the bourgeoisie:

• The new government immediately nationalized the entire Somoza and Somozaist assets in agriculture, real estate, banking, industry, commerce, transport, fishing fleets, shipyard and port equipment, and communications media property.

• It nationalized all domestic banking and imposed strict controls on foreign banks. This is a necessary first step toward channeling resources, directing them to expanding education, housing, hospitals and other such needs, and initiating measures of economic planning.

• It launched an extensive agrarian reform on Somozaist land, bringing under state control some 60 percent of the big landholdings currently under cultivation.[4] In collaboration with the ATC, INRA is transforming these haciendas [large agricultural estates] into state farms on which the agricultural laborers will participate in administrative tasks. Peasant cooperatives are being encouraged on the smaller nationalized holdings, and some land redistribution has taken place in response to the demands of peasants with tiny plots. Debt foreclosure on the farms of small proprietors has been abolished.

• The government took control over all export trade of agricultural cash commodities such as cotton, coffee, sugar, beef, and fish. A state monopoly (ENABAS) has been established for the purchase and sale of all grains and agrochemical products. Similar state monopolies have been set up for the purchase and sale of all other major crops (coffee, cotton, sugar, etc.).[5]

• While pledging to renegotiate and honor Nicaragua's legitimate foreign debt, the government immediately canceled Somoza's army debts to the Israeli and Argentine governments. It then announced it would study carefully all other debts contracted by the dictatorship to determine which ones were illegitimate—that is, had been arranged through corrupt dealings or had simply wound up in private Somocista bank accounts abroad. Meanwhile, given the virtually empty treasury left by Somoza, the new government has declared a de facto moratorium on interest and repayment.

• It nationalized the essential means of land, sea, and air transport. The television system and several of the radio networks have been expropriated and are being used by the FSLN to present its views to the population. The Sandinista daily, *Barricada*, is produced in the plant that previously printed the Somozaist newspaper, *Novedades*.

• It launched programs to reorganize and upgrade education, health care, social security, and other social services.

• The government issued a radical currency reform measure that—under the slogan "Let's take back from Somozaism the money that belongs to the people"—stopped Somozaists or other businessmen abroad from exchanging their córdobas for dollars held inside Nicaragua. All 500 and 1,000 córdoba notes were withdrawn and investigations were begun into many large holdings. This measure helped slow the devaluation of the córdoba and combat capitalist economic sabotage. Deposits under 3,000 córdobas were returned within a few days of the measure; at the end of October, following registration of the bank notes, the government began redeeming the certificates of deposit issued to holders of the notes inside Nicaragua.

• It has adopted an outspoken anti-imperialist stance on vital world political questions such as Indochina, the Mideast, southern Africa, and Carter's war moves against Cuba, the Caribbean, and Central America. The outpouring of more than thirty thousand in Managua to greet Vietnamese premier Pham Van Dong, one of the largest mass demonstrations since the revolutionary victory, was a big blow to the imperialist campaign to isolate Vietnam as an international pariah. U.S. imperialism was condemned for its aggression during the "Soviet brigade" crisis.[6]

Following the October military coup in El Salvador, Moscow was quick to approve the new Washington-backed regime, signaling to the imperialists its willingness to help preserve capitalist stability in the area. The Nicaraguan government, along with the Cuban, refused to do so.

• The new government has continued its efforts to construct a centralized professional army to defend the revolutionary conquests against imperialism, the Somozaist forces, and other class enemies both inside Nicaragua and beyond its borders.

• Having integrated most of the militia fighters into the EPS and Sandinista Police, FSLN leaders have announced their intention to strengthen and reorganize a volunteer national militia on the basis of regular training in the workplace and in high schools and universities. Weapons are to be kept in the factories and controlled by the *milicianos*.

• After decades of tyrannical rule under which even the most elementary bourgeois-democratic liberties were ground into the dust, there has been an enormous expansion of democratic rights, including institutions of workers' democracy, fostered by the new government. The CDSs and other popular bodies operate on the basis of democratic elections. The bill of rights guarantees not only basic freedoms such as speech, press, and assembly, but also the right to unionize and strike and to "organize political parties or groups, or to belong to them." The FSLN has strengthened the Sandinista-led CST trade union federation in political competition with the old union federations led by the Stalinists, Christian Democrats, and bourgeois business-unionists closely linked to the U.S. AFL-CIO bureaucracy. Workers have held democratic assemblies to choose their leaders and decide which federation to affiliate with; this has often resulted in unions previously part of one of the old federations joining the CST.

• The agrarian reform has also included "interventions" (that is, takeovers short of outright nationalization) of some lands owned by members of the bourgeois anti-Somoza opposition. Since there is a top priority on raising crops for food and vital foreign exchange, this most often targets landlords who refuse to cultivate their land.

• There have been further nationalizations and interventions; again including properties of "anti-Somozaist" capitalists. These have been carried out on the basis of economic need or because of illegitimate or antilabor operations by the owners. All insurance companies were nationalized in mid-October. This complements the nationalizations of the banks by giving the government further control over the flow of capital and lays the foundation for future economic planning.

• The FSLN is campaigning to organize peasants and rural laborers into the ATC and workers into the CST. In addition, the Sandinistas are taking steps to prepare and extend workers' control over production in the nationalized sectors.

• At the beginning of November, the first major imperialist property was nationalized: the mines. (Domestic holdings in the mining sector were also taken over.) This further strengthens the government control over the country's natural resources and lays the basis for improving the wretched and extremely dangerous conditions under which Nicaragua's miners were forced to work.

• Sharp reductions in housing rents were decreed on December 19. Rents less than $50 a month were cut by 50 percent and those from $50 to $100 a month were cut 60 percent. Rents over $100 a month were also substantially reduced under the new law, which also stipulates that the Ministry of Housing can reduce rents to below 50 percent of their old rates and can take over slum dwellings that have inadequate sanitary conditions.[7]

• Housing reconstruction aid in the devastated popular neighborhoods has been initiated by the government. State control has been applied in housing developments built or operating in violation of real estate and tax laws. The first major public works projects have been initiated in this sector.

• A big increase in pensions and other social benefits to the aged and indigent has been decreed.

• Price controls have been established on basic food items. The government has authorized the CDSs to operate as price committees to enforce their control, and the CDSs in the big open-air markets of Managua have taken the lead in this task.

• An enormous nationwide drive has been launched to wipe

out illiteracy, a problem that is prevalent throughout Nicaragua but especially widespread among the rural population. All students above the sixth-grade level are to be mobilized in this "crusade for literacy," and the country's schools are to be shut down for four months so that these students and all teachers can fully participate. Material, technical, and personnel aid is coming from Cuba for this campaign, which is being explicitly modeled on the way that country wiped out illiteracy in the early 1960s. As that experience showed, such a literacy drive is an important aid to firmly winning the poor peasantry to the side of the revolution and defending it against counterrevolution.

Workers and peasants government

5. The FSLN-led government, based on Nicaragua's proletarian, semiproletarian, peasant, and radicalized petty-bourgeois masses, has initiated deep-going inroads against capitalist property in agriculture, industry, and finance. It has launched an ambitious program of social and cultural betterment for the Nicaraguan toilers. It has begun to construct a new armed power through the EPS and Sandinista Police. Its radical policies have helped the FSLN spur the development of proletarian organizations through the CDSs, the trade unions, and other mass organizations. It has continued to foster mass mobilizations. The latest—a November 7 demonstration to honor FSLN founder Carlos Fonseca Amador—brought over 100,000 people into the streets of Managua. It was the largest outpouring since Somoza's fall.

The structures and direction of development established through all these measures indicate that this new regime has not only broken the armed might of the bourgeoisie; it has displaced the *political* power of the capitalists, taken decisive steps to block the establishment of a bourgeois government, and refused to subordinate the interests of the exploited to the bourgeoisie's needs either nationally or internationally.

All this points to the conclusion that the Sandinista-led regime in Nicaragua is neither definitively bourgeois nor proletarian at this time. It is a *workers and peasants government*, of the kind described in the Transitional Program as "a government independent of the bourgeoisie"[8] and at the Fourth Congress of the Communist International as a government that is born out of "the struggle of the masses themselves . . . based on working-class organizations that are suited for combat and formed by the broadest layers of the oppressed working masses."[9]

By recognizing the new government in Nicaragua as a workers and peasants government, we signify:

a. its origin in an antidictatorial and anti-imperialist movement with a radical political program;

b. its coming to power as the result of a popular mass struggle, culminating in a civil war and tumultuous urban insurrections;

c. its resoluteness in combating and disarming the counterrevolution;

d. its tendency to respond by practical measures to popular demands for action against the urban and rural exploiters and against imperialism;

e. the capacity of its leading force, the FSLN, with whatever hesitations and political limitations, to undertake measures against bourgeois political and economic power and prerogatives. The exact stage in the development of these measures is not decisive in determining the class character of the regime; the decisive factor is the capacity and tendency of the leadership to move in this direction.

Combined with these factors is the FSLN's explicit identification of the revolutionary process in Nicaragua with the Cuban workers state, and with the anti-imperialist internationalism of the Castro leadership. Cuba's accomplishments under its social system are repeatedly held up as a model—in speeches, in *Barricada,* and over radio and television.

The Nicaraguan workers and peasants government, despite its many unique features, is similar to the regime described by the Fourth International that arose and governed in Cuba from mid-1959 to late 1960 (when the expropriation of the bourgeoisie and the consolidation of the workers state was completed); and in Algeria from late 1963 to mid-1965 (when Boumédienne ousted Ben Bella and restored a stable capitalist regime). The appearance of governments of this type was foreseen in the "Theses on Tactics" adopted by the Fourth Congress of the Communist International and pointed to by Trotsky in the Transitional Program as a possible forerunner of the establishment of a workers state.

While the Nicaraguan workers and peasants government is politically independent of the bourgeoisie, the latter's economic and social power have so far only been weakened. Remnants of the old state structure remain intact. Bourgeois and petty-bourgeois figures hold governmental posts. Capitalist ownership and control over major sectors of industry, commerce, and agriculture has not been broken, which means the class character of the state remains bourgeois.

If this contradiction between workers and peasants government and bourgeois state is not resolved by a thoroughgoing expropriation of the big imperialist and domestic bourgeoisie and repudiation of the foreign debt, the capitalists—backed up by Washington, international finance organizations, and capitalist regimes in Central and South America—will use their economic positions and growing economic hardships to erode the power of the new government, sabotage economic reconstruction, foster division among the toilers, reconstruct their own political and military power, and reverse the revolutionary process initiated by the Nicaraguan masses led by the FSLN.

Cuba and Nicaragua

6. Although the revolutionary process now under way in Nicaragua bears many resemblances to those which occurred under the workers and peasants governments established in Cuba and Algeria, each of these cases has its own particular characteristics.

In Nicaragua the establishment of a workers and peasants government after the fall of the dictatorship was not preceded by a period of rule by an unstable bourgeois coalition regime.

In Cuba and Algeria, on the other hand, the political power and influence of bourgeois governmental figures at the outset of the revolution was greater than in Nicaragua. As a result, in Cuba and Algeria these bourgeois figures felt more confident in openly resisting or balking at purges of the old state apparatus, in opposing the acceleration of mass mobilizations and the accumulation of radical measures aimed at carrying out the programs of the Cuban July 26 Movement and the Algerian FLN (National Liberation Front).

Thus the transition from a bourgeois coalition government to a workers and peasants government in both Cuba and Algeria was marked by changes in the composition of the government as well as by radical measures and mass mobilizations in support of them. In Cuba Osvaldo Dorticós replaced Manuel Urrutia as president. Che Guevara replaced Felipe Pazos as head of the National Bank, and Cuba's ambassador to Washington, José Miró Cardona, defected. In Algeria Mohammed Khider, Ferhat Abbas, and other bourgeois leaders were successively ousted.

In Nicaragua the initial impact of the deepening revolutionary situation was expressed, on the governmental level, in the decisions taken by the FSLN. In light of the class relationship of forces established by the massive urban insurrections, they decided to postpone and restructure the class composition of the Council of State. They created a governmental setup in which all decisive decision-making power from the outset clearly rested in the FSLN's hands, although bourgeois figures participated. This was different from the very first stages of either the Cuban or Algerian postliberation regimes.

In both the latter countries however, as in Nicaragua, bourgeois figures were still in major government posts at the time that the workers and peasants governments came into being. In Cuba some were not purged until the early 1960s; in Algeria some were never purged.

The acceleration of mass mobilizations and the steady accumulation of anticapitalist measures has certainly met with resistance from the greatly weakened bourgeoisie in Nicaragua. But most Nicaraguan capitalists still fear that an open provocation or head-on confrontation at this time would redound to their detriment. Within the government, bourgeois figures try to use de facto veto—as the relationship of class forces allows—over the most radical measures. At some stage this will pass over into denunciatory resignations or recalcitrant obstructionism that will force the FSLN to remove them.

The more consistently radical course of the new Nicaraguan government from its first day (compared to the bourgeois coalition regimes in either Cuba or Algeria) reflects its different nature. Bourgeois figures in those governments carried out anti-labor measures and openly attempted to block progressive ones. The bourgeois Supreme Court, basing itself on the 1940 constitution, resisted the Castro leadership's land reform. There were attempts from inside the government to reestablish a bourgeois army. Such moves by the bourgeoisie spurred the class confrontations in Cuba that led to the workers and peasants government.

The greater speed of events in Nicaragua is accounted for primarily by the broadly insurrectional character of the victory there. It accelerated the development of mass organizations of the urban and rural toilers on a scale unmatched in Cuba. Because of the dramatic shift in the relationship of class forces created by this massive upsurge, the FSLN took the opportunity, which it had not previously expected, to conduct a preemptive purge of capitalist political power and set off along a course that radically diverged from its earlier agreements with bourgeois forces in the anti-Somoza opposition.

In Algeria, in a number of big ways, the revolutionary process was much less advanced during the workers and farmers government there than in Nicaragua today. For example, mineral, banking, and insurance sectors remained in private hands and the FLN government did not implement radical currency or trade controls of the type already imposed by the FSLN-led government in Nicaragua.

In Cuba the conflict between the workers and peasants government consolidated by late 1959 and the bourgeois state was resolved by August-October 1960 with the establishment of a state foreign-trade monopoly, further agrarian expropriations, and the nationalization of virtually all U.S. and Cuban industry. Despite the absence of a Leninist party, the anticapitalist measures carried out by the revolutionary Castro leadership, relying on mass workers' mobilizations, could not have been rolled back short of a full-scale civil war backed to the hilt by the massive intervention of Yankee imperialism. A workers state had thereby been established.

In Algeria, on the other hand, the revolutionary process initiated in 1963 with the emergence of a workers and peasants government under Ahmed Ben Bella was cut short. Unlike the Castro leadership, Ben Bella responded to pressure from the right and accommodated to the demands of French imperialism. The regime turned away from mass mobilizations and from creating a militia and attempted to slow the tempo of change. The foundations of the workers and peasants government began rotting away. When army commander Houari Boumédienne took advantage of the vacillating leadership and declining mobilizations to stage a coup in June 1965, the Algerian government changed direction and reversed many of the earlier progressive measures. A capitalist government was put in the saddle. The capitalist state was preserved and subsequently reinforced.[10]

IN NICARAGUA THE OUTCOME of this fundamental contradiction between the class character of the workers and peasants government and the capitalist state still hangs in the balance. The designation of Nicaragua today as a workers and peasants government in no way implies that a workers state will automatically be the outcome of the process under way. The big class conflicts that will settle that question still lie ahead. As the workers and peasants press forward to win their demands, the imperialists and Nicaraguan bourgeoisie will strike blows. They will have to be met with counterblows. Each new encroachment against capitalist property and prerogatives will meet stiffening resistance by the reaction. Open breaks will occur within the government and all other Nicaraguan institutions.

A workers and peasants government is by its very nature an unstable and transitory formation: It must either *move forward* to the establishment of a workers state, or—failing to decisively break the economic power of the bourgeoisie—*fall back* and open the way to a reassertion of capitalist political power and reinforcement of the bourgeois state. How this unstable situation will be resolved in Nicaragua depends in large part on how well the FSLN responds to the initiatives of the masses and succeeds in educating, organizing, and mobilizing them. They will have to defeat the counterrevolutionary threats. And they must be prepared to face the eventuality of direct U.S. military intervention aimed at preventing the triumph of a second workers state in the Western Hemisphere.

7. The FSLN was formed at the beginning of the 1960s under the impact of the socialist revolution in Cuba. It was able to tap the popular tradition of radical anti-imperialist struggle symbolized by Augusto César Sandino's rebel peasant and worker army in the 1920s and early 1930s.[11]

From its origins, the FSLN was shaped by its strong identification with the experience and Marxist evolution of the Castro-Guevara team and the Cuban revolution. While of similar social composition to the July 26 Movement, it started out with an advantage—the ability to learn from the example of the Cuban workers state and from the further political evolution, experiences, and false starts of the Castro leadership team. In addition, many FSLN cadres were recruited out of the worldwide youth radicalization of the 1960s and early 1970s and gave more serious consideration to Marxist ideas, including those of Lenin and Trotsky, than the early cadres of the July 26 Movement.

Under the impact of the defeats its guerrilla units suffered in the 1960s and the dramatic growth of the urban proletarian and semiproletarian population in the 1960s and the early 1970s, a discussion developed in the FSLN over an assessment of its guerrilla strategy. This led in 1975 to a division into three tendencies that later became three separate public factions. Their differences reflected debates over the relation of armed struggle and mass mobilizations, the respective roles of the urban and rural toilers, the relation between military and political struggle, and the purpose and acceptable limits of pacts with the opposition bourgeoisie.

In the final analysis, these differences boiled down to contending points of view around a decisive question: *How to topple Somoza and throw off imperialist domination of Nicaragua.* The answer was to be given in practice before the decade was over.

The POLITICAL CONTENT of these debates reflected the ripening objective conditions for the overthrow of Somoza and contributed to the overall political education and development of all three tendencies. Challenged to meet the responsibilities posed by accelerating revolutionary developments, the tendencies reached agreement on unity in action in June 1978 and reunified in December of that year. Their leadership bodies fused and old divisions in the ranks broke down, as the tasks posed by the rising class struggle resolved in life many previously disputed questions.

The FSLN leadership was profoundly affected by the largely unanticipated scope and power of the 1978-79 urban mobilizations and by the spread of popular committees and militias—sometimes at the initiative of the FSLN, often through spontaneous mass emulation. The revolutionary process gave a powerful thrust toward bypassing the bourgeois coalition government that the FSLN had, on the eve of the insurrection, considered inevitable.

The actual course of the insurrection caused the FSLN to move in an increasingly anticapitalist direction. This course has demonstrated the FSLN's will and capacity to learn from and react to the actions and aspirations of the workers and peasants. Relying on the organization and mobilization of the masses, the FSLN has led the process that has brought a workers and peasants government into being. This is consistent with its efforts to learn from the Cuban experience.

By learning from the example of the Cuban revolution and

Castro leadership, the FSLN bypassed Stalinism and social democracy and has been able to carry out an intransigent and victorious struggle against Somoza and his imperialist backers,
opening the door to the fight for the second workers state in
the Americas.

The advances already registered under the leadership of the
FSLN, like the July 26 Movement victory in Cuba twenty years
ago, constitute a blow to world Stalinism. The central founder
of the FSLN, Carlos Fonseca Amador, broke from the Partido
Socialista Nicaragüense (PSN), the Nicaraguan Stalinist party,
and the FSLN was built in opposition to the PSN. By bypassing
the Stalinists *in action,* the FSLN further deflated the Stalinists'
claim to be the only current ever to stand at the head of revolutionary mass upsurges. And by unyielding struggle at the head
of the insurrectionary proletarian and plebeian masses, the
Sandinistas provided in practice a living alternative to the Stalinist line of "two-stage" revolution in which the interests of the
toilers are subordinated to the interests of the bourgeoisie.
Thus, the FSLN-led revolution in Nicaragua has strengthened
the revolutionary current within the workers' movement internationally and has shifted the relationship of forces against the
Stalinist camp.[12]

Despite its expressed desire to establish workers and peasants
power in Nicaragua, the FSLN leadership has thus far not organized a mass Leninist party that would best insure the positive resolution of the class contradiction between the government and state.

But the direction of the FSLN shows that it would be a grave
error to think that any a priori limits exist on how far its leadership and cadres can develop and how fast they can act as the
class struggle deepens in Nicaragua.

The FSLN has announced its intention to launch a vanguard party rooted in the masses. The construction of a revolutionary socialist proletarian party within which the political
vanguard of the Nicaraguan working class can democratically
debate and decide the important questions facing the revolution would be a major step in advancing and consolidating the

gains of the toilers and expropriating the remaining bourgeoisie.

U.S. imperialism

8. Yankee imperialism failed in its efforts first to salvage Somoza and then, in the final weeks, to establish Somozaism without
Somoza. Washington's attempts through the governments of
Costa Rica, Venezuela, Panama, and other Latin American ruling classes to insure installation of a bourgeois-dominated government were no more successful than its proposal for a joint
military intervention sponsored by the Organization of American States, or its attempt to base troop-carrying attack helicop-
ters in northern Costa Rica on the eve of Somoza's fall. Dashing
the hopes of the U.S. rulers, the government that was consolidated not only included the FSLN but was one in which the
Sandinistas held decisive political power.

The fall of Somoza and rapid consolidation of a workers and
peasants government in Nicaragua has had a profound impact
in Central America—most dramatically in El Salvador—and the
Caribbean. This was a giant blow to imperialism's efforts to isolate the Cuban revolution and bolster capitalist rule south of its
borders. Today Washington faces increasing isolation in Central and South America and in the Caribbean.

Washington's incapacity so far to directly intervene militarily
in Nicaragua fundamentally reflects two factors: (1) the deep
solidarity of the Latin American toilers with the Nicaraguan
struggle and consequent political cost for any government too
openly identified with U.S. imperialism's counterrevolutionary
policies, and (2) the constraints on the direct use of U.S. military might as a result of the post-Vietnam antiwar attitudes and
suspicion of U.S. foreign policy goals among American workers.

Despite these initial reversals, however, it is precluded that
Washington will passively look on while "another Cuba" is established in its own backyard. It is acutely aware that the deepening of the revolution in Nicaragua has already had profound
ramifications in Grenada and El Salvador and will have further

repercussions throughout the Caribbean and Central America.

Imperialism's goal is to contain, stall, disrupt, and, at the right moment, crush the Nicaraguan revolution. Along with the economic cudgels wielded by world imperialism, its two strongest weapons in achieving these goals are (1) the desire of the Kremlin bureaucracy to avoid any disruption of its diplomatic relations with Washington, the fruit of its overall class-collaborationist policy of peaceful coexistence with imperialism, and (2) Washington's own massive military power.

THE U.S. RULERS initially adopted an openly aggressive stance toward the revolution. They warned the new government against radical measures and against any close association with Cuba. In this way, the imperialists sought to strengthen the hand of what they had hoped would be a politically viable bourgeois wing in the government. When it became clear that the FSLN was in political control of the government, beginning in late August, the big-business media, especially in the United States, made a noticeable shift in its treatment of the Nicaraguan events. This reflected imperialism's tactical judgment that use of open force, or the overt threat of open force, could politically backfire in the short run.

News from Nicaragua virtually dropped out of the papers and news broadcasts. And editors toned down their earlier dire warnings about the dangers of an FSLN-led government.

Imperialism's tactics up until now have revolved around maintaining an outward appearance of fairness and friendliness toward the new government, while exploiting the economic devastation to arrest and prepare to reverse the revolutionary process. Somoza inflicted massive destruction on the country during his final year in power. More than 35,000 people were killed in the last year alone and 100,000 wounded. Damage to schools, hospitals, and social services amounted to $80 million. Agricultural production was severely disrupted and 40 percent of the population goes without adequate food. More than half the active population is unemployed, and a quarter of industrial plants were damaged by Somoza's bombs.

All this was superimposed on the growing misery caused by the 1972 earthquake damage (Somoza stole millions of dollars in international reconstruction aid to expand his personal financial empire), by other consequences of the dictator's grand-scale corruption, and by the blows of the world capitalist economic crisis. These economic problems will be exacerbated as an inevitable food crop shortage develops during the early months of 1980.

Taking advantage of this social and economic dislocation, Washington is seeking to limit the flow of aid into Nicaragua to intensify the pressures bearing down on the FSLN-led government and on the morale of the Nicaraguan masses. The Carter administration promises credits, both loans and aid. But aside from some initially limited food aid, they have not given a single penny. At the same time, a certain amount of the aid from its imperialist allies is funneled not to the government but to projects actually strengthening imperialist links with the private sector, thus reinforcing the remaining points of support for the Nicaraguan bourgeoisie. The policy as a whole revolves around buying time for the Nicaraguan capitalists. Washington is counting on the coming economic pressures to alienate the petty bourgeoisie and parts of the toilers and hopes this will gradually demobilize the masses and divide the FSLN itself.

The imperialists are organizing these pressures on Nicaragua through their international financial institutions; their domination of trade and distribution in the world capitalist market; the Latin American bourgeoisies, who desperately fear a new Cuba; and the international apparatus of the social democracy, which acts as a political tool of world capitalism, especially for the Western European powers.

By avoiding a public propaganda campaign against the Sandinista revolution, Washington at the same time aims to erode international solidarity with Nicaragua. It wants to project the image that adequate aid is being sent and that there is no danger of imperialist-orchestrated military intervention. It even hopes to foster the knee-jerk sectarian reaction among some radicals that if Washington isn't openly yelping, then the Nicaraguan government must be betraying the masses. Unfortunately, the petty-bourgeois left has largely taken the bait in the United States, the country whose government poses the greatest threat to Nicaragua. Those sectarians who are not already advocating the overthrow of the new government and denouncing the FSLN are mimicking the low-key coverage of the bourgeois press and abstaining from solidarity efforts.

Meanwhile, Nicaragua's aid needs are *not* close to being met. And there is a real danger of military intervention connected to the coming conflicts with the Nicaraguan bourgeoisie or explosions over the extension of the Nicaraguan revolution.

The U.S. and Honduran governments are aiding and intimately collaborating with the remnants of the Somocista National Guard. Moreover, Washington has launched an aggressive military buildup in the Caribbean and renewed calls for a Latin American "regional military peacekeeping force." By mid-November 1979, Somocista National Guard units, some integrated into the Honduran army, began incursions into Nicaragua to engage the FSLN in battle. The Honduran air force began illegal overflights of Nicaragua. Nicaraguan diplomats faced intense harassment—including arrests and beatings—in the Honduran capital to such a degree that all personnel but one chargé d'affaires were withdrawn from the Tegucigalpa embassy by the Nicaraguan junta. Washington's silence in the face of the attacks on Managua's emissaries in Honduras stands in sharp contrast to its hue and cry over the events in Tehran in the same period.[13]

Carter's threats

9. Washington launched a new series of threats against Cuba in September on the pretext that a Soviet "combat brigade" was stationed there. This was linked both with their attempts to discredit Cuba's leadership of this year's Nonaligned conference held in Havana and with the squeeze on Nicaragua. The Cuban

government has responded with enthusiastic solidarity and material assistance to Nicaragua. It has issued an embarrassing challenge to the U.S. government for an emulation competition to see who can provide the most aid to reconstruct Nicaragua. Moreover, Washington knows that Cuba is aiding the new government on the island of Grenada and liberation groups throughout Central America. In a September 30, 1979, interview presented for nationwide broadcast over CBS television's "60 Minutes" show in the United States, Castro was questioned about Cuban aid to the opponents of the dictatorship in El Salvador. Castro said: "I neither confirm it nor deny it. I proclaim it as a right; furthermore, as a duty."[14]

Above all, the U.S. rulers know that Cuban aid to Nicaragua helps counteract imperialist pressure and thereby strengthens the ability of the FSLN-led government to reconstruct Nicaragua along socialist lines. They know that the FSLN looks to the Cuban workers state as a model for social and economic development.

Furthermore, in light of Cuba's role in Africa, the imperialists are convinced that Cuba will come to the aid of Nicaragua in the event of a direct U.S. or U.S.-engineered attack, posing a confrontation of international proportions.[15]

Carter's moves in the Caribbean are also a warning to the Soviet Union. Washington is telling the Kremlin that it won't tolerate any substantial Soviet aid to Nicaragua. And it is pressuring Moscow to put the squeeze on Cuba to abandon its internationalist policies, including its aid to Nicaragua.

Cuba has made clear that it won't be intimidated, however. An October 1979 editorial in the Cuban daily *Granma* responded to Carter's moves by asserting that Cuba's "dignity and sovereignty, its right to defend itself by any means it regards as appropriate, as well as its internationalist policy, will remain unshakable." In a speech earlier in the year, Castro pointedly included "our sister socialist nations" in his call for an emulation contest to aid Nicaragua.[16]

In contrast to the anti-imperialist policies of the Castro leadership, the Stalinist bureaucracy in the Kremlin seeks to gain trade and diplomatic concessions from imperialism in return for using its power and influence to sabotage revolutionary struggles. So far, Moscow has heeded Washington's warning to withhold major assistance from Nicaragua. And following Moscow's lead, Stalinist parties around the world have given little coverage to the Nicaraguan revolution in their press and have not used their full influence to mount solidarity campaigns.

The aggressive maneuvers by the Carter administration over the past several months, together with Moscow's refusal to provide aid to Nicaragua and its demonstrative support to the new military regime in El Salvador, show that defending Cuba against imperialist pressure and fighting to lift the economic blockade are intertwined with defense of the Nicaraguan revolution.

10. As yet, the Sandinistas still lack the mass democratic-centralist proletarian party that would best enable them to meet the challenges and opportunities they face. Moreover, the FSLN faces huge obstacles: economic dislocation, which will produce great hardships—and class conflicts—in the early months of the 1980s; a shortage of political cadres; the inexperience of the new mass organizations; cultural deprivation imposed by imperialist subjugation; and maneuvers by imperialism and the indigenous capitalists.

Yet the FSLN's course up to now, together with the growing militancy and political class consciousness of the workers, gives no cause for pessimism.

Faced with the threat of imperialist intervention and counterrevolutionary subversion, the Sandinistas have moved rapidly to build a professional revolutionary army, as well as a new police force under FSLN control. They have also announced plans to construct a large, workplace-based militia and draw the CDSs into the fight against rightist terror.

But direct military threats are not the only danger to the revolution. The economy's fundamental economic laws foster capital accumulation and expanding capitalist economic power on the basis of the large remaining blocs of private property in the means of production.

The economic chaos caused by Somoza is the biggest factor operating to the benefit of the exploiters inside and outside Nicaragua. Despite the measures that the government has already taken in health, education, and other areas of social welfare, an austerity situation has been imposed on the country.

As the government has correctly taken steps to revive a minimum of industrial and agricultural production, in the private as well as the public sector, the economic power of the bourgeoisie and the inevitable dangers associated with that power have become more obvious. The capitalists insist on credit and currency concessions, alleviation of trade controls, and assurances that wage demands resulting from the growing unionization of workers will not undercut profitability. A confrontation is looming over these issues.

The bourgeoisie retain their chambers of commerce and industry, which are supported by their counterparts elsewhere in Central America and by international financial institutions. While the bourgeois political parties—the Social Democrats, Social Christians, Democratic Conservatives, and others—at present have a very narrow popular appeal, they nonetheless serve as a vehicle for organizing propaganda campaigns against the government and mass organizations. The Catholic Church hierarchy retains some credibility among the Nicaraguan masses. Sections of it are another potential support for rebuilding bourgeois political power.

The most important bourgeois propaganda instrument in this regard is the country's largest daily, *La Prensa,* though even this is limited by the necessity, given conditions in Nicaragua, for *La Prensa* to open its pages every day to FSLN leaders laying out the Sandinista perspective or responding to criticisms of policies of the government or FSLN.

The presence of bourgeois figures in the junta and cabinet is not a mere decoration. It is an expression of the fact that the contradiction between the class character of the workers and peasants government and the bourgeois state has yet to be resolved. As the government is buffeted by conflicting class pressures, by the initiatives and counterinitiatives of the toilers and the exploiters, movement toward or away from establishment of a workers state will find its reflection in further alterations in personnel in the junta, the ministries, and the Central Bank.

It would be a blunder to conclude from this, however, that progress toward a progressive resolution of this contradiction can be furthered by action around the slogan "Bourgeois ministers out of the government!" Such a schema ignores the real location of military and political power, the deep-going character of the break in continuity with the old regime, the progression of radical measures by the new workers and peasants government, and the real process through which the masses will advance their consciousness to drive the revolution forward. It would be infantile leftism to deliberately provoke a premature confrontation with the bourgeoisie over the composition of the junta and cabinet. The decisive conflicts will grow out of the intensification of the class struggle, which will be reflected in the government; as the bourgeois forces in the government make themselves known by their deeds, it will then become timely to fight for their ouster.

Revolutionary course

The Nicaraguan capitalists face the growing power of the Sandinista army and police, the CDSs, the CST, the ATC, the women's and youth organizations. The FSLN has sought ways to organize their power, including taking more governmental prerogatives. It encourages the democratic organization of these committees on a neighborhood and district level and has projected the next stage as consolidation on a municipal level. National gatherings of CDS and ATC activists have already been held, and a provisional National Council of the CDSs has been set up. Congresses of CDS and CST delegates are scheduled to be held in early 1980.

The Nicaraguan bourgeoisie, on the other hand, is virulently opposed to attributing any governmental authority to these organizations, insisting that they are merely FSLN bodies. This dispute has become a public debate.

The coordination and centralization of these mass organizations on a municipal, regional, and national level—together with the extension of workers' control over all areas of production and economic activity, both privately owned and nationalized—would further weaken the social and economic power of the capitalists and sharpen the class confrontation. Such steps would prepare the way for the establishment of a workers state based on these mass organizations, and generalized workers control evolving toward workers management, as democratic participation by the toilers in national economic and social planning is established.

Prospects for development toward institutionalized workers democracy along these lines show the sectarian error of placing the demand on the Nicaraguan government to organize the election of a constituent assembly. Those in the radical movement who advance this slogan seek to promote the false idea that the government is a bourgeois coalition regime, or that the FSLN is depriving the masses of their democratic rights in order to reconsolidate capitalist power. However, it is these sectarians themselves who actually counterpose an unfounded schema to the process by which the Nicaraguan toilers have already begun to assert their own power against that of the class enemy. It is no accident that variations on the same theme are one of the complaints hurled by the bourgeoisie against the Sandinistas.

The FSLN's stated intention to develop the mass organizations as the basis for popular power in Nicaragua opens up the most positive framework, as *Barricada* has explained, for the majority to create "their own means of resolving their political, social, and economic problems," "to defend themselves against their enemies, and to consolidate the revolution." It is this dynamic of the revolution that the capitalists will oppose most strongly, demanding that the junta take steps to regulate and hold back the extension of the power of the mass organizations.

11. The success of the FSLN, and the revolutionary workers

who join it, in building a mass-based vanguard party will be an extremely important factor in increasing the chances that the workers and peasants government will culminate in the establishment of a workers state that can effectively fight to defend and extend the revolution. No single element is more important to the consolidation of the gains of the revolution than forging a party of the Nicaraguan working class that takes the political leadership in building a centralized system of democratic workers and peasants councils to assume governmental power.

Combating capitalist sabotage and reconstructing Nicaragua will require an ever-wider exchange of viewpoints within the camp of the toilers over how best to move forward to solve their problems. The greatest possible democracy and the cultivation of an atmosphere encouraging the free expression of ideas can only strengthen the revolution and the commitment of the masses to it. It is the only means to tap the full talents of the workers and peasants, who must be drawn into the revolutionary movement in increasing numbers and become the overwhelming bulk of its cadres and leaders.

It is natural that different currents of thought will emerge, even among the most advanced workers collaborating to build their vanguard party. Various tendencies or parties will arise, reflecting the uneven development of class consciousness among the workers. The Sandinistas know from their own experience that tendencies and political differences, even sharp ones, can develop among revolutionists.

Impatience with the serious political errors and often provocative behavior of some sectarian organizations, however, led the FSLN in September and October to publicly lump these groups together with the Somocistas. During the campaign against right-wing terror launched under the slogan "Control Somozaism—defend the revolution," the "ultralefts" were mentioned in speeches, on the radio, and in *Barricada* as being among the counterrevolutionary forces that had to be smashed. Detentions and other administrative measures were taken against members of some of these organizations, without presentation of proof of any likely or actual crimes that would justify such measures.[17]

By November a modification in the FSLN's approach to the sectarian-led organizations was becoming evident. FSLN leaders announced that evidence now showed that bank robberies previously attributed to MILPAS (Anti-Somoza People's Militias) had been committed by Somocistas posing as radicals. Speeches by some FSLN leaders, while containing contradictory statements, included offers to open a "dialogue" with the sectarian groups. In addition, all of those detained were released.

Nonetheless, there has still been no definitive public political clarification on this important matter by FSLN leaders.

The pro-Moscow Stalinists in Nicaragua, who had always attacked the FSLN itself for being "ultraleft," will continue to push in the direction of stifling workers democracy. Their attacks are in reality aimed at the toiling masses and at all revolutionists—above all the FSLN—since their objective is to arrest the revolution at the "bourgeois-democratic stage." Any policy of repression within the workers movement would play into their hands.

EQUATING SOMOZAISM and counterrevolution with those under the influence of petty-bourgeois pressures and ideas could also lead to an underestimation of the dangers posed by the real class enemy—both among the capitalists who backed Somoza, those who opposed him for whatever reason, and their powerful allies centered in the United States. As the class polarization deepens, it will be the forces of the bourgeoisie that spearhead the counterrevolution.

The revolutionary leadership must be able to distinguish between those in the radical movement who operate within the framework of the revolution and those who—and there will be some—desert to the camp of the class enemy and carry out crimes against the revolution.

The problems the Nicaraguan revolution faces and must immediately cope with are real and cannot be waved aside. It is sometimes necessary to make tactical concessions to the capitalists to avert economic reverses and premature confrontations.

The sectarian groups are wrong in their tendency to view such necessary concessions as incorrect in principle or betrayals of the revolution. They are a vital necessity in Nicaragua. At the same time, however, these organizations can sometimes reflect in a distorted way moods of sections of the masses. In order to effectively lead the masses, the revolutionary vanguard should openly explain its considerations to the workers and peasants when it believes concessions are necessary.

An important part of this process of interaction between the masses and their vanguard is politically confronting the ultra-left sectarians and explaining what is wrong with their infantile proposals. Repression cuts across this political clarification and makes it more difficult to win these cadres to a genuinely revolutionary course.

Furthermore, the workers and peasants will take initiatives that go beyond the leadership's immediate plans. This is one of the keys to all revolutionary uprisings and victories. The leadership's capacity to respond positively to such initiatives to drive the process forward will be a prime element in the consummation of the objectives of the revolution.

The FSLN's contradictory moves in late 1979 toward repression of its opponents on the left stand as an exception to its generally revolutionary course toward the development of mass popular organizations and respect for democratic rights. If this overall tendency prevails, the direction of the Nicaraguan revolution in this important respect will represent a significant advance over revolutionary Cuba. It could also stimulate motion toward the development of democratic forms of proletarian power based on workers and peasants councils in Cuba.

Toward a workers state
12. Given the desperate economic situation in Nicaragua, a pressing objective of the government has been to restore a minimal level of production in the privately owned industries and

on the big and medium-sized farms still in the hands of their owners. It has appealed for aid from all countries to obtain credits and food.

As the example of Cuba has proven, however, the needs of the masses cannot be met if private ownership is maintained in the basic means of production. The laws of capitalist accumulation will distort the country's economy, subordinating real economic development and social betterment to the quest for profits and to imperialist exploitation. This would be the inevitable outcome of the maintenance of a "mixed economy" such as that described in the July 9 GRN program.

Thus the reconstruction of Nicaragua in the interests of the workers and poor peasants makes it necessary to extend workers control of production; shift the tax burden to the exploiters; repulse attempts by the imperialist financial institutions to use foreign debt as a means of pressure; nationalize the remaining privately owned large landholdings, industries, and big firms; develop the CDSs and unions, and widen the scope of their authority; expropriate the imperialist banks and enterprises; and establish a monopoly on foreign trade, thus laying the foundation for real economic and social planning.

It is along this road that the system of capitalist accumulation and labor exploitation can be destroyed. Once the qualitative turning point has been passed and a workers state established, capitalist property relations could be restored only through all-out civil war, requiring ruthless and massive military intervention by imperialism.

These measures, of course, would mark the final showdown with the Nicaraguan bourgeoisie and its backers in Washington and on Wall Street. The FSLN has correctly acted on the recognition that steps in this direction go hand in hand with, and must be preceded by, raising the consciousness and organization of the toilers. The class struggle must be taken into the countryside. The CDSs, CST, ATC, Sandinista army, and the new youth and women's organizations must all be expanded and strengthened. The new militias must be established and trained. The new party must be built. All this requires time, and premature confrontations can set back rather than advance the process.

WHILE IT WOULD BE adventuristic to try to force the rhythm of the class struggle, it is also true that the pace of polarization and confrontation cannot be controlled by preconceived plans. The tempo will be dictated by the blows and counterblows between the masses and the FSLN on one side and the exploiters on the other. With each new encroachment against the property and prerogatives of the landlords and business interests, the likelihood grows that some section of the bourgeoisie will throw down the gauntlet. In addition to radical measures by the government, the workers and peasants—suffering under economic burdens, capitalist sabotage, and social dislocation—will themselves take initiatives on the land, in their factories, and in the barrios. This is the historic record of the Russian, Cuban, and every other socialist revolution; there is an accelerating dialectical interplay between the leadership and the initiatives and responses by the masses, often unforeseen by the leadership.

In revolutionary situations above all, history confirms Frederick Engels's observation that when controlled forces are put in motion, uncontrolled forces are inevitably put in motion as well. No amount of political preparation can annul this consequence of the class struggle. Instead, the aim of such preparation must be to increase the self-confidence and readiness of the masses *to respond* to new turns by defending their conquests and propelling their struggle forward. That is where their consciousness, organization, and mobilization will prove decisive. It is correct to make concessions to the class enemy when the relationship of forces leaves no alternative. But the masses must be told the class truth about such concessions, so that they can be better prepared to ward off the concomitant dangers.

All this highlights the need for a revolutionary Marxist proletarian party to unify and lead the workers and their allies in accomplishing these tasks and defeating their class enemy. Forging the initial cadres of such a party out of the leadership and ranks of the FSLN would not only facilitate the socialist reconstruction of Nicaragua but would mark an advance for the entire international workers movement in the fight to resolve the historic crisis of proletarian leadership.

13. The revolution in Nicaragua and the political evolution of the FSLN present an enormous opportunity and responsibility for the Fourth International.[18] These developments pose new tests for us as we strive to measure up to our historic task of solving the leadership crisis of the world working class and constructing an international party of socialist revolution. The cadres of the world Trotskyist movement are the irreplaceable nucleus of that world proletarian party. We carry forward the Leninist program and transitional method indispensable to the victory of the toilers over the economic and social catastrophe and nuclear annihilation that will otherwise be brought down on humanity by imperialism.

Due to the crimes and obstructions of the social democracy and Stalinism, however, the construction of a mass revolutionary workers' International is a task that is still only at its beginning stage. The development of revolutionary currents that bypass Stalinism such as those in Cuba, and now in Nicaragua, are thus of the greatest importance to the Fourth International and to the further development of our prospects and our revolutionary program.

As Trotsky explained, in the death agony of capitalism *revolutionists of action* will continually emerge out of the class battles provoked by the exploiters' ruthless drive for profits. These fighters will arise not only out of the anti-imperialist struggle but within the labor movement and other organizations of the oppressed in the imperialist countries. History will judge the Fourth International by our capacity to link up with these currents, integrate ourselves in them, learn from them, and help steel them politically in the program of Leninism, and in that process build the world proletarian party that can take on the imperialists in battle and defeat them.

Along this strategic line of march, we recognize in the leadership of the FSLN fellow revolutionists who have already demonstrated their internationalism, their desire to move forward to a socialist Nicaragua, and their intention to build a vanguard party. On that basis, the Fourth International seeks political collaboration with them on all the big questions facing the workers of Nicaragua and of the entire world.

This course runs directly counter to that taken by several organizations that consider themselves Trotskyist—by the Bolshevik Faction, by the Socialist Workers Organization of Costa Rica (OST) and its Nicaraguan sister organization, Revolutionary Socialist Group (GRS), and by the Revolutionary Marxist League (LMR) in Nicaragua.[19] Boiled down to its essentials, the political line of all four of the above has been opposition to the new Nicaraguan government as a bourgeois government and the construction of political parties in opposition to that projected by the FSLN.

The Simón Bolívar Brigade (BSB), established under the direction of the Bolshevik Faction, carried this sectarian line to the point of criminal adventure—sending to Nicaragua and maintaining there an armed unit outside the discipline of the new revolutionary army or the people's militia. The BSB falsely portrayed itself as an FSLN unit in order to win popular sympathy. As a result, the FSLN leadership—after attempting to persuade the BSB to take its place among the forces striving to advance the revolution and respecting revolutionary legality—expelled the brigade's non-Nicaraguan members from the country.

Having been called to order by leading bodies of the Fourth International for its utterly undisciplined and disloyal course, which was not conceived to advance the interests of the workers and peasants of Nicaragua, the Bolshevik Faction organized a split on the eve of the International's World Congress. It has been joined in this walkout by the leadership of the Nicaraguan LMR and the Costa Rican OST, and is now attempting to organize a rump "world conference" with other sectarian groups internationally that call themselves Trotskyist and share a sectarian disdain for and lack of comprehension of the Nicaraguan revolution.

The Fourth International condemns and repudiates the activities of the Simón Bolívar Brigade and rejects the political views on the Nicaraguan revolution of the Bolshevik Faction, the LMR, and the OST. The Fourth International has no organized forces in Nicaragua—the activities of the latter groups have been organized outside the guidance of, or collaboration with, the elected leadership bodies of the Fourth International. As mentioned earlier, these groups have now split from the Fourth International. The policies of these groups are diametrically opposed to those of the Fourth International and can only harm the opportunities to win a hearing for Trotskyist ideas in Nicaragua and advance our international party-building perspective.

Partisans of the Fourth International present their ideas as loyal and hard-working militants in the framework of the organization that led the overthrow of Somoza and is today guiding the revolution forward.

B<small>Y ADVANCING</small> our program and perspectives, the Fourth International places itself firmly on the side of the FSLN's battle to promote and achieve the victory of the socialist revolution in Nicaragua. Our main contributions in this regard are:

• active participation inside and outside Nicaragua in efforts to reconstruct the country and defend the revolution from all its enemies, above all U.S. imperialism;

• advancing the development of the unions, of mass organizations and of democratic workers and peasants councils to bring the masses into decision making and strengthen the revolution; and

• loyal participation in the FSLN's efforts to construct a revolutionary proletarian party, putting forward the fundamental program of Leninism in order to advance toward the mass world party of socialist revolution whose construction will be decisive in the defeat of exploitation and oppression on an international scale.

Aid to Nicaragua

14. Outside Nicaragua, the Fourth International and its sections will mobilize all their forces to build broad, united solidarity and aid campaigns with the Nicaraguan revolution and help defend it against the threat of imperialist-orchestrated counterrevolution. Part of this will be a campaign against the blockade and other hostile acts against revolutionary Cuba. We will energetically work with others to involve the labor movement, farmers organizations, organizations of oppressed national minorities, women's groups, youth organizations, and others in a vast effort to publicize the truth about what is happening in Nicaragua and mobilize solidarity and aid with the Nicaraguan people.

This is an especially important responsibility for members of the Fourth International in Latin America, where the direct impact of the Nicaraguan revolution is the greatest, and in the United States, which not only installed and maintained the Somoza tyranny in power but today represents the most powerful enemy of the revolution. In placing ourselves in the front ranks of such a solidarity and aid campaign, the Fourth International will help revive the example of proletarian internationalism demonstrated by the worldwide movement against the imperialist war in Vietnam.

We will demand that the imperialist governments provide whatever economic, agricultural, and medical aid is asked for by the Nicaraguan government—channeled through the official government and mass organizations and with no strings attached. We will back up Commander Daniel Ortega's proposal before the United Nations that Nicaragua's burdensome debt should be assumed "by the developed countries, by the economically powerful countries, and especially those that fed Somozaism with financing." That means demanding that the imperialist governments and all imperialist financial institutions cancel all of Nicaragua's debts.

The Fourth International calls on the mass workers and farmers organizations throughout the world to make resources available to aid their Nicaraguan brothers and sisters.

We know that political and material solidarity can be decisive to the outcome of the revolutionary process in Nicaragua. The FSLN's steps to encourage the development of such an international campaign show that it too recognizes this fact.

The Fourth International also understands that the socialist revolution that has begun in Nicaragua is an important breakthrough in combating the isolation of Cuba and hastening revolutionary prospects throughout Central and South America and in the Caribbean.

Finally, we know that the establishment of the second workers state in the Western Hemisphere would further weaken world imperialism, inspire and educate the oppressed and exploited around the world, and buy precious time for the workers in the advanced capitalist countries to take political power out of the hands of the war makers and exploiters and open the road to a peaceful and prosperous socialist future for all humanity.

15. The outcome of the deepening confrontation of class forces in Nicaragua will profoundly affect the Cuban workers and peasants and the outlook of their leadership. The future of the two revolutions is now inextricably linked.

The establishment of a workers state in Nicaragua would make possible another huge step forward in the struggle to resolve the crisis of leadership of the world proletariat. It would have an immediate, positive impact inside Cuba, and its weight would be felt throughout the Caribbean and Central America. It would spur the development of revolutionary forces and strengthen them in their conflict with Stalinist and social democratic betrayers, and centrist vacillators.

As a result, the door would be opened further to a process that could lead the Castroist leadership, the FSLN, and other revolutionists linking up with the Fourth International in steps toward building a mass world party of socialist revolution.

The Fourth International must prepare for the showdown that is approaching in a matter of months. Decisive moves toward the establishment of a workers state in Nicaragua will entail a head-on confrontation with the Central American bourgeoisies and the power of Yankee imperialism. The leadership of the Cuban revolution will face one of its biggest tests since the missile crisis of 1962.[20] Every current claiming to be revolutionary will be tested to the end.

Today it is the heroic workers and peasants of Nicaragua who are on the front lines of the advancing world socialist revolution. We will be tested by our capacity to respond with courage and decisiveness, to throw our forces into this struggle without hesitation or delay, to mobilize and lead all those we influence. Only along that road can we advance the construction of the world party of socialist revolution.

Carlos Fonseca Speaks

Building Nicaragua's Sandinista National Liberation Front, 1960-1976

Learning from the example of the Cuban revolution, Carlos Fonseca broke from the Stalinist movement in Nicaragua in 1961 and successfully brought Marxism to Central America. His political writings formed the foundation of the movement that toppled the Somoza dictatorship in 1979. Available October 1994. $17.95

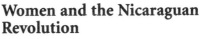

Sandinistas Speak

by Tomás Borge, Carlos Fonseca, Daniel Ortega, and others

The best selection in English of historic documents of the FSLN and speeches and interviews from the opening years of the 1979 Sandinista revolution. $13.95

Nicaragua: The Sandinista People's Revolution

by Tomás Borge, Daniel Ortega, and others

Speeches, articles, and interviews on the fight against Washington's contra war, the campaign for literacy and education, the fight for equality by the peoples of the Atlantic Coast, and more. $21.95

Women and the Nicaraguan Revolution

by Tomás Borge

In the early years of the Nicaraguan revolution, a central leader describes the challenge before the FSLN in beginning to lead, organize, and educate around the fight for women's equality. Booklet. $2.50

Proletarian Leadership in Power

What We Can Learn from Lenin, Castro, and the FSLN

by Mary-Alice Waters

When the great masses of men and women march onto the stage of history and take command of their own destinies, Waters explains, proletarian leaderships are put to the ultimate test: will they be "as bold and resolute as the million-strong who are fighting with unparalleled tenacity because they see a possibility of building society on a new foundation?" Waters reviews the experiences of the Russian and Cuban revolutions, and the opening year of the Nicaraguan and Grenada revolutions. $8^{1}/_{2}$ x 11 format. $6.00

Maurice Bishop Speaks

The Grenada Revolution and Its Overthrow, 1979-83

Speeches and interviews by the central leader of the workers and farmers government in the Caribbean island of Grenada. With an introduction by Steve Clark. $20.95

One People, One Destiny

The Caribbean and Central America Today

Edited by Don Rojas

The fight against economic and social backwardness and imperialist bullying in the Caribbean and Central America, as presented in speeches and articles by political leaders from the region in the late 1980s. $11.95

Panama: The Truth about the U.S. Invasion

by Cindy Jaquith, Don Rojas, Nils Castro, Fidel Castro

Booklet. $3.50

PATHFINDER

See page 2 for distributors

THE COMING SHOWDOWN
IN THE CARIBBEAN

A HISTORIC CONFRONTATION is shaping up in the Caribbean and Central America. On one side are millions of workers and peasants who have said "Enough!" to the poverty and tyranny imposed on them for decades by Washington and Wall Street. On the other side is the U.S. government, speaking for the business interests whose profits are bloated by the superexploitation of the peoples of Latin America. Washington is urgently seeking to free its hands to use massive military force against the advancing revolutionary fighters.

The socialist revolution that dawned in the Americas with the Cuban victory in 1959 is now being extended in Nicaragua. A revolutionary-minded government has come to power on the island of Grenada. The Salvadoran workers and peasants are rising, arms in hand, determined to take the same road.

These freedom struggles challenge the right of U.S. big business to grow fat off the labor and natural resources of the peoples south of the U.S. border. As a result, Washington is determined to prevent Nicaragua from becoming another Cuba, and El Salvador from becoming another Nicaragua.

Washington's stubborn refusal to allow the peoples of the Caribbean and Central America to run their own governments,

---

This public statement was issued by the National Committee of the Socialist Workers Party on May 24, 1980.

control their own resources, and chart their own destinies carries a grave threat of war. Because the imperialists know that in the final analysis they *must* throw U.S. military might into the battlefield—or face the "loss" of El Salvador and other countries to the people who live and work there. Arming subservient local dictators is not enough, as shown last year when the shah of Iran and Washington's puppet Somoza in Nicaragua fell before massive popular insurrections.

Three big obstacles stand in the way of Washington's war plans:

• the unwillingness of American workers to fight and die in another Vietnam;

• the overwhelming opposition of working people throughout Latin America to bullying by Yankee gunboats; and

• the solidarity pledged by Cuba's revolutionary government and people to all those under fire from imperialism.

So, while escalating the U.S. military presence in the Caribbean and Central America, President James Carter has launched a propaganda offensive to slander Cuba, to convince working people that the extension of the Cuban revolution is a threat to freedom.

For its part, revolutionary Cuba has responded with the biggest mobilizations ever held in Latin America. The latest—the May 17 March of the Fighting People—brought out some five million people, half the island's population. "Like Cuba, Vietnam, and Nicaragua—El Salvador will win," they declared. "We will never surrender." And, "Fidel pitch, because Carter can't hit."

For sure, Carter cannot get five million Americans—or even a fraction of that number—to demonstrate for his policy toward Latin America. And it's no wonder.

Why should U.S. workers fight our brothers and sisters in Latin America? *We* own no sugar refineries, no plantations, no copper mines, no factories there. The profits coined from the sweat and blood of Latin American workers and peasants never find their way to *our* pockets. The plunder of imperialist exploitation serves only to strengthen the same giant U.S. corporations that attack our wages, jobs, and union rights here at home.

Why should U.S. Blacks go to war against Cuba—the only society in the Americas that has uprooted racism; against Grenada—the first free Black land of the Caribbean; or against Nicaragua—which is treating its national minorities with equality and dignity for the first time?

Why should U.S. youth serve as cannon fodder against these revolutionary societies, where literacy and education are given top priority and where youth are shaping a future free from exploitation and injustice?

To see where working people in the United States should stand, we must dispel Washington's smokescreen of lies and look at what has really been happening in the Caribbean and Central America.

Socialist revolution opened

Twenty-one years ago, Cuba broke the chains of imperialist domination. The socialist revolution has made possible sweeping economic and social advances—jobs for all, free medical care, free education for all, low rents, the outlawing of racist discrimination, and big strides toward equality for women. These despite Washington's blockade and the horrible poverty that Cuba, like all countries in Latin America, had been reduced to by U.S. imperialism.

Cuba became a beacon for workers and peasants throughout the hemisphere, proving what could be accomplished by throwing off foreign domination and eliminating capitalism. It has won further prestige among the oppressed by sending brigades of teachers, doctors, and technicians to help other countries combat the bitter fruits of imperialist oppression, and sending internationalist fighters to help countries such as Angola combat the troops of imperialism.

Military invasion, sabotage, assassination plots, and attempts at economic strangulation have proved unable to roll back this revolution. Nor has Washington been able to crush the revolutionary spirit of the Cuban workers and peasants and their leadership.

Extension of the revolution

For two decades the Cuban government has carried out an internationalist foreign policy. It has sought to *defend* Cuba by *extending* the socialist revolution.

Today, Cuba no longer stands alone in the Americas. As Fidel Castro recently put it, "Grenada, Nicaragua, and Cuba are three giants rising up to defend their right to independence, sovereignty and justice, on the very threshold of imperialism."

The government brought to power by the Nicaraguan workers and peasants last summer, under the leadership of the Sandinista National Liberation Front (FSLN), is pressing forward social and economic measures to improve the lives of the vast majority of people. The biggest effort throughout the country right now is a literacy crusade that aims to teach more than half the population to read and write.

The FSLN-led government has consistently put the interests of the workers and peasants first, despite resistance from the capitalists. The Sandinistas have relied above all on the mobilization, organization, and class-conscious education of the toilers.

The FSLN leaders, standing on the shoulders of their Cuban forerunners, are consciously charting a course toward consolidating the second workers state in the Western Hemisphere.

In Grenada, the government led by the New Jewel Movement has defended its right to take Cuba as a model. It has adopted the same internationalist positions as the Cubans on the big questions of world politics. The deepening revolution in Grenada is having a special impact among the millions of Blacks in the Caribbean as well as among Blacks in the United States.

These revolutionary victories have raised political consciousness, self-confidence, and combativity throughout the region—from Honduras and Guatemala to St. Lucia and Dominica, from Guadeloupe and Martinique to Puerto Rico and Belize. The strongest movement has developed in El Salvador, where today the working class and rural poor are fighting to overthow the murderous U.S.-backed dictatorship.

Events are educating and bringing forward new class-struggle leaders. Thousands of revolutionists are trying to learn the lessons of Nicaragua and apply them to making the socialist revolution in their own countries.

As Fidel has explained, the extension of the socialist revolution in this hemisphere is also profoundly felt inside Cuba. No longer alone and isolated, the vast majority of Cubans are inspired with new hope, confidence, and revolutionary commitment.

Washington threatens war

These same events inspire only alarm, fear, and hatred among the U.S. rulers. Throughout this century, big business in the United States has considered the Caribbean its private lake. U.S. corporations claim the right to strip the natural resources of these countries and to appropriate the wealth produced by the labor of the Central American and Caribbean masses. The profits of the corporate overlords are swelled at the expense of the health, welfare, and democratic rights of the millions of people who live there.

The drive to protect capitalist profits at all costs is behind the escalated U.S. military threats and the media barrage of lies and slanders against Cuba.

Last fall the Carter administration raised a demagogic hue and cry over an alleged Soviet "combat brigade" in Cuba. The capitalist politicians and big-business press never mentioned, of course, the outrageous violation of Cuban sovereignty by the U.S. Navy's occupation of Guantánamo against the explicit demand of the Cuban people and the Cuban government that these forces get off Cuban soil.

Next came U.S. military maneuvers in the Caribbean, including the landing of U.S. marines on the beaches of Guantánamo, clearly a practice invasion of the island. Spy flights by Washington's SR-71 reconnaissance planes, violating Cuban airspace, were stepped up. And a special Pentagon command center was set up in Key West, Florida, to centralize U.S. military

124 SWP statement (1980)

operations for the purpose of intervening in Central America and the Caribbean.

Then, in April of this year, Washington began winding up its Big Lie machine around the events at the Peruvian embassy in Havana and the subsequent emigration of thousands of Cubans.[1] The U.S. rulers sought to convince the oppressed around the world that the Cuban economy is in shambles, that social conditions are unbearable and getting worse, and that a brutal dictatorship tyrannizes the Cuban people. The imperialists hoped to tarnish the moral appeal of the Cuban revolution and undermine solidarity with it.

Naturally the big-business press covered up the fact that millions of impoverished victims of imperialism throughout Latin America seek entry into the United States every year because of the higher living standards here. In Cuba, thousands have left while millions voluntarily choose to stay. If Washington opened the doors to immigration from any other country in Latin America as Fidel has pointed out, it would "empty out overnight."

THE CUBAN GOVERNMENT turned the tables on Carter. It exposed, before the whole world, that the obstacle to Cubans who want to leave the island is Washington's refusal to grant visas. Cuba reaffirmed its position that any Cuban is free to emigrate. As Fidel declared on May Day in Havana, "the building of socialism is a task for absolutely free men and women and is absolutely voluntary."[2]

By opening the port of Mariel, the Cuban government put Washington on the spot. Would it accept the thousands of Cubans arriving by boat? Carter's abrupt reversal from offering "open arms" to cracking down on those who bring Cubans here, and his announced intention to deport thousands of the Cubans who have arrived, are sure to contribute to the radicalization of

ENDNOTES FOR THIS ARTICLE BEGIN ON PAGE 310.

Cubans in this country and their disillusionment with capitalism's "land of the free."

Washington's hypocrisy was further underlined by its treatment of thousands of Haitians who have been refused visas and political asylum by the Carter administration. The racist double standard toward these Black immigrants has been put under a national spotlight.

The attempt to tar the Cuban revolution got another jolt when Blacks in Miami rose up in rebellion against police brutality and racism. In the very city where tens of thousands of Cubans are arriving, they have been starkly confronted with the reality of life in capitalist society.[3]

Along with its propaganda blitz, Washington also launched the "Solid Shield 80" military exercises in the Caribbean. This operation was even more extensive and provocative than the U.S. maneuvers last fall. This time, however, after the April 19 demonstration of more than one million in Cuba, Carter backed down from the planned practice invasion of Cuba at Guantánamo.

Right now, Washington is stepping up its military intervention in El Salvador to shore up the dictatorship there against a developing armed uprising of the workers and peasants. Washington has poured in millions of dollars in military aid, along with hundreds of U.S. "advisers." With the assistance of the dictatorships in Honduras and Guatemala, preparations are being laid for a military invasion if necessary.

To prevent El Salvador from following the Nicaraguan road, the U.S. government is prepared to slaughter tens of thousands, just as it backed Somoza's bloodbath during his last year in power.

Washington is also deploying economic weapons in the Caribbean. Next to the vindictive blockade of Cuba, the harshest measures have targeted the people of Jamaica. Washington has sought to "destabilize" the Manley regime there because it has had friendly relations with Cuba.

Under pressure of the world economic crisis, Jamaica has had to borrow tens of millions of dollars at high interest from the imperialist banks. Now the bankers are withholding further loans because the Manley government has refused to accept austerity conditions dictated in Washington.

The bankers have seized the toiling masses of Jamaica by the throat, and hope to bring the government down and replace it with one more directly serving imperialist interests. But the draconian measures may backfire, bringing about a revolutionary explosion of the Jamaican masses.[4]

Mobilizations to defend revolution

The people of Cuba, Nicaragua, and Grenada are preparing to defend themselves and their gains. Fidel has said that if imperialism invades, it will face "another Vietnam." And every Cuban knows, as they pledged so often during that war, "For Vietnam, we will give even our own blood."

The Sandinistas and the New Jewel Movement have likewise declared that they view an attack on each other, on El Salvador, or on Cuba as an attack against themselves.

Cuba, Nicaragua, and Grenada are all strengthening popular militias and organizing their entire populations to repel invading forces.

The series of three mass mobilizations in Cuba in a single month has shown the entire world the overwhelming support for the revolutionary government. By these class-struggle methods, the Cuban leadership has maximized the possibilities for sympathy and solidarity from working people in other countries.

Stakes for U.S. working people

Washington's aggressive moves in the Caribbean and Central America pose a deadly threat to working people in the United States and throughout the world. Workers here are the ones who would be fighting and dying for corporate profits in any new Vietnams.

We have no interest in maintaining a military base on Cuban soil. We gain nothing from the U.S. Navy's use of the Puerto Rican island of Vieques for bombing and shelling practice. Our needs are not served by sending American soldiers to try to crush fellow workers and farmers in El Salvador and Nicaragua.

Rather, the social gains won by working people in Cuba, Nicaragua, and Grenada offer an inspiring example to workers here. Our interests lie in fighting here—as they have done—to bring to power a government that represents *our* class and meets *our* needs, not those of big business.

When the Cuban and Nicaraguan fighters strike a blow against Yankee imperialism, they strike a blow against the same monopolies that we are up against in this country. Their gains are our gains. Their conquests are our conquests. And their struggles *strengthen* our struggles against our common enemy.

This is the challenge before the labor movement, the Black and Latino organizations, antidraft and antinuclear organizations, students, and all those in this country who support the right of the peoples of Latin America to determine their own destiny:

We have a responsibility to expose and refute the lies churned out by Washington and the media.

We have a responsibility to organize the broadest possible solidarity campaign of material aid to help our Nicaraguan brothers and sisters reconstruct their war-torn country.

We have a responsibility to mobilize united emergency protest actions whenever Washington escalates its threats or begins to deploy its interventionist forces.

The unions and organizations of the oppressed should be in the forefront of this effort.

We should join with the revolutionary peoples throughout Latin America in demanding:

U.S. out of Guantánamo!

Stop the spy flights!

End the blockade against Cuba!

U.S. hands off Central America and the Caribbean!

Books by Farrell Dobbs

Writings by a leader of the communist movement in the U.S. and organizer of the Teamsters union during the rise of the CIO

THE TEAMSTER SERIES

Four books on the 1930s strikes and organizing drives, led by a class-struggle leadership, that transformed the Teamsters union in Minneapolis and much of the Midwest into a fighting industrial union movement. Manuals of revolutionary politics, organization, and trade union strategy.

Teamster Rebellion
The 1934 strikes that built a fighting union movement in Minneapolis and helped pave the way for the CIO. 195 pp., $15.95

Teamster Power
The 11-state Midwest over-the-road organizing drive. 255 pp., $17.95

Teamster Politics
Rank-and-file Teamsters lead the fight against antiunion frame-ups and assaults by fascist goons; the battle for jobs for all; and efforts to advance independent labor political action. 256 pp., $17.95

Teamster Bureaucracy
The class-struggle Teamsters leadership organizes to oppose World War II, racism, and government efforts to gag revolutionary-minded workers. 304 pp., $18.95

REVOLUTIONARY CONTINUITY
Marxist Leadership in the United States

Dobbs explains how successive generations of fighters took part in struggles of the U.S. labor movement, seeking to build a revolutionary leadership to advance the class interests of workers and small farmers.

Revolutionary Continuity: The Early Years, 1848-1917
221 pp., $16.95

Revolutionary Continuity: Birth of the Communist Movement, 1918-1922
240 pp., $16.95

THE HISTORIC PROGRAM OF THE FSLN

by Carlos Fonseca

T HE SANDINISTA NATIONAL LIBERATION FRONT (FSLN) arose out of the Nicaraguan people's need for a vanguard organization. That is, it grew out of the need for an organization capable of taking political power through direct struggle against its enemies. It emerged from the need for a formation capable of establishing a social system that eliminates the exploitation and poverty our people have suffered throughout their history.

The FSLN is a political and military organization. Its strategic objective is to take political power by destroying the dictatorship's military and bureaucratic apparatus. It seeks to establish a revolutionary government based on an alliance of workers and peasants and a convergence of all patriotic forces opposed to imperialism and the oligarchy.

The people of Nicaragua live under the reactionary regime of a fascist clique imposed by U.S. imperialism in 1932, the year Anastasio Somoza García was named commander in chief of the National Guard.

The Somozaist clique has reduced Nicaragua to a neocolony exploited by U.S. monopolies and the oligarchic groups.

The present regime is politically unpopular and has no legal foundation. The recognition and aid it receives from the United States is irrefutable proof of foreign interference in Nicaragua's affairs.

After seriously and responsibly analyzing the situation in our country, the FSLN has resolved to confront the dictatorship arms in hand. We have concluded that the triumph of the

---

This manifesto was first published in 1969.

Sandinista people's revolution and the overthrow of the regime that is an enemy of the people will take place through the development of a hard-fought and prolonged people's war.

No matter what maneuvers and resources U.S. imperialism deploys, the Somozaist dictatorship is condemned to total defeat as it confronts the unstoppable advance and development of the people's forces, headed by the Sandinista National Liberation Front.

At this historic moment the FSLN has drafted the political program that follows. The aim of this program is to strengthen our organization and inspire the people of Nicaragua to march forward. Together we will fight until the dictatorship is overthrown. We will resist the intervention of U.S. imperialism. And we will forge a free, prosperous, and revolutionary homeland.

I. A revolutionary government

The Sandinista people's revolution will establish a revolutionary government that will eliminate the reactionary regime placed in power through rigged elections and military coups. People's power will create a Nicaragua that is free of exploitation, oppression, and backwardness. It will create a free, progressive, and independent country.

The revolutionary government will apply the following measures of a political character:

A. It will give revolutionary power a structure that allows the entire nation to participate fully, nationally as well as locally (province, municipality, neighborhood).

B. It will guarantee all citizens full exercise of individual freedoms and it will assure respect for human rights.

C. It will guarantee the free exchange of ideas, which is essential to vigorously broadening the rights of our people and nation.

D. It will guarantee freedom for the labor movement to organize in the city and countryside. It will guarantee freedom to organize peasant, youth, student, women's, cultural, sporting, and similar groups.

E. It will guarantee the right of emigrant and exiled Nicaraguans to return to their native soil.

F. It will guarantee the right to asylum for citizens of other countries who are persecuted for participation in revolutionary struggle.

G. It will severely punish the gangsters who are guilty of persecuting, informing on, abusing, torturing, or murdering revolutionaries and the people.

H. Those individuals who occupy high political posts as a result of rigged elections and military coups will be stripped of their political rights.

The revolutionary government will apply the following measures of an economic character:

A. It will expropriate the landed estates, factories, companies, buildings, means of transportation, and other enterprises fraudulently acquired by the Somoza family through theft and plunder of the nation's wealth.

B. It will expropriate the landed estates, factories, companies, means of transportation, and other enterprises stolen by politicians, military officers, and their accomplices who have taken advantage of the present regime's administrative corruption.

C. It will nationalize the holdings of all foreign companies that exploit mineral, forest, maritime, and other natural resources.

D. It will establish workers control over the management of factories and other enterprises that are expropriated and nationalized.

E. It will centralize mass transit service.

F. It will nationalize the banking system, which will be placed solely at the service of the country's economic development.

G. It will establish an independent currency.

H. It will refuse to honor the loans imposed on the country by the U.S. monopolies or those of any other power.

I. It will establish commercial relations with all countries, whatever their economic system, to promote the country's economic development.

J. It will establish an appropriate policy of taxation, which will be applied with strict justice.

K. It will outlaw usury. This prohibition will apply to Nicaraguan nationals as well as to foreigners.

L. It will protect the small and medium-size owners (producers, merchants) while restricting the excesses that lead to the exploitation of workers.

M. It will establish state control over foreign trade, with an eye to diversifying it and making it independent.

N. It will rigorously restrict the importation of luxury items.

O. It will plan the national economy, putting an end to the anarchy characteristic of the capitalist system of production. A major focus of such planning will be industrialization and electrification.

II. The agrarian revolution

The Sandinista people's revolution will put forward an agrarian policy based on a genuine agrarian reform. This means an immediate and massive distribution of land, taking what was stolen by the big landlords and giving it back to the toilers (small producers) who labor on it.

A. It will expropriate and eliminate the big landlords, both capitalist and feudal.

B. It will turn land over to the peasants free of charge, in accordance with the principle that land should belong to those who work it.

C. It will carry out a program of agricultural development aimed at diversifying agriculture and increasing its productivity.

D. It will guarantee peasants the following rights:
1. Timely and adequate agricultural loans.
2. Marketing (a guaranteed market for their products).
3. Technical assistance.

E. It will protect patriotic landowners who collaborate with the guerrilla struggle. They will be compensated for their holdings that exceed the limits established by the revolutionary government.

F. It will encourage and provide incentives to peasants to organize themselves in cooperatives. In this way they can take their destiny into their own hands and participate directly in development of the country.

G. It will abolish debts the peasantry has incurred to the landlord and to any type of usurer.

H. It will eliminate the forced idleness that exists most of the year in the countryside, and it will ensure the creation of jobs for the rural population.

III. Revolution in culture and education
The Sandinista people's revolution will lay the groundwork for developing our country's culture, the education of our people, and the reform of our universities.

A. It will organize a massive campaign to immediately wipe out illiteracy.

B. It will develop our country's culture and will root out neo-colonial penetration of it.

C. It will rescue progressive intellectuals, and the works they have created throughout our history, from the neglect to which they have been consigned by the antipopular regimes.

D. It will promote the development and advancement of education at all levels (primary, intermediate, technical, university, etc.). Education will be free at all levels and compulsory at some.

E. It will grant scholarships at all levels of education to students with limited economic resources. These scholarships will include housing, food, clothing, books, and transportation.

F. It will train more and better teachers. It will equip them with the scientific knowledge the present era requires, enabling them to meet the needs of our entire student population.

G. It will nationalize private educational facilities that have been immorally turned into industries by merchants who hypocritically invoke religious principles.

H. It will adapt teaching programs to the needs of the country; it will apply teaching methods to meet the country's needs in science and research.

I. It will carry out a university reform that will include, among other things, the following measures:

1. It will rescue the university from the domination of the exploiting classes, so it can serve the real creators and shapers of our culture: the people. University instruction

must be oriented around the human being, around the people. The university must stop being a breeding ground for bureaucratic egoists.

2. It will eliminate the discrimination against youth from the working class and peasantry that deprives them of access to a university education.

3. It will increase the state budget for the university in order to provide the economic resources required to address the problems it confronts.

4. It will ensure majority student representation on the boards of the various departments, keeping in mind that the student body is the main component of the university population.

5. It will eliminate neocolonial penetration of the university, especially the influence exercised by the U.S. monopolies through donations by pseudophilanthropic foundations.

6. It will encourage free, experimental, scientific investigation that will help unravel national and universal questions.

7. It will strengthen the unity of students, faculty, and researchers with the whole people, by perpetuating the selfless example of the students and intellectuals who have given their lives for the sake of patriotic ideals.

IV. Labor legislation and social security

The Sandinista people's revolution will eliminate the injustices in living and working conditions suffered by the working class under circumstances of brutal exploitation; in their place it will institute labor legislation and social assistance programs.

A. It will enact a labor code that will establish, among other things, the following rights:

1. It will adopt the principle that "those who do not work do not eat." Exception will of course be made for those who are unable to participate in the process of production due to age (children, the elderly), medical condition, or other reasons beyond their control.

2. Strict enforcement of the eight-hour workday.

3. The income of workers (wages and benefits) must be sufficient to satisfy daily needs.

4. Respect for the dignity of the worker, prohibiting and punishing unjust treatment of workers in the course of their labor.

5. Abolition of unjust firings.

6. Obligation to pay wages in the period required by law.

7. Right of all workers to regular vacations.

B. It will eliminate the scourge of unemployment.

C. It will extend the social security system to all workers and public employees. Coverage will include illness, physical incapacity, and retirement.

D. It will provide medical care free of charge to the entire population. It will set up clinics and hospitals throughout the country.

E. It will undertake massive campaigns to eradicate endemic illnesses and prevent epidemics.

F. It will carry out urban reform, which will provide each family with adequate shelter. It will put an end to usurious speculation in urban land (subdivisions, urban development, rental housing) that exploits the need of working families for adequate shelter.

G. It will initiate and expand the construction of adequate housing for the peasant population.

H. It will reduce the charges for water, light, sewers, and the upkeep of public urban areas; it will implement programs to extend such services to the entire urban and rural population.

I. It will encourage participation in sports of all kinds.

J. It will eliminate the humiliation of begging by implementing the measures above.

V. Honesty in administration

The Sandinista people's revolution will uproot governmental corruption and will establish strict administrative honesty.

A. It will abolish the criminal trafficking in vices (prostitution, gambling, drugs, etc.), exploited by the privileged sector of the National Guard and foreign parasites.

B. It will establish strict controls over the collection of taxes to prevent government officials from profiting personally, thus eliminating what has become an everyday practice in governmental agencies under the present regime.

C. It will put a halt to the arbitrary actions of members of the National Guard, who plunder the population under the guise of collecting local taxes.

D. It will stop military commanders from appropriating funds allocated to the care of common prisoners, and it will establish rehabilitation centers for these prisoners.

E. It will put an end to the smuggling that is practiced on a large scale by the gang of politicians, officers, and foreigners who are the regime's accomplices.

F. It will severely punish persons who engage in crimes against honest administration (embezzlement, smuggling, trafficking in vices, etc.), acting with the greatest severity when individuals active in the revolutionary movement are involved.

VI. Reincorporation of the Atlantic Coast

The Sandinista people's revolution will put into practice a special plan for the Atlantic Coast. It seeks to incorporate into the nation's life a region that has been abandoned to total neglect.

A. It will end the unjust exploitation the Atlantic Coast has suffered throughout its history by foreign monopolies, especially U.S. imperialism.

B. It will help bring into production land in the region that is suitable for agriculture and cattle raising.

C. It will seek to take advantage of favorable conditions to promote commercial fishing and forestry.

D. It will encourage and promote local cultural values that flow from specific aspects of the region's tradition.

E. It will wipe out the odious discrimination to which the indigenous Miskitos, Sumos, Zambos,[1] and Blacks of this region are subjected.

ENDNOTES FOR THIS ARTICLE CAN BE FOUND ON PAGE 311.

VII. Emancipation of women
The Sandinista people's revolution will abolish the odious discrimination that women have been subjected to compared to men. It will establish economic, political, and cultural equality between women and men.

A. It will pay special attention to the needs of the mother and child.

B. It will eliminate prostitution and other social scourges, thereby helping to raise the dignity of women.

C. It will put an end to the system of servitude that women suffer, reflected in the tragedy of the abandoned working mother.

D. It will grant children born out of wedlock equal protection under revolutionary institutions.

E. It will establish day-care centers for the children of working women.

F. It will establish a two-month maternity leave, spanning the period before and after birth, for women who work.

G. It will raise women's political, cultural, and occupational levels through their participation in the revolutionary process.

VIII. Respect for religious beliefs
The Sandinista people's revolution will guarantee those who hold religious beliefs the freedom to profess any religion.

A. It will respect the right of citizens to profess and practice any religious belief.

B. It will support the work of priests and other religious figures who defend working people.

IX. Independent foreign policy
The Sandinista people's revolution will put an end to the foreign policy of subservience to U.S. imperialism. It will establish a patriotic foreign policy that is based on absolute national independence and seeks genuine and universal peace.

A. It will put an end to U.S. interference in Nicaragua's internal affairs. With respect to other countries, it will follow a policy of mutual respect and fraternal collaboration between peoples.

B. It will expel the U.S. military mission, the so-called Peace Corps (spies disguised as technicians), and similar military and political elements whose presence constitutes barefaced intervention in our country.

C. It will accept financial and technical aid from any country so long as no political strings are attached.

D. Together with other peoples of the world it will promote a campaign in support of genuine and universal peace.

E. It will abrogate all treaties, signed with any foreign power, that undermine national sovereignty.

X. Central American people's unity

The Sandinista people's revolution supports the true union of the peoples of Central America in a single nation.

A. It will support genuine unity with our sister peoples of Central America. This unity will prepare the way for coordinating efforts to achieve national liberation and establish a new system free of imperialist domination and national betrayal.

B. It will eliminate the economic policy known as "integration." The aim of this policy is to deepen Central America's subservience to U.S. monopolies and local reactionary forces.

XI. Solidarity among peoples

The Sandinista people's revolution will put an end to the use of our nation's territory as a base for U.S. aggression against our sister peoples. It will extend militant solidarity to sister peoples fighting for their liberation.

A. It will actively support the struggle of the peoples of Asia, Africa, and Latin America against both traditional and modern forms of colonialism, and against the common enemy: U.S. imperialism.

B. It will support the struggle of the Black people and all the people of the United States for genuine democracy and equal rights.

C. It will support the struggle of all peoples against the establishment of U.S. military bases in foreign countries.

XII. People's patriotic army

The Sandinista people's revolution will abolish the armed forces known as the National Guard, which is an enemy of the people. In its place, the revolution will create a patriotic, revolutionary, and people's army.

A. It will abolish the National Guard. This force is an enemy of the people created under U.S. occupation in 1927 to hunt down, torture, and murder Sandinista patriots.

B. In the new people's army, professional soldiers who were members of the old army will be able to play a role providing they have observed the following norms of conduct:

1. They have supported the guerrilla struggle.

2. They have not participated in murder, plunder, torture, and persecution of the people and revolutionary activists.

3. They have rebelled against the despotic Somoza dynasty.

C. It will strengthen the new people's army, raising its fighting ability and its tactical and technical level.

D. It will instill in the consciousness of the members of the people's army the need to rely on their own forces to fulfill their duties, and the need to develop their creative potential to the fullest.

E. It will deepen the revolutionary ideals of the people's army. It will reinforce the army's patriotic spirit and firm conviction to fight until victory is achieved, overcoming obstacles and correcting errors.

F. It will forge a conscious discipline in the ranks of the people's army and will encourage the close ties that must exist between the combatants and the people.

G. It will establish compulsory military service and will arm the students, workers, and farmers who—organized in people's militias—will defend the rights won against inevitable attack by the reactionary forces here and U.S. imperialism.

XIII. Veneration of our martyrs

The Sandinista people's revolution pledges eternal gratitude to and veneration of our homeland's martyrs; it will continue the shining example of heroism and selflessness they have bequeathed to us.

A. It will educate the new generations in eternal gratitude and veneration toward those who have given their lives in the struggle to make Nicaragua a free country.

B. It will establish a college to educate the children of our people's martyrs.

C. It will instill in the entire people the imperishable example of our martyrs, defending the revolutionary ideal: *Hasta la victoria siempre!* [Ever onward to victory!]

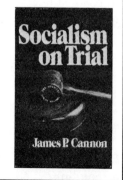

FIDEL CASTRO
speeches & interviews

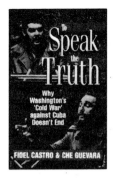

To Speak the Truth
Why Washington's 'Cold War' Against Cuba Doesn't End
BY FIDEL CASTRO AND CHE GUEVARA

Why the U.S. government is determined to destroy the example set by the socialist revolution in Cuba and why these efforts will fail. Introduction by Mary-Alice Waters. $16.95

In Defense of Socialism
Four Speeches on the 30th Anniversary of the Cuban Revolution

Not only is economic and social progress possible without the dog-eat-dog competition of capitalism, Castro argues, but socialism is the only way forward for humanity. Also discusses Cuba's role in the struggle against the apartheid regime in southern Africa. $13.95

Selected Speeches of Fidel Castro
Speeches from the 1960s and 1970s

Includes 1961 speech, "I Shall Be a Marxist-Leninist to the End of My Life," explaining why only a socialist revolution could bring about the profound changes Cuban working people had overthrown the Batista dictatorship to achieve. 8½x 11 format. $14.00

The Second Declaration of Havana
"It is the duty of every revolutionist to make the revolution." A call issued in 1962 for revolutionary struggle throughout the Americas. Booklet. $3.00

War and Crisis in the Americas
The stakes in the looming showdown with Washington in Central America and the Caribbean, and the explosive social consequences of the foreign debt in Latin America. Speeches and interviews from 1984-85. $17.95

'Cuba Will Never Adopt Capitalist Methods' (1988), $2.50

Cuba's Internationalist Foreign Policy, 1975-80, $20.95

PATHFINDER   *See page 2 for distributors*

Writings of
ERNESTO CHE GUEVARA

Che Guevara and the Cuban Revolution
Writings and Speeches of Ernesto Che Guevara

The most complete collection in English. Guevara discusses the revolutionary war that brought the workers and farmers to victory; Cuba's efforts to overcome economic backwardness; developing "the new man and woman" in a society on the road to socialism; and Cuba's commitment to freedom struggles around the world. $21.95

Che Guevara: Economics and Politics in the Transition to Socialism
CARLOS TABLADA

"To build communism," Guevara wrote in 1965, "it is necessary, simultaneously with the new material foundations, to build the new man." This book, based on Guevara's extensive writings and speeches, explains why. Also available in Spanish and French. $17.95

Che Guevara Speaks
Selected Speeches and Writings

"A faithful reflection of Che as he was, or, better, as he developed"—from the preface by Joseph Hansen. Includes works by Che not available elsewhere in English. $12.95

See page 2 for addresses   **FROM PATHFINDER**

2. WASHINGTON'S CONTRA WAR AND THE CHALLENGE OF FORGING PROLETARIAN LEADERSHIP

By the end of 1987, the U.S.-organized contra armies had been
defeated in a revolutionary war, opening the way to new advances by
workers and peasants. Above, a member of the Sandinista People's
Army on patrol in northern Nicaragua, November 1987.

PHOTO: ROBERTO KOPEC / MILITANT

WAR AND REVOLUTION IN CENTRAL AMERICA AND THE CARIBBEAN: THE CENTER OF WORLD POLITICS

1. REVOLUTIONARY VICTORIES IN CENTRAL AMERICA AND THE CARIBBEAN

T HE TRIUMPH in 1979 of the Grenada and Nicaraguan revolutions came after the Socialist Workers Party had decided to make the turn to get a big majority of our members into the industrial unions.[1] The decision on the character and timing of this turn was not, and could not have been, built around anticipation of these revolutionary victories in Central America and the Caribbean, nor of the advance of the Cuban socialist revolution that was accelerated by these new triumphs in the Americas. Rather, the turn flowed from the concrete evolution of the class struggle on a world scale and its manifestation inside the United States, which portended intensified class battles nationally and internationally.

While the turn was not begun in response to these revolutionary advances, the concrete working-class outlook we gained by being based in industry oriented us to respond as a proletarian internationalist party to the revolutionary advances being registered by workers and exploited rural producers in the Americas. As a party whose energies were focused on constructing fractions in the industrial unions, we could see more clearly and respond more fully to new opportunities to move forward

---

This is excerpted from the resolution "The Revolutionary Perspective and Leninist Continuity in the United States," adopted by a January 1985 convention of the Socialist Workers Party. The entire resolution can be found in New International, *no. 4 (spring 1985).*

ENDNOTES FOR THIS ARTICLE BEGIN ON PAGE 311.

in resolving the historic crisis of proletarian leadership. The turn helped us to recognize enthusiastically, and without sectarian hesitation, the revolutionary capacities of the leaderships that were being forged in Central America and the Caribbean.

The turn to the industrial unions has been equally decisive to placing the party in a position to act effectively in the class battle in the United States over the deepening imperialist war against the workers and peasants of Central America and the Caribbean. The triumphs in Grenada and Nicaragua, and the battles being waged in El Salvador, have deeply affected class-conscious working people in the United States. This is true despite the imperialists' efforts to hide the truth about these revolutions—and despite the souring toward these revolutions and toward Cuba by a layer of petty-bourgeois critics as imperialist war pressures mount. The pessimism of these fainthearted radicals about the course of events in Central America and the Caribbean reveals their own recoiling from the fight in the face of Washington's power and deadly intent.

The governments in Nicaragua and—until its overthrow in October 1983—in Grenada have provided workers and farmers in the United States with inspiring new examples of what can be accomplished once the alliance of workers and rural producers succeeds in overthrowing a landlord-capitalist regime and placing power in the hands of the working people of the city and countryside, organized by a revolutionary regime. These examples have taken their place beside and have reinforced the powerful beacon that Cuba represents, illuminating the road forward for all the exploited and oppressed.

The multinational character of the U.S. working class magnifies the impact of these revolutions on working people in this country. Working people who are Black, and the growing number of workers who are Latino, are particularly inspired by the courage and accomplishments of the Central American and Caribbean peoples. They have seen working people of their color, and who speak their language, establishing popular revolutionary dictatorships in nearby countries and using that power to win genuine national liberation, to defend and advance the class interests of those who labor for a living, and to begin transforming economic and social relations. They can see more clearly what a revolutionary worker-farmer alliance means for their own struggles in this country.

A party with its roots in the industrial working class can take advantage of these living examples of revolutionary conquests to strengthen the organized working-class vanguard in the United States, and to deepen the consciousness of those workers and farmers who are attracted to and encouraged by the revolutions in Central America and the Caribbean. It can explain the importance of the Cuban revolution, and the turning point it represented in modern history for the continuing development of Marxist leadership.

Working-class axis in the fight against imperialist intervention
Basing the party in the industrial unions is essential to meet the political challenge posed by the need to draw the labor movement into a fight against the war U.S. imperialism is waging today.

The Vietnam War took place during a period of prolonged economic expansion, when there was substantial improvement in living standards for large sections of the U.S. working class. The opposite is now the case. The Central American war is being escalated at a time when the offensive against the working class is producing a deepening class polarization, making it easier to see the class forces that will confront each other in coming battles.

Part of the labor movement has been involved from the beginning in opposing Washington's war moves and will become increasingly so. This will be the case even though the initiative in organizing antiwar actions will initially be held by pacifists, solidarity groups, and others with no particular orientation to the labor movement or the working class.

Under current conditions, calls for action in the streets against the imperialist war will be initiated largely outside the labor movement. Revolutionists actively participate in organizing such protests and seek to build them and guide them insofar as possible along lines that can maximize drawing in union forces and oppressed nationalities. Such an orientation is essential for a revolutionary workers party if opportunities are to be utilized to deepen and broaden the fight in the labor movement against the U.S. war, and build an antiwar movement that will become increasingly proletarian and multinational in its composition and leadership.

By actively participating in all initiatives that mobilize opposition in the streets against the U.S. war in Central America and the Caribbean, the party sets a leadership example for all opponents of that war. We will attract to our ranks young fighters, both inside and outside the unions, who become politicized through the experience of taking to the streets in opposition to a war being waged by their own imperialist government.

Proletarian strategy in the struggle for power

The turn to the industrial unions has also been essential in placing the SWP in a position to be able to learn from the revolutionary experiences in Central America and the Caribbean, and to relearn and absorb the lessons from twenty-five years of experience of socialist revolution in Cuba. These lessons have helped to enrich our own understanding of how the working class will advance along its line of march toward power in the United States and on a world scale. They have helped us more firmly reknit our continuity with the early years of the Communist International, when the Bolsheviks sought to advance the construction of parties in each country oriented to leading the working people in the fight to take power.

In doing so, we are clarifying our understanding that the strategic questions the Cubans, Nicaraguans, Grenadians, and Salvadorans have had to confront are also questions that a revolutionary party in the United States must answer: How does the proletariat solidify and make lasting its alliance with other working people, especially the exploited farmers? With what kind of government do we propose to replace the capitalist government now in power? How do we prevent day-to-day tactics from becoming separated from, and over time counterposed to, the strategic objective of leading working people in a revolutionary struggle for power?

2. IMPERIALIST WAR DRIVE IN CENTRAL AMERICA AND THE CARIBBEAN

WASHINGTON'S EFFORTS to hold back the world revolution now focus on Central America and the Caribbean. This region is today at the center of the battle of our epoch—the battle between the efforts by workers and farmers to establish their own revolutionary regimes in new countries, and the imperialists' determination to prevent this.

In Nicaragua the workers and peasants have taken power away from a landlord-capitalist tyranny, and have established a workers and peasants government. They are advancing—as Cuba did twenty-five years ago—toward the expropriation of the capitalist class, which will open the socialist revolution. That is the road the exploited producers of El Salvador are also fighting to embark on. It is in Central America and the Caribbean that the political example of the revolutionary Marxist leadership of socialist Cuba has its greatest influence among fighters for national liberation, land reform, and workers' rights.

It is for these reasons that Central America and the Caribbean are at the very center of world politics today. The imperialists have no alternative but to fight to reverse this altered relationship of class forces brought about by the revolutionary advances in the region.

With the support of both political parties of U.S. imperialism, the Pentagon is steadily deepening its military intervention in El Salvador, attempting to defeat the forces of the Farabundo Martí National Liberation Front and block a revolutionary victory by the FMLN and Revolutionary Democratic Front (FDR). The U.S. government is fielding a Somocista mercenary army to weaken and if possible overthrow the workers and peasants government in Nicaragua. Advances and setbacks for either side in either country deeply affect the struggle in the other.

Washington is trying to convert Honduras into a virtual U.S. military base. It is pushing to transform the entire region, including the U.S. colony of Puerto Rico, into a military staging ground for its counterrevolutionary war.

The October 1983 invasion of Grenada, which followed the overthrow of the Bishop-led workers and farmers government by the Stalinist forces headed by Bernard Coard, marked the first direct use of U.S. military power in the Americas in nearly twenty years. Not since U.S. marines landed in the Dominican Republic in April 1965 to put down a popular revolution had Washington sent large numbers of U.S. troops into combat in the Americas.

The Coard coup, culminating in the murder of Maurice Bishop and other revolutionary leaders, overthrew the workers and farmers government and handed Grenada to Washington on a silver platter. This was a harsh defeat for the workers and farmers of the entire hemisphere. The reconquering of Grenada by imperialism marks the most important victory Washington has attained in the sustained offensive it has been waging since the 1979 victories for worker-farmer power in Grenada and Nicaragua.

In the half-decade since 1979 there has been no new revolutionary conquest of power by the workers and farmers anywhere in the world. The pace of the advances in the international struggle against imperialism that marked the latter part of the 1970s—from Indochina to Iran, from Zimbabwe to Nicaragua and Grenada—has not continued. Moreover, in a number of cases the imperialist counteroffensive has registered gains, pushing back earlier advances. In Central America, for example, the 1979 victories initially impelled a step-up in mass struggles by the Guatemalan workers and farmers, as well as progress toward unification of revolutionary forces there. In recent years, however, the escalation of U.S.-backed repression by the Guatemalan regime has resulted in important setbacks for the mass movement in city and countryside.

Nonetheless, Washington has not accomplished its goal of restoring the relationship of class forces that existed prior to 1979 in Central America and the Caribbean. The easy victory for the imperialist invaders of Grenada will not be duplicated in Nicaragua, let alone Cuba. Despite the massive military aid being poured into El Salvador to prop up the regime there, the revolutionary forces—now organized in the FMLN-FDR—remain stronger than they were before the Nicaraguan victory opened a new and more favorable political situation for the Salvadoran workers and peasants.

Imperialism's escalating intervention in El Salvador

The imperialists are determined to prevent a revolution in El Salvador that smashes the landlord-capitalist forces and brings to power a popular revolutionary dictatorship—a workers and peasants government. Washington is escalating its intervention in El Salvador to prevent another such historic advance in national liberation from imperialist domination. The U.S. government is propping up the tyranny with arms, military advisers, and money to prevent just such an anticapitalist revolution. It has drawn the Honduran regime into this counterrevolutionary effort. The Israeli government is also a major supplier of arms and ammunition to the Salvadoran generals, serving as a conduit for Washington and at the same time advancing its own imperialist interests in that part of the world.

U.S. imperialism has put to work a team of public relations experts whose job is to paint a democratic mask on the face of the bloody Salvadoran regime. The essential character of this dictatorship has not changed despite the U.S.-organized elections— in which the popular forces are excluded from participation by state-organized terror, and the people are compelled to vote by law backed by assassination squads and empty pledges by U.S.-picked president José Napoleón Duarte to end repression.

The imperialists' surrogate armies cannot do the job. Nor can all the most advanced military technology at their disposal. Nor can faked elections or "land reforms" carried out against the peasantry. The democratic electoral facade imposed by Washington on the Salvadoran oligarchy is part of the political preparation for more direct U.S. military intervention—with more arms and, when necessary, U.S. combat troops.

Somocista armies incapable of accomplishing objective

The U.S. imperialists are escalating their efforts to weaken and eventually overthrow the Sandinista-led workers and peasants government in Nicaragua. They are intensifying their diplomatic pressure and blackmail against the Nicaraguan government, with increasing help from their imperialist allies in Western Europe and compliance from neocolonial bourgeois regimes in Latin America. They are organizing and financing the self-proclaimed "democratic" and "labor" opposition forces inside Nicaragua, especially those that rally around the Catholic Church hierarchy and the reactionary newspaper *La Prensa*. And they are arming, financing, training, and supplying a large mercenary army of counterrevolutionaries.

The imperialists, however, are face to face with the fact that their hired army of Somocista forces has failed to take and hold a single city or town that it could use as a center for declaring a provisional government. They have not succeeded in mobilizing a mass following in the urban areas. They have not even been capable of maintaining anywhere in Nicaragua a base of operations in a section of the countryside where they exercise control and can move at will. In short, the imperialists have failed to accomplish their objective of transforming their mercenary war into a civil war that could bring down the Sandinista government.

The CIA-backed contras have been prevented by armed workers and peasants from accomplishing any of these objectives, despite abundant U.S. arms and supply shipments, and despite the military advantage of being able to operate with impunity from staging grounds in Honduras and Costa Rica within striking distance of a number of Nicaraguan population centers.

Instead, the contras' activities revolve around terrorist raids on economic targets, inflicting heavy economic damage on the Nicaraguan people. The cost in lives and economic resources has been high, but the Somocista army is being defeated militarily, while failing politically.

The bourgeois opponents of the revolution inside Nicaragua have been emboldened by imperialist support. But they have been unable to take and hold the political offensive, despite the severe economic problems imposed by the CIA-organized terror attacks and the massively financed "disinformation" and destabilization campaigns carried out by the bishops, in the pages of *La Prensa,* and in other ways.

This relationship of forces was clearly registered in the Nicaraguan elections of November 1984. Despite the fact that the Nicaraguan bourgeoisie retains significant property in land and industry and the economy is one in which capitalist property relations remain predominant, it is the workers and peasants who hold the political initiative. As part of its efforts to carry out the bourgeois-democratic tasks of the revolution, the FSLN-led government organized elections for a president, vice president, and constituent assembly. The Sandinistas challenged the proimperialist forces on the terrain these forces claim as their own, that of liberal bourgeois democracy, and won. The capitalist opposition forces who refused to participate were discredited further. The confidence and organization of the workers and peasants were strengthened.[2]

Defeating the U.S. imperialist aggression remains the overriding task confronting Nicaraguan working people today. The FSLN continues to make advances in organizing the workers and peasants to maintain production, combat the effects of the war, and defend their revolution. The vanguard Nicaraguan workers and peasants are displaying iron determination. They are defending the gains of their revolution against the efforts of their class enemies to restore the rule of the landlords and capitalists, whose hated regime they overthrew on July 19, 1979. And they are prepared to fight to defend their country—as their parents and grandparents did—against any invasion by the armed forces of U.S. imperialism.

Cuba: permanent target of imperialism
The imperialists retain their goal of reversing the socialist revolution in Cuba. That island remains a permanent target of U.S. economic warfare and military might. The Cuban people are subjected to a continuing economic blockade, assassinations and other acts of terror against Cubans abroad, internal sabotage, biological warfare, destabilization efforts organized and inspired by the CIA and their gangs of hired counterrevolutionary Cuban *es-*

coria,[3] and military provocations and pressure from Cuban territory still occupied by the U.S. government at Guantánamo. At all
times the Cubans face the reality of this overwhelming military
power of Washington, including its nuclear arsenal.

Despite these pressures, the Cubans have refused to retreat
from their course of extending aid and solidarity to the peoples
of the region who are fighting arms in hand to defend their
country, as in Nicaragua, or to overthrow the tyranny under
which they live, as in El Salvador and Guatemala. The Cubans
understand that every victory against imperialist domination and
landlord-capitalist oppression—whatever countermoves by imperialism may be entailed—strengthens the Cuban revolution as
well, and enables it to play an even stronger internationalist role.

War and revolution

The imperialists will fail in their efforts to turn the tide in Central America and the Caribbean in their favor short of using
U.S. combat troops. But Washington fears the political consequences of this move as long as the revolutionary forces continue to advance, making a quick military victory, such as that
in Grenada, unobtainable. A protracted ground war, pitting
U.S. troops against the mobilized workers and peasants of Nicaragua or El Salvador, will set uncontrolled forces in motion
throughout Latin America and the Caribbean—and right here
in the United States.

Such a war will not be restricted to a single country. It will become regional, with unpredictable consequences for imperialist-
dominated regimes throughout the Americas. It will become, as
the revolutionary leaders of Central America and the Caribbean
have warned U.S. imperialism, another Vietnam War.

What is more, as the dead and wounded U.S. soldiers are
shipped home, the class conflicts inside the United States over
this war will sharpen rapidly and become polarized and radicalized in a way never before seen here in this century.

In addition, the pace of revolutionary struggles elsewhere in
the world directly affects what Washington can accomplish in its
drive to crush struggles by the workers and peasants of Central

America and the Caribbean. As the Cuban leaders explain, their revolution survived its first decade in large part because of Vietnam's tenacious revolutionary struggle against U.S. imperialist domination, which bought crucial time for the Cubans. A worker-farmer victory or major advance by revolutionary forces in Asia, Africa, or elsewhere in the Americas today would again force U.S. imperialism to devote more of its energies and resources to other fronts of the international class struggle.

The imperialists must take these factors into account as they push forward their war drive against the revolutions in Central America and the Caribbean.

3. OBJECTIVE CHANGES BROUGHT ABOUT BY 1979 VICTORIES

T HE 1979 victories in Grenada and Nicaragua, the deepening of the Cuban revolution in response to these triumphs, and the gains in El Salvador have changed the relationship of class forces in the Americas.

The existence of the Nicaraguan bastion of worker-peasant rule right in the middle of Central America is an impulse to revolutionary organization and action throughout the entire area— from Panama north to Guatemala. It is an inspiring example to anti-imperialist fighters throughout the Americas. While the objective conditions and subjective factors in each of the countries of Central America vary widely, the existence of the Sandinista workers and peasants government on the Central American isthmus changes the framework in which each of these struggles will unfold. The conquest of state power by the Nicaraguan workers and peasants, led by the Sandinista National Liberation Front, means that in order to push back the revolution the imperialists have to do more than just isolate or wear down a mass movement—they must succeed in *overthrowing a state power,* a mighty weapon in the hands of the exploited classes of Nicaragua.

There has also been an objective change in the Caribbean, progress that has been pushed back but not eliminated by the overthrow of the workers and farmers government in Grenada. An advance has been registered in beginning to tie together revolutionary developments in the Spanish-speaking Caribbean with struggles in the English- and French-speaking islands, whose populations are predominantly Black or East Indian. The Grenada revolution was the biggest single factor in this process.

This transformation has brought to bear the revolutionary influence of the Cuban revolution in a new way on a part of the world previously less affected by it than the Spanish-speaking Americas. The blockade of revolutionary Cuba has been breached at another spot.

The Coard faction's betrayal of the Grenada revolution and imperialism's subsequent invasion and occupation of the island have set back this progress in the Caribbean. Nonetheless, the economic squeeze of international capital on the Caribbean nations will continually undermine social and political stability for proimperialist regimes such as those in Jamaica, Barbados, and throughout the region. As working people resist their imperialist and domestic oppressors and exploiters, the most class-conscious fighters will continue to learn from the lessons of the Grenada revolution and the example of Maurice Bishop. They will look to socialist Cuba.

The advances in the Caribbean have also led to new interest within the United States in the revolutions in the Americas. Through the Caribbean peoples living in the United States, and because of the interconnections between the U.S. Black movement and the struggles of the Black people of the Caribbean islands, these struggles have had greater impact in the United States.

Reaffirmation of the Cuban road

The 1979 victories in Nicaragua and Grenada were led by forces that shared the revolutionary perspective advanced by the leadership of the Cuban Communist Party: that the road forward is the road to workers and farmers power. The result has been to establish on a broader scale throughout Latin America and the Caribbean the political authority and attractiveness of Marxism among revolutionary-minded fighters who are striving to find a proletarian strategy.

These victories have been widely seen as a reaffirmation of the "Cuban road"—the revolutionary mobilization of the workers and peasants, led by a conscious vanguard formation, to resolve the central question of every popular revolution in our epoch: the seizing of power and the inauguration of a revolutionary government of the workers and farmers.

For its first twenty years, revolutionary Cuba stood alone in the Americas, the first government to emerge from a successful anticapitalist revolution in this hemisphere. This changed with the victories in 1979. Cuba now stood with Grenada and Nicaragua, and together the "three giants" pointed the way forward for the peoples of all the Americas. This weakened the position of the social democrats, who condemn Cuba as "totalitarian" while trying to dismiss the revolutionary victory there as an exception. It was also a blow to the Stalinists, who combine fulsome public praise for the Cuban revolution with advice to the workers and peasants of their own countries to follow a different road. They also say that the Cuban revolution was possible only due to exceptional circumstances.

The imperialists deliberately seek to misrepresent the influence of revolutionary Cuba's *example* on workers and farmers beyond its borders, and its unselfish *aid* to many in other countries, as efforts by the Cuban government *to export* its revolution. This lie, used by the imperialists to justify their aggression toward Cuba, was forcefully answered in the Second Declaration of Havana in 1962:

"To the accusation that Cuba wants to export its revolution, we reply: Revolutions are not exported, they are made by the people.

"What Cuba can give to the people, and has already given, is its example.

"And what does the Cuban revolution teach? That revolution is possible, that the people can make it, that in the contemporary world there are no forces capable of halting the liberation movement of the peoples."[4]

4. STRENGTHENING PROLETARIAN INTERNATIONALIST LEADERSHIP

T HE VICTORIES in Central America and the Caribbean in 1979 have shown that the Cuban revolution was not unique, but rather the first successful conquest of power by the workers and farmers in the Americas. So too they have shown that the leadership forged by the Cuban revolution was not a historical exception, but a vanguard component of a new leadership of the working class, fighting to apply in practice the principles of communism, converging historically with all those who have attempted to continue along the road charted by the Comintern under Lenin's leadership. Other parties have now emerged from the revolutionary struggles of the masses of workers and peasants and have proven their capacity to lead those forces to power.

These events have confirmed the historic character of the turning point signaled by the development of the Cuban leadership team. For the first time since the degeneration of the Russian revolution, the world revolution made a mighty advance under the leadership of revolutionary forces that developed outside the Stalinist Communist parties. The battle against the class-collaborationist policies of the Stalinists that the leaders of the July 26 Movement began when they launched their revolutionary struggle more than thirty years ago has continued to this day. The development of internationalist leaderships in Grenada, Nicaragua, and El Salvador has confirmed that the leadership breakthrough represented by the Cuban victory was—like the Cuban revolution itself—not an exception. A historic stride is being taken toward resolving the crisis of proletarian leadership on a world scale. As the Fourth International anticipated at its founding in 1938, new revolutionary leaderships are developing outside of, and in political counterposition to the strategy of, Stalinist-dominated organizations.

The victories in Cuba, and then in Nicaragua and Grenada, ended the period in which the only parties in power claiming to be proletarian and internationalist were Stalinist parties. This has made it qualitatively harder for the Stalinist movement on a world scale to claim the sole continuity with the revolutionary leadership of the Bolsheviks and the Comintern in Lenin's time. The breach of this claimed monopoly has opened the door to our movement, and to others, to be recognized as legitimate components of the worldwide communist movement that must be built. There is a political convergence between our world current and other revolutionists in the Americas, in the first place the leadership of the Communist Party of Cuba, who are charting a course in practice that leads to reestablishing continuity with the internationalist program and strategy of the Communist International in Lenin's time.

The emergence of these leadership forces has dealt a blow to the imperialists' anticommunist propaganda, which equates communism with Stalinist repression of the workers and farmers, and with the narrow national interests that the Stalinist regimes and parties take as their framework.

In Nicaragua, the FSLN, with its immense mass support, has won authority among a wing of former and some present members of the Nicaraguan Socialist Party (PSN—the traditional Stalinist party in Nicaragua). In El Salvador, a component of the Communist Party there has integrated itself into the FMLN. These processes are similar in some ways to what happened earlier in Cuba, when a majority of the Cuban Popular Socialist Party was politically won after the revolutionary victory to recognize the unchallengeable authority of the central leadership of the July 26 Movement.

These gains in the fight for revolutionary leadership have been furthered by the Cubans' policy. They have set an example of proletarian internationalism in action in order to point the way forward and mobilize maximum support for revolutionary struggles and regimes.

At the same time, the Cubans have resolutely combated those, even among their "friends," who fail to understand the decisive role of economic and military aid to the Cuban revolution from the Soviet Union and other Warsaw Pact countries. They have refused to allow a wedge to be driven between Cuba and the Soviet and Eastern European workers states.

Deepening proletarianization of leadership

In the first two years following the January 1959 insurrectionary triumph in Cuba, the leadership there successfully mobilized and educated the broad popular masses, leading the revolution forward to the expropriation of capitalist property—the decisive step in consolidating a durable worker-farmer alliance. Since then, the Cuban leadership has gone through a process of deepening proletarianization. It has gained greater political clarity on communist strategy in the fight of the workers and peasants to take power and then institutionalize it, as they advance the construction of socialism in their own countries and carry out a selfless internationalist course.

Part of this process in Cuba was the fusion of revolutionary proletarian forces, as well as differentiation from those whose trajectory led in a nonproletarian direction. The July 26 Movement went through a number of splits with petty-bourgeois forces who had earlier supported the revolution but who later turned against it, and then politically defeated and split with the petty-bourgeois Stalinist forces around Aníbal Escalante.

The FSLN and the FMLN have had the advantage of benefiting from the earlier experiences, including mistakes, that the Cuban leadership lived through and learned from.

In Nicaragua, the fusion of the three wings into which the FSLN had split was an essential prerequisite for the successful leadership of the insurrection and revolution. The FSLN, too, has seen petty-bourgeois components break away and turn against the revolution. The best known of these is the traitor Edén Pastora, who has been notably unsuccessful in his attempt to lead a "non-Somocista" counterrevolutionary army to drown the revolution in blood. There will be more defections as the Nicaraguan revolution advances and the class polarization deepens.

In El Salvador, there has been progress toward the fusion of the five groups making up the FMLN. This process was advanced with the decisive rejection by the FMLN of the political and organizational trajectory of Salvador Cayetano Carpio (Marcial). Carpio's followers have now split from the FMLN and are hostile to it.

In each case these fusions and the splits necessary to accomplish them have been part of deepening the roots of these vanguards in the working class, making them more proletarian in composition as well as orientation.

This process has also been part of developing a more thoroughly and consistently proletarian strategy. This includes greater clarity around the need for the working class to lead the broadest possible forces in fighting for a revolutionary-democratic program, participating in the daily struggles of the masses with a constant orientation of advancing toward the conquest of power.

In Nicaragua the Sandinista leaders have deepened their understanding of the lessons to be learned from the experiences of other proletarian revolutionaries in power. They have learned from the experience of the Cuban revolution in the 1960s, including what Fidel Castro has aptly called the "utopian" errors that were made by the Cuban revolutionaries. In correcting these errors, the Cubans absorbed and generalized lessons that have similarities to those the Bolsheviks drew from the period of "war communism," including the mistakes that were analyzed and corrected when the Bolsheviks adopted the New Economic Policy in 1921. The Nicaraguan revolutionaries, too, have sought to benefit from the lessons of the NEP; the Sandinista-led trade unions have printed and circulated pamphlets containing some of Lenin's articles and speeches from this period.[5]

By absorbing these lessons, the Cuban leadership, and now the Nicaraguan leadership, have deepened their understanding of the importance of maintaining and strengthening the class alliance between the workers and other exploited producers, especially the peasants.

Proletarianization has also meant a deepening internationalism. Such an internationalist policy includes understanding the importance of workers and farmers governments establishing solid links with the Soviet Union and with the other workers states. The Cuban leadership has repeatedly and publicly insisted on the responsibility of the more economically developed workers states to provide generous material aid and preferential terms of trade to the workers and farmers governments and workers states that are fighting to overcome the legacy of imperialist domination and develop their national economies, as well as to other countries in Asia, Africa, and Latin America that are suffering economic blackmail by international finance capital.

Proletarian internationalist policy is, above all, built on subordinating the narrow national interests of any single country to the advance of the world revolution. It is built on the repudiation of any form of national chauvinism, of selfishness with regard to the struggles of the workers and farmers in other countries, and of efforts to purchase détente with imperialism at the price of renouncing active solidarity with revolutionaries fighting to defeat imperialism.

5. OBJECTIVE WEIGHT OF THE LEADERSHIP QUESTION—EL SALVADOR AND GRENADA

A T THE CENTER of this deepening proletarianization is a consciousness of the importance and weight of revolutionary working-class leadership. The construction of a proletarian internationalist leadership is essential for the success of the revolution in overturning capitalist political rule, bringing to power a workers and farmers government, and subsequently carrying through the decisive and irreplaceable steps necessary to establish a workers state through the expropriation of the capitalist class and the establishment of a planned economy. Without a sufficiently strong vanguard, united around a proletarian strategy, revolutionary opportunities will be lost.

The experiences of the revolution in El Salvador and in Grenada provide graphic illustration of the decisive weight of leadership in the advance of the revolutionary process.

In El Salvador the different groupings that united to form the FMLN have set the goal of creating a single, united vanguard party committed to the mobilization of the workers and peasants behind a revolutionary-democratic program in a struggle to topple the landlord-capitalist government. The goal of the guerrilla struggle being waged by the FMLN is to maximize the conditions for a mass insurrectionary upheaval in which the workers and peasants will overthrow the government, destroy its repressive apparatus, and bring to power a popular revolutionary regime, one representing their class interests.

This strategic perspective is the same as the one that guided the central leadership of the July 26 Movement in Cuba. The guerrilla struggle waged by the Rebel Army there helped set the stage for a mass mobilization of the population when the army of the Batista dictatorship began disintegrating as a result of its inability to continue a losing war against the rebel fighters.

In Nicaragua the armed struggle in the countryside rallied mass support for the FSLN and showed that armed action against the dictatorship was possible. It opened the door to broader urban organization. This prepared the way for the insurrection, when the Nicaraguan masses took history into their own hands and overthrew the government.

Implementing this perspective in El Salvador necessitates a vanguard organization of the working class—a revolutionary party—that is united around this perspective and capable of clearly projecting the road forward to the conquest of political power, while leading the day-to-day struggles of the peasants and workers to constantly clarify and advance toward this objective.

Clarification of the differences with Carpio

An essential step forward in the process toward unification of the big majority of the leadership and cadres of the FMLN into a united vanguard with a revolutionary proletarian perspective has taken place in the last two years. The majority of the People's Liberation Forces (FPL), the largest of the components that formed the FMLN, rejected the political line defended by Salvador Cayetano Carpio, the FPL's central founding leader. Two groups, the Revolutionary Workers Movement (MOR) and the Clara Elisabeth Ramírez Front, which still cling to Carpio's line, subsequently responded to their political defeat by splitting from the FPL and FMLN.

The strategic orientation of the Carpio supporters who have split from the FMLN is to prepare for decades of guerrilla war against the regime. In contrast, the FMLN leadership, while recognizing that an insurrection that can topple the regime is not an immediate prospect, rejects the notion that preparation by the workers and peasants to achieve this goal should be put off to the remote and distant future. It seeks to carry out activity on a day-to-day basis, including renewing mass activity in the urban areas, in order to advance toward the insurrectionary upheaval that can overthrow the U.S.-backed dictatorship.

The Carpio supporters reject this strategy as a guide to action today. They warn against what they call the FMLN's "short-termist" strategy toward taking power prematurely, before the masses can be organized and educated sufficiently to prepare them to run the country. They counterpose to it what they refer to as the strategy of "prolonged people's war." This term has been used by various organizations in many different countries to refer to quite distinct strategies, but the content given to it by the splitters from the FMLN is an ultraleft and sectarian one. It points away from implementing a strategy today that will hasten the resolution of the central question of the revolution in El Salvador: leading the workers and peasants in an insurrectionary struggle to bring a workers and peasants government to power.

The Carpio loyalists also accuse the FMLN and FDR of preparing to sell out the revolutionary struggle by negotiating a deal that would keep in power a bourgeois government in San Salvador.

On the organizational plane, Carpio and his supporters fought against the process of fusion within the FMLN. While giving lip service to the need for unity, in practice they insisted on maintaining their own political organization and military forces at the expense of the fusion process, thus becoming a barrier to actually moving toward unity. A small layer of these factionalists went so far as to organize the brutal and sadistic assassination of Mélida Anaya Montes (Commander Ana María), who had broken politically with Carpio and was helping to lead the fight for unity of the revolutionary vanguard.

Carpio subsequently committed suicide, after being confronted with the fact that the Nicaraguan government had proof of his involvement in the murder. The FMLN's repudiation of these acts and this line of Carpio's followers marks an advance for the FMLN in clarifying its political line and progress in the unification of its forces.

Grenada: the decisive weight of leadership

The experience of the Grenada revolution from 1979 to 1983 also confirms the decisive weight of revolutionary leadership for the working class and its allies. The example provided by the leadership of Maurice Bishop has not been diminished since his assassination by the betrayers of the Grenada revolution, headed by Bernard Coard. Bishop was both a genuine popular leader of the working people and a Marxist whose political understanding of the line of march of the Grenadian workers and farmers was a decisive element in the victory over the dictatorship of Eric Gairy, and in leading the revolution forward for four years.

In contrast, the political line and practice of the Coard faction within the New Jewel Movement was Stalinist. This faction favored use of bureaucratic and administrative measures in place of the organization and mobilization of the working people, in an attempt to leap over objective problems facing the revolution. It built itself on and attracted those who had lost, or never had, confidence in the capacity of the toilers of Grenada to defend their revolution and those for whom revolutionary victories elsewhere appeared an increasingly remote possibility.

The Coard group functioned as a secret faction, consolidating its position through favoritism and distribution of material privileges. It based itself not on the most oppressed and exploited layers of the working people of the towns and countryside but on a layer of the governmental and army apparatus and a milieu of their hangers-on.

More than a year prior to the October 1983 events, Coard and his backers had begun engineering the removal of central

NJM leaders from leadership positions in the party, replacing them with individuals from their faction. This grouping also fastened its hold on the leadership structures of the National Women's Organisation, National Youth Organisation, and sectors of the trade union movement.

In order to discredit those in the party leadership who resisted their bureaucratic course, Coard's faction claimed that the Grenada revolution under Bishop's leadership had reached a point of perilous social, economic, and political crisis.

Of course, as a former colonial nation oppressed by imperialism, the revolution faced substantial objective difficulties. These included the small size and relative lack of revolutionary political experience of the working class in Grenada; the economic vulnerability of the island to the imperialist-orchestrated campaign to deny loans and financial aid and to curtail important economic income from tourism; the world economic crisis, which compounded the problems of economic development essential to the advance of the revolution; and the calculated work of the CIA to discredit and corrupt.

D ESPITE THESE OBJECTIVE obstacles, however, the Grenada revolution was not sliding into a social catastrophe. Actually, the revolution was making important progress. Its economic growth rate was among the highest in the Western Hemisphere and unemployment was declining. The social conditions and living standards of the working people were improving. Bishop and other revolutionists in the NJM were seeking to institutionalize further the mass organizations and other forms of democratic participation that had emerged in the first years of the revolution. The revolutionary government enjoyed broad popular support as a result of these achievements.

Nonetheless, the narrow political outlook and administrative methods employed by Coard's followers in the New Jewel Movement and in the mass organizations, together with their bureaucratic practices in various government departments and programs, were taking a mounting toll on the workers and farmers, especially during the last year of the revolution. Sectors of the population, including revolutionary activists, began to become disoriented and demoralized. Participation in the mass organizations began to stagnate or decline, as did the level of popular mobilization in support of the revolution.

In the weeks leading up to its counterrevolutionary bid for power the Coard faction sought to pin the blame for these problems on Bishop. At the same time, Coard recognized that the big majority of workers and farmers supported the revolution, and that they associated their own conquests and interests with the policies advanced by Bishop.

Thus, Coard's followers systematically organized ways of further demobilizing the revolutionary masses, regardless of the domestic and international consequences for Grenada. They used their position in the army, government, and party to accomplish this, including—in the final weeks before the coup—disarming the militia. Having taken these steps, the Coard faction on October 12, 1983, carried out the coup, placing Maurice Bishop under house arrest. When other leaders of the revolution organized popular resistance, they too were placed under house arrest.

Though demobilized, the working people who had made the revolution were not yet defeated. Protests began to be organized in the streets against the Coard faction's moves. On October 19, twenty-five to thirty thousand people, more than a quarter of Grenada's population, turned out to demand Bishop's release—proof of the mass backing for the revolution and Bishop's political course. A section of the crowd freed Bishop from house arrest.

Bishop and the leaders who looked to him made an effort to lead this uprising of the people in order to call the Coard clique to order and restore to office the women and men who had led the workers and farmers government and had inspired the construction of a new Grenada. But this effort was drowned in blood. The Coard faction ordered armed units to fire into the crowd, killing many. Then in cold blood it murdered Bishop and other leaders of the revolutionary government.

The workers and farmers government that had come to

power in March 1979 was overthrown.

The Coard coup, with its heinous culmination, was the decisive act that opened the door to the U.S. invasion of Grenada and the ongoing imperialist occupation of that country. The imperialists' goal was to establish their domination of the island and claim a "victory" that would make it politically easier to introduce U.S. troops into combat in Central America in the future. Without the Coard-organized counterrevolution, the U.S. rulers could not have achieved this goal in October 1983. Had the workers and farmers government not been overthrown from within, a U.S. invasion as part of the deepening imperialist war in the region would have met the resistance of Grenada's working people and their internationalist Cuban allies.

The Coard faction, in pursuing its counterrevolutionary course, had gained room to maneuver because of the relatively small size of the revolutionary proletarian leadership team around Bishop in the New Jewel Movement.

This limitation could have been overcome only by drawing into the leadership of the government and the party the most conscious and combative leaders stepping forward in the mass organizations and in the workplaces. However, the Coard faction organized to block this by imposing drastic restrictions on recruitment to the party. This had prevented the party from growing much beyond three hundred full and candidate members at the time of the overthrow. The Coard group thus guaranteed that the emerging revolutionary vanguard of the workers and farmers would be only minimally integrated into the leadership of the revolution, thereby consolidating its own position in the party and government apparatus.

The overthrow of the government and the subsequent invasion by the imperialists was not the necessary outcome of the revolution. The Grenada revolution was not a utopian adventure that could have ended only in defeat. It is precisely because the outcome was not inevitable that vanguard fighters have emphasized so strongly the criminal role played by the Stalinist faction headed by Bernard Coard, whose treachery was decisive for the imperialist victory.

However, once the Coard faction carried out its counterrevolutionary coup against the workers and farmers government, almost completely demobilizing and demoralizing the big majority of the Grenadian workers and farmers, it *was* inevitable that the imperialists would invade the island. They succeeded in brutally putting down the scattered, unorganized, and ineffective resistance from the courageous but leaderless Grenadian defenders of the revolution, as well as the heroic and disciplined resistance of the Cuban construction workers.

The current preparations for a show trial of Coard and other former members of the New Jewel Movement by the U.S.-backed government of Grenada are aimed at discrediting the Grenada revolution, justifying the criminal invasion and occupation, and strengthening the legitimacy of the puppet government.[6]

Acid test for revolutionaries on a world scale

The events in Grenada have been an acid test for all revolutionaries on a world scale. For many petty-bourgeois radical currents in the imperialist countries, the events in Grenada are of passing interest at most. This giant revolution in a small island inhabited by Black people did not appear to them to have much to do with the main line of march of the world revolution. They could not have been more mistaken. They reacted to the overthrow of the workers and farmers government led by Maurice Bishop as unfortunate confirmation of their view that not much could be hoped for from the Grenada revolution.

Some Stalinist parties in the Americas responded to the Coard coup and the murder of Bishop and other Grenadian leaders by defending the course of the Coard faction, with which they were identified politically and which they had helped to promote and organize. Some even identified themselves with the anti-Bishop slanders used to cover up the assassination of the leadership. Others remained cautiously silent for a number of days.

In face of the revulsion among the international working-class vanguard at the murder of Bishop, however, these forces have shifted their approach. While still echoing the charges against Bishop and covering up the role played by the Coard faction, they now seek to identify themselves with the legacy of Bishop.

In sharp contrast, the Cuban leadership has spread the truth about the events in Grenada on a world scale. They have explained the role played by the Coard faction. They have educated about the accomplishments of the Grenada revolution under the leadership of Bishop.

At the same time the Cubans have taken the lead in organizing a united-front campaign to demand that U.S. imperialism end its occupation of Grenada. They have worked to prevent even the deepest disagreements over evaluation of the events in Grenada from being used to precipitate the kind of public clashes that would narrow this united front.

The Cubans have provided leadership to the defenders of the Grenada revolution in helping them to understand and draw political lessons from the defeat, and helping to provide a perspective for continuing the fight, beginning with opposition to the continuing U.S. occupation of the island. In Grenada itself, this political course by the Cuban Communists has been important for those survivors of the New Jewel Movement leadership team around Bishop who are today organizing to build the Maurice Bishop Patriotic Movement. This organization places the demand for an immediate withdrawal of all U.S. forces in the forefront of its program.

Central to the considerations of the Cuban leadership in responding to the U.S. invasion was exacting the biggest political price possible from the imperialists for their invasion. The goal was to buy time for the fighters in El Salvador, for the revolutionary government in Nicaragua, and for Cuba itself by slowing down the imperialist move toward direct military intervention in Central America and the Caribbean. The Cuban workers on Grenada fought heroically to accomplish this objective. They refused to surrender even though they were hopelessly outnumbered and outgunned. They gave up their lives in order to give the imperialists—and the world—a taste of what U.S. forces will face should they decide to invade Nicaragua or Cuba, where workers and farmers governments are organizing and leading the revolutionary population in arms.

Echo of early years in Cuba

The functioning of the Coard faction was similar to that of a Stalinist faction that had been formed in the early years of the Cuban revolution. Headed by Aníbal Escalante, it had tried to seize control of the party and government apparatus, using bureaucratic and administrative methods against the workers and peasants, and dispensing privileges to its supporters. Had the Cuban revolutionary leadership not been able to smash this factional operation, what happened in Grenada would have happened in Cuba twenty years before.

The importance with which the Cubans view this political question is indicated by the unusual step taken by Fidel Castro in publicly criticizing the Cuban embassy staff in Grenada for failure to accurately assess and report what was happening in Grenada. In an interview with a *Newsweek* reporter, Castro said that "with all the personnel we had in the embassy there, we did not know the split was taking place. That is the greatest criticism that we must make of our own political, diplomatic, and military aid personnel. We did not have any idea what was happening."[7]

As a result of their response to the Grenada events, the Cuban leaders won international respect and admiration. Many working people today, especially throughout the Caribbean, understand more clearly than before the revolutionary role of the Cuban leadership in world politics. This has increased the authority of the Cuban revolution in the Caribbean, in sectors of the Black movement in the United States, and among internationalist workers everywhere.

Pathfinder Press included the major public statements on the Grenada events by Fidel Castro and the Cuban CP in the book *Maurice Bishop Speaks,* published in December 1983. Our movement acted rapidly to get out this collection and circulate it as widely as possible in order to provide a political weapon for all those working to explain the truth about Grenada. In addition to speeches by the outstanding central leader of the revolution, the book also contains an introduction explaining the accomplishments of the Grenadian workers and farmers government and some key lessons to be drawn in light of its overthrow.

BUILDING FIGHTING INDUSTRIAL UNIONS

The Eastern Airlines Strike
Accomplishments of the Rank-and-File Machinists
BY ERNIE MAILHOT, JUDY STRANAHAN, AND JACK BARNES

Tells the story of the 686-day strike and how a rank-and-file resistance by Machinists prevented Eastern's antiunion onslaught from becoming the road to a profitable nonunion airline and a beacon to profitable union-busting. "Anyone involved in the wide trade union and labour movement should find this account of the 1989-91 strike against the union-busting efforts of Frank Lorenzo instructive"—*T & G Record,* magazine of the Transport and General Workers Union of Britain, December 1993. 91 pp., $9.95

Labor's Giant Step
The First Twenty Years of the CIO, 1936-1955
BY ART PREIS

How the political struggle of the major currents in the workers movement marked the rise of the Congress of Industrial Organizations (CIO) in the 1930s. And how it continues to pose the issues that must be resolved today by the labor movement as it is transformed by its struggles with the employers. 538 pp., $26.95

Trade Unions in the Epoch of Imperialist Decay
BY LEON TROTSKY, KARL MARX

What are the tasks of trade unions under capitalism? What is their relationship to workers' fight for economic justice and political power? Includes "Trade Unions: Their Past, Present, and Future" by Karl Marx. 156 pp., $14.95

Available from Pathfinder. See page 2 for distributors

Karl Marx, Frederick Engels

PARIS COMMUNE, 1871

Collected Works of Karl Marx and Frederick Engels

The complete writings. Now available: vols. 1-34, 38-46. $1,075 set (43 vols.), $25 per volume.

The Communist Manifesto

Founding document of the modern revolutionary workers movement, written in 1847 by Marx and Engels. Explains how capitalism arose as a specific stage in the economic development of class society and how it will be superseded through the revolutionary action on a world scale of the working class. 47 pp. Booklet. $2.50

Socialism: Utopian and Scientific

by Frederick Engels Modern socialism is not a doctrine, but a working-class movement growing out of the establishment of large-scale capitalist industry and its social consequences. Engels explains why. 63 pp. Booklet. $3.00

On the Paris Commune

"Storming heaven," Marx wrote, the "proletariat for the first time held political power" in Paris for three months in 1871 and the international workers struggle "entered upon a new stage." Writings, letters, and speeches by Marx and Engels on the Paris Commune. 356 pp. $15.95

Available from Pathfinder See page 2 for distributors

'Socialism can be built only by free men and women'

Che Guevara and the Fight for Socialism Today
Cuba Confronts the World Crisis of the '90s
BY MARY-ALICE WATERS

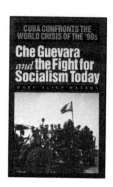

Socialism can be built only by free men and women working together to lay the foundations for a new society and transforming themselves in the process. That practical commitment was championed by Ernesto Che Guevara in the early years of the Cuban revolution. It remains central for Cuban working people today as they organize a retreat in face of defeats in the 1980s in Grenada and Nicaragua. 37 pp. Booklet. $3.50

Dynamics of the Cuban Revolution
BY JOSEPH HANSEN

To understand new developments in Cuba's socialist revolution, Hansen says, "it is not necessary to begin from zero—the problems presented to Marxist theory by the uniqueness of the events was solved at the time. One of the purposes of this compilation is to present those theoretical conclusions." 393 pp. $20.95

The Leninist Strategy of Party Building
The Debate on Guerrilla Warfare in Latin America
BY JOSEPH HANSEN

In the 1960s and '70s, revolutionists in the Americas and Europe debated how to apply the lessons of the Cuban revolution to struggles elsewhere. A record of that debate. 608 pp. $26.95

PATHFINDER
See page 2 for distributors

THE 1987 PEACE ACCORDS:
A NEW SITUATION IN NICARAGUA

1. THE FSLN LEADERS ARE DETERMINED to take advantage of the peace process they set in motion by signing the Guatemala accords and rapidly moving toward the lifting of the state of emergency.[1] The restoration of full civil liberties in Nicaragua will create the best conditions for waging the "political-ideological battle" necessary to lead the revolutionary process forward. Their goal is to minimize administrative measures, which are an obstacle to advancing the political education, orientation, and organization of the working people in the city and the countryside as the class struggle deepens in Nicaragua.

This opens a new stage in the Nicaraguan revolutionary process, one that marks significant progress by the workers and farmers government there.

2. This step forward is made possible by the two decisive victories that the toilers in Nicaragua have won in the past year: first, the strategic defeat of the contra mercenary army; and second, the political victory on the Atlantic Coast with the adoption and the beginning of the implementation of the autonomy plan.[2]

The strategic defeat of the contras has opened the door inside Nicaragua to this political initiative; until that was achieved, this course was precluded. At the same time, the strategic defeat of the contra army has created a crisis for Washington's policy and for the pro-U.S. regimes in Central America. It is this crisis that has compelled the governments in Guatemala, Honduras, Costa Rica, and El Salvador to embark on the road

---

This resolution was adopted by the Socialist Workers Party Political Committee September 22, 1987.

ENDNOTES FOR THIS ARTICLE BEGIN ON PAGE 313.

that has led to the Guatemala accords.

The strategic defeat of the contras by itself was not enough to make this initiative possible, however. The victory on the Atlantic Coast was also essential because it confirmed in life the correctness of the decision made several years ago to move to replace military and other administrative methods of government with a political battle to lead forward the peoples of the Atlantic Coast along the lines charted by the Autonomy Plan, and to neutralize and divide opponents. The significance of this political approach to resolve the potentially fatal problems confronting the revolution on the Atlantic Coast goes far beyond the Atlantic Coast itself. It has been, as Tomás Borge says, a premonition of the course now being implemented for the country as a whole.

3. The steps now being taken by the Nicaraguan government toward ending emergency measures are presented in the bourgeois press in this country as primarily moves being made for international consumption, as concessions extracted from the FSLN as the price for the Guatemala accords, or as attempts to influence votes in Congress on contra aid. In large measure this explanation is mirrored in the radical press. This is fundamentally false.

It is true, of course, that the Nicaraguan government is being forced by the criminal war policy of the United States to make decisions, including concessions, under duress from the contra war and the extensive trade restrictions by the United States. It is particularly important for defenders of the Nicaraguan revolution in the United States to keep pointing this out and not cede an inch to the claimed right of the United States to dictate, directly or indirectly, *any* policies to the sovereign government of Nicaragua.

But the course of the FSLN leadership in relation to the internal opposition and the restoration of civil liberties is being followed because the FSLN leadership has concluded that it is the best way to advance the revolutionary process, that is, to strengthen the mobilization, organization, and education of the workers and peasants of Nicaragua to fight for their class interests. This is being explained by the FSLN leaders as they seek to win support for this new course, beginning with the cadres of the FSLN itself.

Overcoming administrative obstacles

4. The use of administrative measures to deal with political opposition carries an overhead price. It is an obstacle to winning new layers of the exploited and the oppressed to the revolution. It cannot answer the arguments of the opponents of the FSLN—whether they be the bourgeois opposition or the ultraleft currents. It does not eliminate the ideas of these opponents, nor reduce their support. It merely drives them into various indirect channels, where it is more difficult to deal with them by clarifying them, answering them, and educating the toilers about the consequences of the policies proposed by the FSLN's opponents. Moreover, to the degree that the FSLN cadres come to rely on administrative measures to answer criticisms, this can become a serious obstacle to class consciousness and to the political education and development of the FSLN itself.

The "political-ideological struggle" that is needed can be waged most effectively—in the countryside, in the factories, in the mass organizations—with a minimum of emergency laws and a maximum of political organization, mobilization, discussion, and debate led by the FSLN cadres.

5. This new course, combined with measures to disintegrate the contra army and heighten the military preparedness of Nicaragua, will strengthen the weight of, and give encouragement to, the most class-conscious elements among the working people and the most politically conscious forces in the FSLN itself.

It will reduce the weight of those in Nicaragua who argue that the need for national unity in the war against the contras is sufficient reason to postpone until the indefinite future further advances in the distribution of land, driving forward concretely on women's rights, and similar questions. It will also reduce the weight of those who prefer, for whatever reasons, to rely on administrative measures to respond to challenges instead of leading the working people to fight politically to win over those who are confused, disoriented, or alienated from the revolutionary process.

It is here that the experience of the Atlantic Coast project is decisive in giving broad layers of the FSLN the confidence that political leadership can successfully advance the process by broadening the base of support for the revolution among the toiling classes and neutralize, divide, and isolate the opponents.

6. This approach has not been, and will not be, greeted with unanimous support among the cadres of the FSLN. The FSLN leadership is now trying to win as many cadres as possible to this approach. The "old" cadres of the FSLN who led the fight to mobilize the workers and peasants in the battle for political power were trained to do this kind of political work. Many of the newer cadres, however, who have joined and been educated in the period of the contra war and consequent heavy use of state of emergency restrictions, will have to learn. This new situation will be reflected in a new differentiation and advance among the FSLN cadres. This will pose the question of the next steps forward in the development of proletarian leadership in the FSLN, which will become a less heterogeneous organization.

7. For the last decade, the Nicaraguan revolution has confronted the horns of a dilemma imposed by the objective situation and relationship of forces: one horn has been the course of maintaining national unity against the imperialist-backed war; the other has been the need for emergency measures on the political, economic, and military fronts, a kind of "war communism" without the economic foundations of a workers state.[3]

The Guatemala accords—and the victories that made them possible—can open the way to allowing the FSLN to lift itself off the horns of this dilemma and chart a new course. In the period ahead we will see more clearly, with fewer disguises, what it means to be a workers and farmers government—not a workers state, and not a capitalist regime. The essential fact that the class struggle between the working classes and the exploiting classes is the spring, the dynamic, of change in Nicaraguan society will be more visible both inside and outside Nicaragua.

In this way, the Nicaraguan revolution will advance toward the next qualitative leap forward in historical terms, the establishment of a workers state. The advances that will prepare the establishment of a workers state will be the growing self-confidence and organization of the working people and the deepening of the communist education and preparation of the vanguard.

To the degree that the Nicaraguan government can continue to push back the contras militarily and accelerate their decline by eroding their morale through such measures as the amnesty offer combined with hitting them hard in the field, if necessary, the direct use of military might by the United States will continue to be pushed back because the price Washington would have to pay for it will keep going up.

Washington's policy in crisis

8. The strategic defeat of the contras and the events that this has set in motion in Central America pose a tactical crisis for Washington's policy. This crisis has not been, and will not be, resolved in the short term. The United States cannot and will not come to an "accommodation" with the Nicaraguan revolution as long as it remains a revolution. Nicaragua cannot "buy peace" through measures relating to maintaining the mixed economy, restoring civil liberties, or other similar moves. It is the existence of the bastion of workers and farmers political power on the American continent and the example it sets that the rulers in Washington cannot be reconciled to.

9. No wing of the U.S. ruling class is putting forward any coherent alternative to replace the contra war policy of the Reagan administration. It also remains the case that the strategic defeat of the contras and the fact that they continue to be pushed back in the field does not mean that the U.S. rulers have given up on the use of military force to accomplish their goal of overthrowing the Nicaraguan workers and farmers government.

Until the past year, the Reagan administration had been able to maintain the initiative, pushing hard on the right flank of the rightward-shifting bipartisan consensus around the need to over-throw the Nicaraguan government. That initiative has now shattered following the Iran-contra exposures[4] and the Guatemala accords. However, this has not given way to a new tactical course of accommodation with substantial consensus in the ruling circles.

WHEREVER THEY FIND the opportunity the U.S. rulers continue to push such methods as piracy, blockades, and gunboat diplomacy, as they are doing today in the Persian Gulf war. The use of U.S. military power in the Persian Gulf—and the resort in the eastern Mediterranean to the high-seas kidnapping of a citizen of another country—without substantial opposition and reaction in this country poses a danger to Nicaragua.[5] Washington's success—even if it turns out to be only temporary—in enlisting active participation by major imperialist allies in Europe in its world-cop operations in the Persian Gulf also marks a danger.

This ties in directly with the debate within the framework of bourgeois politics over how far, how fast, and through what methods to drive forward the rulers' offensive against the rights and living standards of the working people in the United States. This battle is reflected today in the confrontations over the Bork nomination, which has at this moment become part of the fight over such fundamental acquisitions as the strengthened right to privacy won by working people through struggles for civil rights and women's rights; the conquests of affirmative action; and political and union rights in general.[6] There is no broad consensus in the ruling class on when and at what pace to begin using the rougher methods and new tactics against the working class that will be needed to drive forward their offensive in the attempt to renew a rout.

The sharp battles over U.S. policy toward Nicaragua and the rulers' offensive at home coincide in time and will increasingly interpenetrate.

10. The key task of defenders of the Nicaraguan revolution in

this country is to continue to seek to convince opponents of U.S. intervention in Central America that actions taken now are decisive in affecting the course of the battle. Action needs to be initiated in opposing any more contra aid, in spreading the truth about the Nicaraguan revolution to working people and youth in this country, and in increasing the number of those visiting Nicaragua to see for themselves and pitch in to help reconstruct the country devastated by the Washington-backed aggression.

11. With regard to the new situation unfolding today in Nicaragua, the task of our movement is a double one. First, to accurately report and analyze what is unfolding there. This includes publishing the explanations being offered by the leadership of the FSLN, as well as coverage of the class struggle as it develops throughout the region. The *Militant* and *Perspectiva Mundial* are, and will be to an increasing degree, the only source of accurate information on these developments in Nicaragua. Connected to this will be the publication, as resources allow, of further Pathfinder books on the Nicaraguan revolution: collections on topics such as the Atlantic Coast and its lessons, the land question, and the fight for women's liberation, as well as a book of writings by Carlos Fonseca, the founder of the communist movement in Central America.

Second, we should take advantage of the new situation to do what we can to help increase the traffic on the "Managua trail," to expand the numbers of workers, farmers, and youth from the United States and around the world who travel to Nicaragua on work brigades and other delegations. We can also be confident that within this growing flow of people, in light of increasing discussion, there will be an increase in those who are attracted toward communism and therefore are potential recruits to our movement.

Nelson Mandela Speaks

Forging a Democratic, Nonracial South Africa
President of the African National Congress
tells the story of the struggles that are opening
a deep-going transformation of political,
economic, and social conditions in the
former land of apartheid. 296 pp. $18.95

Thomas Sankara Speaks

The Burkina Faso Revolution, 1983-87
The leader of the Burkina Faso revolution
recounts how peasants and workers in this
West African country began confronting
hunger, illiteracy, and extreme capitalist
underdevelopment prior to the 1987 coup in
which Sankara was murdered. 260 pp. $18.95

Cosmetics, Fashions, and the Exploitation of Women

BY JOSEPH HANSEN, EVELYN REED,
AND MARY-ALICE WATERS
How big business uses women's second-
class status to generate profits for a few and
perpetuate the oppression of the female sex
and the exploitation of working people. 138 pp.
$12.95

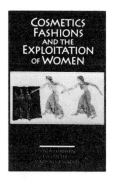

The Revolution Betrayed

What Is the Soviet Union and Where Is It Going?
BY LEON TROTSKY
Classic study of the degeneration of the Soviet workers state under
the brutal domination of the privileged social caste whose
spokesman was Stalin. Illuminates the roots of the Russian crisis of
the 1990s. 314 pp. $19.95

PATHFINDER—See page 2 for distributors

3. THE POLITICAL DEGENERATION OF THE FSLN AND THE DEMISE OF THE WORKERS AND FARMERS GOVERNMENT

By the close of the 1980s, the Sandinista leadership had largely transformed the FSLN into a radical bourgeois electoral party. Above, billboard at February 1990 FSLN election rally urges vote for presidential candidate Daniel Ortega. It reads, "We are winning. Everything will be better!"

DEFEND REVOLUTIONARY NICARAGUA: THE ERODING FOUNDATIONS OF THE WORKERS AND FARMERS GOVERNMENT

1. THE POLITICAL AND ECONOMIC course carried out since early 1988 by the government of Nicaragua has been based on increasing long-term reliance on the workings of the capitalist market. This leads away from deepening inroads on the property and social prerogatives of the exploiting classes and away from increasing class consciousness, confidence, organization, and mobilization of the workers and peasants. Effective defense of the historic gains of the Nicaraguan revolution from the unremitting hatred and pressure from U.S. imperialism is being weakened.

As always, the more the market system is extended, the more capitalist social relations of production are reproduced and entrenched. Social inequalities and differentiation increase, and bourgeois values are promoted. The burden of the capitalist crisis in Nicaragua is shifted more onto the backs of the workers and peasants, especially the worst-off layers. The cumulative result is growing depoliticization, demoralization, and divisions within the working class and peasantry. The worker-peasant alliance that forms the class base of the workers and farmers government is weakened.[1]

Leadership's turn has already occurred
2. Unless there is a reversal of this fundamental course being

---

This resolution was adopted by the National Committee of the Socialist Workers Party in July 1989 and by the August 1990 SWP national convention. ENDNOTES FOR THIS ARTICLE BEGIN ON PAGE 315.

pursued by the government and by the leadership of the Sandinista National Liberation Front, the class relationship of forces will continue to shift against the exploited and oppressed. The social and political foundations of the workers and farmers government will continue to erode. The door will be opened for restructuring and reconsolidating the government on the basis of capitalist social relations and state machinery. The opportunity will have been missed to establish the second workers state in the Americas and join Cuba in the difficult but historically necessary effort to begin the construction of socialism.

The turn in policy direction by the government and FSLN leading toward such an outcome has already occurred; it does not lie in the future. Without a sharp political reorientation that reasserts an anticapitalist direction to the revolution, this course will result in the demise of the workers and farmers government.

3. It is not possible to predict the ways that such a qualitative change in the class character of the government of Nicaragua might occur. Since the victory of the Cuban revolution, workers and farmers governments have been reversed in Algeria (June 1965) and Grenada (October 1983). The counterrevolutionary coups in these two cases, organized against the central public leadership figure of the revolution, are not the only form through which the destruction of the worker and peasant character of such a government could occur.[2]

Should a new government displace the workers and farmers regime in Nicaragua, it may well be an FSLN government or a coalition headed by the FSLN. The regime that emerged from the overthrow of the Algerian workers and farmers government, for example, remained under the leadership of the National Liberation Front (FLN), and continued for a substantial period to be looked to by the workers and peasants of Algeria as a revolutionary regime representing their interests.[3] Even the counterrevolutionary government established by Bernard Coard's supporters in Grenada, while hated by the masses of working people for its murder of Maurice Bishop and dozens of others, retained the backing of the big majority of the New

Jewel Movement, its leading committees, and the armed forces it dominated.

Prospects opened by defeat of contras

4. The accelerating erosion of the worker and farmer character of the government is the product of the policy course chosen and deepened by the leadership of the FSLN in the aftermath of the defeat of the U.S.-instigated and -financed counterrevolutionary war.

The hard-fought military victory over the contras brought renewed confidence to the toilers of Nicaragua and opened new opportunities to deepen and advance not only the anti-imperialist but also the anticapitalist development of the revolution. With the end of the war thousands of young, tested, and disciplined cadres from the Sandinista army became available to take on new leadership responsibilities on other fronts. Their enthusiasm and determination needed only to be directed and led.

Simultaneously, the political consciousness of the revolutionary cadres was deepened by the other decisive victory that the toilers of Nicaragua have won in the past half decade: the political victory on the Atlantic Coast registered in the adoption and initial implementation of the autonomy plan. The capacity of the revolutionary leadership to correct previously disastrous policies on the Atlantic Coast and win the majority of the *costeño* population away from the counterrevolution raised the political confidence of the Nicaraguan vanguard.

But the potential opened by these victories for deepening popular mobilizations and powerful new steps forward has not been realized. The momentum has been dissipated by the policies chosen by the FSLN leadership in the period since the end of the contra war.

5. The Sandinista leadership has rejected constructing a mass revolutionary party in Nicaragua growing out of the continuity of the FSLN's Historic Program, a party that is proletarian in the composition of its cadres and communist in program.[4] While many workers and peasants have been brought

into FSLN membership over the first ten years of the revolution, the organization itself retains its top-down military structure. The ranks have no decision-making control over the political course of the FSLN or the selection of its leadership. As the 1990 elections approach, the FSLN leadership models the public face of the organization more and more on that of a radical bourgeois electoral party, with a mass following but no meaningful membership rights, and thus limited responsibilities, and with no political accountability of the leadership to the actual vanguard of a social class.

Under political and historical circumstances such as those inherited from the Somoza tyranny, a revolutionary organization may have to substitute itself for a working-class vanguard in order to carry out revolutionary action and lead the working people to power over an oppressive regime. The opening created by the conquest of power, however, must then be consciously used to transform the revolutionary organization into a communist party whose membership and leadership is increasingly composed of working people. In the absence of such a step, workers and poor peasants have no instrument to block the reproduction and reinforcement of capitalist social relations, fostered by the FSLN's current policy course, and the inevitable economic and political consequences of these relations.

6. The only development that can open the possibility of once again placing the Nicaraguan government on an anticapitalist course is a major revolutionary victory that directly affects Latin America and the Caribbean—whether generated by a mass uprising somewhere in the Americas, by a successful popular counteroffensive by workers and peasants to an aggressive use of U.S. military power in the region, or other circumstances.

Such an advance for the world revolution could rupture the relatively recent consensus in the FSLN leadership rejecting the lessons of the modern communist movement from Marx to Guevara. By common accord, FSLN leaders are today pursuing instead the goal of a long-term social pact based on "national unity," a goal that, if reached, institutionalizes class collaboration and is self-defeating for the workers and peasants.

A political initiative from sections of the FSLN leadership in the face of a major revolutionary victory in the Americas could, however, still galvanize proletarian and peasant forces in Nicaragua to struggle to defend the conquests of their revolution and in the process to place their class stamp on its course.

Despite the toll taken by the current course of the government on the political self-confidence and political class clarity and morale of broad layers of working people, revolutionary-minded Nicaraguan workers and peasants have rich experiences from years of determined struggle. Their spirit and capacity to fight have not been broken.

Need for socialist course

7. A renewed forward march by a workers and farmers government in Nicaragua would lead in the direction of mobilizing the exploited and oppressed in a fight to end capitalist domination of the economy. It would result in a qualitative extension of workers control of production and workers democracy in city and countryside, in combination with the defense of the broad democratic and social rights conquered during the first decade of the revolutionary government. This course points toward the expropriation of major capitalist holdings in industry and agriculture; establishment of a state monopoly of exports and imports; and the institution of economic planning on this foundation. This would register the establishment of a workers state.[5]

The advances made possible by such a course in Nicaragua would add further evidence to the conviction expressed by Fidel Castro and Ernesto Che Guevara—a conviction now backed by thirty years of experience of the Cuban revolution—that the building of socialism not only *can* begin in the countries of Latin America and the Caribbean following a genuine revolution, but offers the *only* way out of imperialist domination, economic devastation, and superexploitation of the masses of working people, as well as the only way to defend the gains of the democratic and anti-imperialist revolution.[6]

To accomplish this, however, the goal of the revolutionary leadership has to be to organize the toilers to advance toward a workers state, not, as in Nicaragua today, toward the consolidation of a bourgeois republic, however radical and anti-imperialist its pronouncements, and however firm its intention to defend Nicaragua's sovereignty and independence.

Origins of workers and peasants government

8. A concrete analysis of the course of the struggle of the toilers in Nicaragua over the past decade, both advances and setbacks, is necessary to understand the crisis now facing the workers and peasants and their government.

In July 1979 the Nicaraguan toilers, led by the FSLN, swept aside the capitalist-landlord tyranny headed by Anastasio Somoza and seized political power. They established a workers and farmers government—the form of government that can be expected to rapidly appear as the result of a successful anticapitalist revolution.

The actions of the new FSLN-led government, responding to the pressures of the workers and peasants, and taking leadership initiatives in an anticapitalist as well as a popular and anti-imperialist direction, determined its character as a workers and farmers government. The class foundations of such a government are established by the revolutionary displacement of the bourgeoisie from political power, the assumption of that power by an administration based on the popular masses and that commands a new army, and the initiation of far-reaching changes in property relations.

9. The establishment of a workers and farmers government opened the possibility for Nicaragua's toilers and their allies to become the second people in the Americas to establish a workers state and begin the construction of socialism. It opened the door to Nicaraguan working people, in the process of transforming their social relations, to begin transforming themselves into new women and men.

As the resolution adopted by the Socialist Workers Party National Committee in January 1980 explained:

Given the desperate economic situation in Nicaragua, a pressing objective of the government has been to restore a minimal level of production in the privately owned industries and on the big and medium-sized farms still in the hands of their owners. It has appealed for aid from all countries to obtain credits and food.

As the example of Cuba has proven, however, the needs of the masses cannot be met if private ownership is maintained in the basic means of production. The laws of capitalist accumulation will distort the country's economy, subordinating real economic development and social betterment to the quest for profits and to imperialist exploitation. . . .

While it would be adventuristic to try to force the rhythm of the class struggle, it is also true that the pace of polarization and confrontation cannot be controlled by preconceived plans. The tempo will be dictated by the blows and counterblows between the masses and the FSLN on one side and the exploiters on the other. With each new encroachment against the property and prerogatives of the landlords and business interests, the likelihood grows that some section of the bourgeoisie will throw down the gauntlet. In addition to radical measures by the government, the workers and peasants—suffering under economic burdens, capitalist sabotage, and social dislocation—will themselves take initiatives on the land, in their factories, and in the barrios. This is the historic record of the Russian, Cuban, and every other socialist revolution; there is an accelerating dialectical interplay between the leadership and the initiatives and responses by the masses, often unforeseen by the leadership.

In revolutionary situations above all, history confirms Frederick Engels's observation that when controlled forces are put in motion, uncontrolled forces are inevitably put in motion as well. No amount of political preparation can annul this consequence of the class struggle.

Instead, the aim of such preparation must be to increase the self-confidence and readiness of the masses *to respond* to new turns by defending their conquests and propelling their struggle forward. That is where their consciousness, organization, and mobilization will prove decisive. It is correct to make concessions to the class enemy when the relationship of forces leaves no alternative. But the masses must be told the class truth about such concessions, so that they can be better prepared to ward off the concomitant dangers.

All this highlights the need for a revolutionary Marxist proletarian party to unify and lead the workers and their allies in accomplishing these tasks and defeating their class enemy. Forging the initial cadres of such a party out of the leadership and ranks of the FSLN would not only facilitate the socialist reconstruction of Nicaragua but would mark an advance for the entire international workers movement in the fight to resolve the historic crisis of proletarian leadership.[7]

Part of rise in world revolution

10. The Nicaraguan toilers triumphed over the Somoza dictatorship at the time of a rising worldwide wave of revolutionary victories. As 1979 began, the U.S.-backed monarchy in Iran was overthrown, and the Pol Pot charnel house in Kampuchea [Cambodia] was toppled. In March 1979 a workers and farmers government, led by the New Jewel Movement of Maurice Bishop, came to power on the Caribbean island of Grenada. Spurred by the triumph in Nicaragua, the revolutionary movement in El Salvador surged forward in city and countryside. The mass struggles of workers and peasants in Guatemala received new impetus. These advances followed by only a few years:

 • the revolutionary overthrow of the landlord-based monarchy in Ethiopia in 1974;

 • the victory over the U.S. imperialist–installed regime in Vietnam in 1975;

 • the triumph over Portuguese colonialism in southern Africa in 1974-75, which inspired fighters for liberation from the Caribbean to Asia and the Pacific islands;

• the defeat—with decisive aid from Cuban volunteer forces—of the South African effort to block an independent Angolan government in early 1976;

• the explosive entry of a new generation of revolutionary youth into the struggle against apartheid in South Africa, registered by the Soweto uprising later in 1976; and

• the defeat in 1978—by an armed force led and largely made up of Cuban internationalist volunteers—of the U.S.-backed Somalian invasion aimed at smashing the Ethiopian revolution.

These victories gave a powerful new impulse to the Cuban revolution. Hundreds of thousands of Cubans volunteered for internationalist duties in Ethiopia, Angola, Nicaragua, Grenada, and elsewhere, and the Cuban government provided unstinting internationalist solidarity as well as generous and unconditional material aid. In September 1979 Cuba assumed the chairmanship of the Movement of Nonaligned Countries, registering a substantial setback to Washington's unceasing efforts to isolate the Cuban revolution. In response to escalating U.S. military pressure in the wake of the revolutionary gains in Central America and the Caribbean, millions of Cubans in 1980 mobilized for the Marches of the Fighting People and joined the newly established Territorial Troop Militia that transformed the defense strategy of the revolution into one based on the military preparedness and mobilization of the entire people.[8]

The Nicaraguan workers and farmers government was part of this revolutionary advance, contributed mightily to it, and drew strength and encouragement from it.

Anticapitalist course in opening years

11. In the opening years of the revolution the FSLN government, responding to the massive mobilizations and expanding organization of the toilers, carried out a series of expropriations and other measures against capitalist property and social prerogatives.

Nicaraguan working people were armed, trained, and organized on a mass scale to fight to defend the revolutionary power. In addition to building the Sandinista People's Army, popular militias were advocated, and in some cases began to be formed, in the factories, workplaces, and in the countryside. Neighborhood Sandinista Defense Committees (CDSs) took on nightly "vigilance" patrols in many areas and were initially presented by the FSLN as bodies that would be organized to help deepen the political mobilization and active involvement of working people in the revolution.

Government power was used to help launch and strengthen unions and other organizations of urban and rural workers and of toiling peasants—the Sandinista Workers Federation (CST), the Association of Rural Workers (ATC), the National Union of Farmers and Ranchers (UNAG), and others.

Poor peasants and farm laborers pressed their demands for land through land occupations and other direct action. They appealed for and won the support of the government in many cases. The ATC and UNAG supported these demands for land. The ATC pressed for improved wages and safer and healthier working conditions for agricultural laborers on both private and state-owned farms, and the government took measures to respond to these demands.

Workers, often organized through locals of the CST, demanded confiscation of large enterprises in order to halt decapitalization and other forms of economic sabotage of the revolution by capitalist owners. Demonstrations were held and factory occupations organized by the toilers to press their proposals for swift and firm government action. In many cases they were successful in impelling the government to expropriate capitalist enterprises.

These mass actions were accompanied by an intensification of the fight by women for equal rights, and the awakening of new struggles by the indigenous peoples and peoples of African origin on the Atlantic Coast against the forms of national oppression, racial discrimination, and political isolation historically imposed on them.

12. In following this course of action during the opening years of the revolution, the FSLN was acting in harmony with the line of its 1969 Historic Program, drafted by Carlos Fonseca. This program, elaborated and presented to the Nicaraguan toilers in many forms during the struggle against the Somoza tyranny, pointed to the socialist road opened for all the Americas by the Cuban revolution. It reknit continuity with the anti-imperialist struggle of Nicaragua's workers and peasants under Sandino's leadership.

It was to this communist perspective that the cadres of the FSLN who led the revolutionary struggle in city and countryside were recruited. As Tomás Borge later explained, Fonseca brought Marxism to Central America.[9]

13. Without dissent within the FSLN leadership, the revolutionary government declared from the time it was brought to power that the maintenance of a "mixed economy" constituted a strategic feature of the Nicaraguan revolution.

In and of itself, this was not an obstacle to the advance of the revolution. In a country of the economic and social structure inherited by revolutionary Nicaragua from its history of imperialist domination and landlord-capitalist exploitation, some mix of petty commodity production by peasants and artisans, expropriated industry and wholesale trade, and capitalist farming would be necessary. What that "mix" was, and how it was to evolve, would be determined in the course of the struggle between classes in Nicaragua. The FSLN responded positively to mass mobilizations and took initiatives that challenged capitalist prerogatives and expropriated capitalist property, and it was this course of action that was decisive.

Class polarization and leadership retreats

14. The July 1979 triumph completely destroyed the armed power of the old regime. In its place, the revolution established a new executive dominated by the FSLN to whom all military and police powers are responsible. This leadership and government have not led the workers and peasants forward to overturn capitalist property relations, however.

Not only does capitalist domination of the economy remain intact but representatives of opposing classes and the expression of contradictory class perspectives maintain a presence within the government and within the FSLN. This is true notwithstanding the fact that neither the government's cabinet nor the FSLN's nine-member National Directorate contain defenders of Nicaragua's wealthiest capitalist interests with their imperialist connections.

15. The clashing class pressures within the government of Nicaragua were already present when Washington initiated, in late 1981, the contra military actions that would be expanded into a full-scale mercenary war by 1983.

The destruction wrought by the imperialist-organized and -financed contra armies accelerated the crisis of capitalism in Nicaragua. The workers and farmers government was faced with an escalating war and its terrible toll, including the deaths of thirty thousand Nicaraguans; the U.S. embargo on trade and aid; devastation caused by several large-scale natural disasters; and failure to obtain aid from other countries—either from the imperialist countries or the workers states—on the scale needed to begin reconstruction or maintain existing production levels. These conditions forced the government to cut back or abandon many social programs and development projects, interrupting the course it had charted to improve the living standards of working people and begin the process of developing Nicaragua.

The contra war, however, did not alter the main lines along which the revolution needed to advance: deepening the organization, mobilization, self-confidence, and class consciousness of the workers and peasants, and strengthening the worker-peasant alliance under working-class leadership, in the struggle to eliminate the rents and mortgages system,[10] do away with capitalist property relations, and on that foundation to begin economic planning.

16. Because of the predominance of capitalist property relations, the weight of the economic and social crisis in Nicaragua continually tends to be shifted onto the backs of the workers and poor peasants. It hits disproportionately hard at those

already on the bottom.

Wage differentials are increasing. The social wage of workers has been reduced relative to the living standards of the middle classes as a result of cutbacks in government spending on subsidies of food and other necessities, health care, education, and housing. These laws of motion of capital also increase and accelerate differentiation among the peasantry.

Worker-peasant alliance weakens

17. One particularly critical manifestation of the capitalist crisis has been the continuing migration to Managua, where some one-third of the entire population of the country now resides. Growing numbers of working people in the capital city are currently not receiving even minimal social necessities, such as running water and electricity, let alone decent housing, education, and health care. Moreover, there are few jobs for these migrants. With falling industrial production and cutbacks in government budgets, there is today no prospect of productive employment for the big majority of working people in Managua.

Only by improving the conditions for the toilers in the countryside and building a fighting mass movement of peasants and farm laborers linked with the urban workers can this deepening social crisis be reversed. This requires deepening the land reform, providing working people with the wherewithal to make a living on the land, as well as prioritizing social programs for the rural areas in order to benefit the worst-off sections of the toilers. This would provide the basis for a political and social effort to inspire large numbers of the toilers in Managua, in particular the youth, to move to the countryside where they can participate in productive work and help rebuild the country. If the totality of class relations were explained clearly and unambiguously to working people and a revolutionary perspective were offered to them, there would be a response to such a national mobilization.

No successful effort to accomplish these goals is possible, however, without simultaneous progress toward the nationalization of basic industry and the beginning of economic planning. The

maintenance of capitalist domination of manufacturing inevitably reinforces the tendency of the prices for agricultural inputs
that the peasants must buy to rise faster than the prices they receive for the crops they produce. Moreover, with a substantial
percentage of agricultural production still in capitalist hands,
previous government measures to provide cheap credit and farm
supplies have often boosted the profits of wealthy landowners
while neither increasing agricultural investment and output nor
substantially improving the lot of toiling peasants.

The economic policy course that the government and FSLN
leadership are pursuing places a mounting burden of indebtedness and material want on the mass of toiling peasants and undermines the worker-peasant alliance on which the revolution
is based.

Crisis of urban toilers

18. As the economic and social crisis has deepened, the FSLN has
resisted mobilizing working people in city and countryside to extend workers' control over capitalist production or distribution, a
step that would challenge the prerogatives of private ownership in
these areas. Such steps, however, are necessary even to protect the
current living standards of workers and peasants.

The rationing of essential foods and other basic items in increasingly short supply is the only way to guarantee that every
resident of the country has fair access to such necessities. Instead of moving in this direction, however, the government has
been moving away even from earlier policies that sought to provide certain basic commodities at subsidized prices to every
Nicaraguan through neighborhood outlets.

Government control over foreign trade has also been weakened in areas where a significant degree of state domination
had been established earlier. This retreat has been made in
the face of threats from capitalists to further reduce investment in the production of agricultural commodities for export. Pressure to weaken state control over foreign trade has
also come from imperialist and other capitalist governments
and banking consortia dangling the always-conditional offer

of aid and loans. In response, the Nicaraguan government has increased the payment of "incentives" in dollars for export crops (which are dominated by capitalist landowners); relaxed currency controls; lifted many restrictions on imported goods, including luxury items; and widened the range of products that can be exported directly by capitalists. This further reduces the ability of the government to allocate export earnings to finance social programs and development projects. It also undermines efforts to control inflation and establish a stable currency unit, without which any effective economic planning is impossible.

The punitive expropriations of some capitalist holdings decreed by the government from time to time in response to provocations by individual bourgeois figures do not constitute a step away from this overall course. They are administrative measures, often applied in anger or frustration, aimed at pressuring the capitalists to go along with the government's social-pact policy.

These nationalizations, carried out largely without political preparation of, or even participation by, the workers, substitute state managers for private managers. Some layers of workers have initially welcomed these measures, anticipating that they will open the door to bettering their conditions and increasing workers' control over production. In fact, however, these nationalizations have done nothing to advance a course of mobilizing and increasing the class consciousness and confidence of the working class or drawing workers into decisions on production and organization of work.

Working class and trade unions
19. Attempts by unionized workers to gain a measure of control over decisions on production and conditions of work have been stalled or pushed back as the government has adjusted to threats and pressure from capitalists. The FSLN has charted a policy of trying to convince workers that in the interests of reviving "the economy" (conveniently ignoring or denying its capitalist character), they should not resist increased exploitation of their labor by those capitalists whom Sandinista leaders call "patriotic produc-

ers." This policy has also strengthened the hands of capitalist-minded managers of state-owned factories and farms.

FSLN leaders have responded to strikes by workers protesting worsening conditions by condemning them for permitting themselves to be manipulated by "pseudorevolutionaries," "agents of imperialism," or "instruments of the CIA." During the construction workers' strike in spring 1988, President Daniel Ortega, in a speech to Managua workers, broadcast over Radio Sandino, referred to the strikers as "small groups of disoriented and confused workers who are being directed by people who are conscious elements of U.S. and counterrevolutionary policy," and "a minority group of ignorant workers—some of whom claim they are revolutionaries—[who] do not know who the enemy is." Some strikers were fired. In November 1988 FSLN commander Jaime Wheelock told workers at the recently nationalized San Antonio Sugar Mill that "if anyone raises the banner of a strike here, we'll cut off his hands because it would be a crime against the people."[11]

The FSLN's course has undermined steps taken during the first years of the revolution to increase working-class and trade union unity and to politically win workers away from pro-imperialist and Stalinist union leaderships to the Sandinista Workers Federation and other prorevolution unions. These policies have politically strengthened rather than weakened the hand of antigovernment bureaucrats in the leadership of some Nicaraguan unions, who have sought to exploit the effects of the economic crisis on workers to organize political confrontations with the FSLN. Bourgeois opponents of the revolution have hypocritically sought to portray themselves as champions of workers' rights against government policies.

Land reform slides backwards
20. The struggle of the exploited peasants and agricultural laborers for a thoroughgoing agrarian reform has at times made substantial progress, at other times been pushed back. The peasants have been fighting for distribution of land to those who have none. They have also mobilized to demand adequate

low-interest credit, technical aid, marketing assistance, cheaper supplies and equipment, and crop price guarantees without which they cannot make a living on the land.

The initial expropriations of capitalist estates owned by the Somoza family and its close allies, implemented right after the July 1979 triumph, were followed in 1980 and 1981 by growing mobilizations, including land occupations, by landless peasants. Despite strong resistance from landowning capitalists, the government decreed an agrarian reform law in 1981, providing for confiscation of idle land and its distribution to landless peasants, and nationalized many of the lands that had been occupied by peasants and farm laborers.

From the second half of 1981 through 1984, however, the distribution of land proceeded at a relatively slow pace despite continuing peasant demands. Moreover, the land that was distributed was often conditioned on the agreement of the recipients to organize cooperative, and in some cases collective, farms.

By 1985, however, with the contra war a couple of years into full swing, peasant demands and pressure for land, including demonstrations and land takeovers, had grown again. In some parts of the country, the government also faced the problem of contra political influence on poor peasants who had not benefited from the land reform program. In response the government accelerated the pace of confiscations of capitalist holdings and distribution of land in 1985 and 1986. It also eased the policy limiting land distribution to those who agreed to establish collective farms or cooperatives. In 1986 a revised and strengthened agrarian reform law was adopted.

Land distribution slowed sharply toward the end of 1986, however, once peasant mobilizations eased and the military tide turned decisively against the contras in favor of Nicaragua. In 1987 the number of families benefiting from land distribution dropped to the lowest level since 1982, and in 1988 the number fell still further. In January 1989 the government announced a halt to any further confiscations of land from capitalist farmers. In his January 30 speech to the National Assembly, President Daniel Ortega declared that "enough land has been distributed already" and "there is no reason to take an inch of land from anyone." Any further distribution of land to the landless would have to be met out of properties already in the hands of the state or existing cooperatives, Ortega said.

As a result of the government's land, credit, and related policies, some poor peasants, including some who have benefited from land distribution programs, are once again being forced into increasing debt and dependence on selling their labor power just to be able to survive.

Without deepening the land reform, including among other things, nationalization of the land, and without strengthening the alliance with the urban workers to fight for such a course, not only will capitalist relations be reinforced in the countryside but the rents and mortgages system itself will be reimposed. Social differentiation will increase among toiling peasants, and between peasants and farm laborers and other rural wageworkers. Renewed land concentration and landlessness will result, as more and more peasants are driven off the soil by indebtedness. That some of the old landowning families may not return, their places now taken by newly enriched ones, does not change the fact that the semiproletarian layers in the countryside are left to the mercy of the workings of the laws of capitalism.

Working peasants have no organized voice

21. The decisive challenge of aiding the formation of fighting organizations of the poor peasants has not been met. The National Union of Farmers and Ranchers (UNAG) was organized in 1981 as an organization based on small and medium peasants. In 1984, however, the FSLN made a turn toward encouraging large capitalist farmers to join UNAG as their organization. Their spokesmen and their class interests increasingly have dominated the organization since then, effectively blocking the development of UNAG as an organization based on the toilers as well as undermining the politicization and self-confidence of poor peasants.

The capitalist farmers, the exploiters of agricultural workers, have been able to increasingly speak in the name of "the agricultural producers," leaving the poor peasants vulnerable to the antiworker and anticity demagogy of the capitalist farmers. This undermines the worker-peasant alliance.

Rights of Blacks, Indians on Atlantic Coast

22. The initial impact of the 1979 revolution on the Atlantic Coast had been to inspire demands for equality and against discrimination by the Black and Indian peoples of that region. But the first steps by the new government to bring social programs to the Coast were marred by administrative methods, insensitive at their best and brutally repressive at their worst. Such practices were compounded by the ignorance about Coastal social relations on the part of mestizos from the Pacific and the legacy of anti-Black and anti-Indian prejudice that could only be shed through common struggle and experience in advancing the revolution. The Sandinistas' actions played into the hands of enemies of the revolution and aroused deep suspicion and bitter opposition among the indigenous peoples and among substantial numbers of Blacks.

At the time of the 1979 victory, the FSLN had few Black cadres and even fewer Indian cadres. Nonetheless, it initially avoided its responsibility to politically organize and lead the indigenous populations and to bring *costeños* into FSLN membership and leadership. This default strengthened the political influence of Indian leaders who had not been won to the revolution, many of whom rapidly turned against it.

The widening of the contra war deepened the crisis. Once again, the initial response of the FSLN and the government was to deepen their reliance on military and other administrative methods directed against the population. This only stiffened opposition on the Atlantic Coast, however, and set the stage for a full-scale military and political disaster that, if not reversed, would have given the imperialists the opening they needed for direct military intervention.

Autonomy process

23. In December 1984 the government reversed its initial reac-

tionary opposition to autonomy for the peoples of the Atlantic Coast and began to champion this demand. This was a response to growing pressures from Black and Indian supporters of the revolution and to the fact that thousands of Miskitos and other Indians, as well as some Blacks, had joined armed groups allied with the contras.

The government and FSLN began to replace repression with efforts to draw the toilers of the Coast into politically resolving the conflicts that had arisen and organizing to exercise control over their own future. The government initiated discussions on a new autonomy statute, which helped inspire a stepped-up political campaign for autonomy by Coast residents themselves, taking the form of meetings, rallies, discussions, and debates from 1985 to 1987.

The decision to champion the fight for autonomy made it possible to negotiate an end to the fighting with the armed groups of Miskitos and other Indians fighting in alliance with the contras, an essential element in defeating the contra military threat.

The new course also amounted to a historic rejection of the radical petty-bourgeois, social democratic, and Stalinist policies toward oppressed nationalities that have done so much damage to the world revolution. It pointed back toward the example set on this question by the Bolshevik-led Communist International in its early years.[12] As such, the autonomy process marked a revolutionary advance for the world workers movement as a whole, as well as an inspiring example for revolutionary-minded fighters of the oppressed nationalities in the Caribbean and Latin America and around the globe—especially indigenous peoples and those of African origin. The FSLN sought to spread the international impact of this turn in policy by sponsoring conferences of indigenous peoples from throughout the Americas and encouraging these and other visitors to Nicaragua to visit the Atlantic Coast.

By rejecting the course of approaching the toilers as a problem to be administered, rather than as the makers of history to be drawn into governing and remaking society, the autonomy project also pointed the way forward for the revolution through-out Nicaragua. This turn and the victories it led to provided a substantial element of revolutionary political momentum to the class struggle as a whole, up to and through the adoption of the autonomy statute by the National Assembly in 1987.

The autonomy process, however, is a concrete reflection of the class struggle in Nicaragua and could not get too far out ahead of the development of the revolution as a whole. Its fur-ther development and concretization, as well as the political education of mestizos both in the Atlantic and Pacific regions about the necessity of autonomy and the fight against anti-*costeño* prejudice and racial discrimination throughout Nicara-gua and Central America, could only be possible with a new advance in the revolutionary process. Without such an ad-vance, substantial further progress in the fight for autonomy will be impossible, and the gains that have been won will be eroded.

Women organize to advance equal rights

24. The establishment of the workers and farmers govern-ment in 1979 gave an impulse to the struggle of Nicaraguan women for equality and against oppression. Peasants and workers who were women began taking up the fight for their right to participate on an equal basis in all aspects of eco-nomic and social life, seeking to win the CST and other unions and mass organizations to this cause. Members of the ATC in particular stepped into the forefront of these strug-gles. Women began to organize in the factories where they worked. The fight was also initially taken up at the national level by the Nicaraguan Women's Association–Luisa Amanda Espinoza (AMNLAE), the Sandinista-led national women's rights organization.

With the support of the government and the FSLN, these fighters began to make progress in changing consciousness among women and men, and scoring victories such as the ad-vancement of literacy among women, especially during the lit-eracy campaign in 1980; the 1979 decree outlawing the exploitation of women in advertising; the construction of child-care facilities in some factories and large state farms; changes in divorce procedures to the benefit of women; the adoption of stronger child-support laws; the right of women to own land and join cooperative farms; the right of female agricultural workers (rather than their husbands) to the wages paid them for their labor; provisions in many union contracts and in the 1986 constitution requiring equal pay for men and women doing the same work; and the increasing incorporation of women into the militias and armed forces, including some combat units. With the advance of the fight for women's liberation came greater participation of women in many aspects of political life, particularly in the unions, in UNAG, and in the CDSs.

25. The fight for access to abortion as a woman's right, a decisive issue in the struggle for equality, has not been successful. In 1985-86 a public debate broke out on whether to repeal the law barring almost all abortions. This law, dating back to the Somoza period, had been left intact by the FSLN-led government. As a result thousands of women each year were dying or suffering serious injuries from back-alley or self-induced abortions. Botched, illegal abortions had become, and remain, the leading cause of maternal death. Without conquering the right to decide whether and when to bear children, which is impossible unless abortion is legal and accessible, the way is blocked for workers and peasants who are female to take another qualitative step toward full equality. Nonetheless, no cabinet-level government official or any of the nine members of the FSLN National Directorate has ever come out in defense of legal abortion.

In March 1987 the FSLN issued a Proclamation on Women, which did not mention the right to abortion or birth control. This document registered the decision of the FSLN leadership to end the discussion on this question and—despite its strong words against machismo—sounded a retreat on the concrete fight for women's rights. On September 26, 1987, Daniel Ortega, the chief executive officer of the FSLN and president of the republic, made his first major public statement on abortion rights, using the most reactionary rationalizations to oppose legalization and speaking out against other aspects of women's fight for equality as well. In the same speech Ortega also declared that Indians and Blacks had never suffered racial discrimination in Nicaragua, either under the Somoza regime or afterward.

Earlier gains won for women's rights, such as the establishment of child-care centers and the breakthrough of women into jobs previously closed to them, became more vulnerable to erosion under the impact of budget cuts and large-scale layoffs. This political retreat continued in 1988, symbolized by the FSLN-backed decision to reinstate beauty contests despite protests from many women fighters, and by the fact that the newly elected national leadership of the Sandinista Youth did not include a single woman.

In early 1989 the AMNLAE leadership announced plans to introduce legislation into the National Assembly in the summer to legalize abortion, outlaw wife beating, and stiffen legal penalties against rape. By the middle of the year, however, AMNLAE leaders had bowed to pressures by the FSLN leadership, which openly argued that raising issues such as abortion rights, wife beating, or rape would—in the words of AMNLAE co-coordinator Mónica Baltodano—"only create confusion" and hurt the FSLN's candidates "in an electoral period." Among the AMNLAE figures advocating this course are FSLN cadres who at an earlier stage were outspoken about violence against women and strong defenders of abortion rights.

Evolution of FSLN leadership
26. By the time the newly elected Nicaraguan government took office in early 1985, those leaders of the revolution least attracted to a *socialist* course had become dominant in the government's executive branch and in the FSLN leadership. Nevertheless, the leadership of the government responded to pressure from the masses and took initiatives to advance important *anti-imperialist* and *democratic* tasks of the revolution.

First and foremost, the FSLN led the mobilization of the toilers of Nicaragua to defeat the imperialist-organized and -financed war. In addition, the Atlantic Coast autonomy process was set in motion in late 1984, and peasant mobilizations for land in 1985-86 led to an acceleration of land distribution and a stronger agrarian reform law.

With the signing of the Guatemala peace accords in August 1987[13] and the subsequent cease-fire with the contras in March 1988, the FSLN and the government faced new opportunities and new challenges to mobilize the toilers to strengthen their class-struggle organizations to lead forward the fight for the establishment of a workers state. The victory over the contras set back the imperialist plans to overthrow the workers and farmers government. It heightened the self-confidence of the Nicaraguan toilers.

27. In February 1988 the Nicaraguan government enacted a large devaluation of the córdoba, which led to sharp increases in prices of basic foodstuffs and consumer goods. This was followed in June 1988 by another series of economic measures: abolition of the national wage and productivity scale, which meant, among other things, abandoning the minimum wage and other attempts to benefit the lowest-paid sector of the workforce, curtailing government spending to maintain the prices paid to farmers for food staples, changes in credit policies to the detriment of the poorest peasants especially, further cutting back on government subsidies of basic foods sold through neighborhood stores, and expanding concessions to capitalist growers and processors of export commodities.

Further changes announced in December 1988 and January 1989, including the proclamation that there would be no further land expropriations, continued and deepened this policy course.

It is not primarily the economic hardships that have deepened the disorientation and demobilization of the Nicaraguan toilers in the face of these policy shifts in the aftermath of the victory over the U.S.-backed contras. It is the leadership default by the FSLN and the absence of any course projected for working people *to act* collectively against their exploiters and, drawing on their own labor and energies, *to alter* the course of their lives.

Declining weight of unions, mass organizations

28. During the two years since the peace accords confirmed the victory over the contras, the weight of the Sandinista-led unions and mass organizations in influencing government policy has been reduced, their scope of responsibilities narrowed, membership participation diminished, and their political level consequently lowered.

Leaders of the CST and other prorevolution trade unions continue to implement and justify the government's policies, striving to convince workers that it is in their interests, and in the interests of the revolution, to sacrifice more while the capitalists get a bigger share of Nicaragua's wealth. The national leadership of the ATC, which had been in the vanguard on social policies such as land reform and women's rights, has also largely gone along.

Since the policies of the government and FSLN place an ever-greater burden of the crisis on the shoulders of working people, the prorevolution union leaders must increasingly subordinate efforts to mobilize the membership in a fight to advance workers' class interests. The necessary process of bringing forward into the leadership of the unions younger workers from the ranks—leaders experienced in organizing and mobilizing the union membership not only to fight for their own needs, but for land reform, a stronger worker-peasant alliance, women's rights, against anti-*costeño* prejudice, and to advance Nicaragua toward socialism and development—is blocked.

29. The place of the neighborhood CDSs, already in decline by the mid-1980s, has been qualitatively downgraded. To the extent they still exist, they function largely as neighborhood committees to carry out routine civic tasks. They are no longer projected by FSLN leaders as units of a mass organization with the responsibility to politically mobilize working people to defend and advance the social goals of the revolution.

Armed militias set up in some factories and urban workplaces in the first year or so of the revolution were not sustained into the second half of the 1980s. They declined, as army reserve units and the implementation of the draft took on greater centrality in the effort to defend Nicaragua against the contra forces. In the countryside, however, militia units were decisive to the defense of the state farms, collective farms, and cooperatives. Since the cease-fire, there has been a de facto reduction in the weight and place of even these armed militias in rural areas. By early 1989 the Sandinista army and Ministry of the Interior were ordering all CST, ATC, and UNAG units to turn in their weapons except for those in areas of the country where contra bands still operate.

A historic opportunity rejected

30. The class battles opened by the 1979 triumph and the sustained mobilization of armed workers and peasants to defeat the contra army brought forward new generations of young revolutionary proletarian and peasant fighters, including a large layer of potential leaders. The decisive military defeat of the contras in the latter half of 1987 opened the possibility to draw these battle-tested cadres into revitalizing the leadership of the FSLN, the unions, other revolutionary organizations, and many government institutions and programs.

The Nicaraguan toilers, arms in hand, had crushed a counterrevolutionary mercenary army financed and organized by the mightiest imperialist power in history, which aimed at gutting Nicaragua's sovereignty and destroying the most basic gains of the revolution. There could have been no better opportunity than this triumph to organize, mobilize, and lead working people to begin the reconstruction and development of war-torn Nicaragua and to deepen the struggle to advance their class interests.

The FSLN leadership, however, has done the opposite. The revolutionary momentum among vanguard workers and peasants coming out of the defeat of the contras has been dissipated. To justify their policy course, FSLN leaders insisted for a year that the war was not over. The slogan of national unity, necessary to fight a successful war to defend Nicaragua's sovereignty, has been transformed into a call on working people to subordinate their interests to those of the exploiters in the name of rebuilding Nicaragua. No substantial section of the army has been reoriented toward productive labor on socially useful development projects, even while remaining mobilized to meet emergency defense needs. The best cadres, steeled and disciplined by their service in the Sandinista armed forces, are not being forged into a communist leadership of the Nicaraguan toilers.

This squandering of the revolutionary momentum and commitment of new generations of Nicaraguan toilers in the aftermath of the victory over the contras is the most important manifestation of the political failure of the course being charted by the FSLN leadership.

Slowing pace of revolutionary advances

31. This leadership retreat in Nicaragua takes place in a world political framework in which no new workers and farmers governments have come to power since 1979. The pace of advances in the international struggle against imperialism that marked the latter half of the 1970s has not continued. Outside of Cuba, there has been no advance toward communist policies among revolutionary and anti-imperialist forces in Latin America or the Caribbean.

In Central America the post-1979 upsurge in El Salvador did not succeed in conquering power, and following the bloody assault by the U.S.-backed government in 1981, the revolutionary struggle there was pushed back. Despite its failure to deal a decisive defeat to the revolutionary forces or maintain stability amid deepening economic and social crisis, the U.S.-armed and -financed Salvadoran rulers have nonetheless been able to hold on to power and further consolidate a repressive bourgeois regime. The Farabundo Martí National Liberation Front (FMLN), which groups together the major revolutionary organizations, has not been able to chart a clear and united political course to mobilize the workers and peasants to remove this regime.[14]

In the Caribbean the murderous Stalinist overthrow of the

workers and farmers government in Grenada in 1983 further shifted the international relationship of forces to the detriment of the toilers in the region. It opened the door to the first large-scale direct assault by U.S. military forces in the Americas since the invasion of the Dominican Republic in 1965.[15]

The U.S.-organized contra war against Nicaragua, which was organized on a large scale beginning in 1983, was part of this counteroffensive by imperialism.

By the end of 1985 the opportunity had also been missed for the governments of Latin America, as well as Africa and Asia, to take up the proposal of Cuban president Fidel Castro to join together in repudiating further payments on the sky-rocketing Third World debt. Since then the imperialist governments and financial institutions have been able to play their game of divide and conquer with ever more devastating effectiveness, draining wealth and wresting concessions from Third World regimes one by one. In a growing number of Latin American and Caribbean countries, bourgeois-nationalist, "populist," or social democratic regimes have become harsh debt collectors for the big imperialist banks. The governments of Michael Manley in Jamaica and Peronist leader Carlos Saúl Menem in Argentina are only two of the most recent examples of this phenomenon.[16]

The formation in 1984 of the Anti-Imperialist Organizations of the Caribbean and Central America registered a step forward for revolutionary forces in the region. Despite setbacks in Grenada and elsewhere, its founding was a product of the revolutionary momentum toward internationalist solidarity and anti-imperialist unity coming out of the 1979-80 advances. In the absence of any further revolutionary victories since that time, however, the Anti-Imperialist Organizations, too, has politically stagnated.[17]

These negative developments weigh heavily on the Nicaraguan revolution, strengthening the hand of those who would continue to retreat from the perspective outlined in the Historic Program, and quieting the voices of those who see the road forward in Nicaragua as inextricably tied to the perspective of extending the anticapitalist and anti-imperialist revolution in the Americas.

Capitalist social crisis in Americas

32. The economic and social plight facing the toilers of Nicaragua is part of the broader devastation throughout the Americas caused by the deepening world crisis of capitalism. Latin America is burdened by more than $400 billion in debts to imperialist banks, financial institutions, and governments. Nicaragua itself has a debt of $6.7 billion, representing largely unpaid interest on past borrowing, not substantial new loans, which have not been forthcoming from most imperialist governments and agencies.

Throughout Latin America and the Caribbean massive unemployment, runaway inflation, land dispossession, the growth of miserable urban shantytowns, rampant environmental destruction, and multiple other social ills afflict growing numbers of toilers. The effects of the crisis have been particularly acute in Central America; one consequence is that the number of refugees in this region is rivaled only by Southeast Asia and some of the most famine-stricken parts of Africa.

All these conditions have continued to worsen during a conjunctural upturn in the capitalist business cycle in the major imperialist countries. The coming recession at the opening of the 1990s will magnify the crisis throughout the Americas and the rest of the semicolonial world. A policy direction by the Nicaraguan government based on the prospect of international capitalist expansion and increased aid and trade with the imperialist countries, rather than on the reality of a coming world depression and intensified social crisis, is set on a headlong course toward disaster.

Promoting a 'social pact'

33. The course being pursued by the FSLN leadership has disoriented, demoralized, and demobilized large numbers of Nicaraguan workers and peasants. Many are not convinced that simply being told they must sacrifice even more is a strategy to

advance the goals for which they made the revolution a decade ago.

FSLN leaders, however, are waging a political fight to win vanguard workers and peasants to their policy course. They hope to convince working people to subordinate their class interests and demands to the strategic need to strengthen capitalist production and market relations (the "mixed economy") as the only realistic road forward for Nicaragua today. The FSLN leadership argues that only by maintaining a social pact with "patriotic" capitalists—that is, only by seeking to freeze the class struggle—will it be possible to ease the devastating social effects of the world capitalist economic crisis, permit a stabilization and improvement in living standards in the medium term, and lead toward socialism somewhere down the road.

34. No member of the FSLN National Directorate, or any other national leader, has stated disagreement with the government's current strategic course or argued for an alternative, communist course. This leadership consensus was confirmed in March 1989, when the recent government measures were endorsed in a major two-part interview in *Barricada* by Tomás Borge, a founder of the FSLN and the most senior member of its National Directorate.

Borge sought to provide a theoretical justification for this policy course, arguing that market mechanisms are an expression of "objective relations" and "general economic laws" that transcend capitalism and socialism and can be used to "serve specific class interests." "From the beginning," he said, "the theories of scientific socialism discarded the idea of associating market relations with capitalism alone, as if they were alien to socialism."[18]

Contrary to these arguments, however, the consequences of maintaining capitalist relations of production are neither socially nor politically neutral. The market is not a fact of nature but a social relationship that arises with class society and becomes generalized with the worldwide spread of capitalist domination and exploitation.[19] Nicaragua's economic backwardness, and the conditions of its working people, are the product of their historic place in the social relations of production in the imperialist system, not simply the inadequacy of Nicaragua's forces of production. Only a qualitative change in those social relations of production can unleash the energies of Nicaragua's workers and peasants to begin developing the forces of production to their maximum on the basis of economic planning for the benefit of the many.

Maintaining the capitalist market system and its domination of industrial and agricultural production in Nicaragua strengthens the exploiting classes, deepens divisions and inequalities among the toilers, blocks progress toward economic and social development, and promotes the spread of bourgeois values. The FSLN government can no more guide a capitalist economy toward recovery and expansion than can the government of any other poverty-stricken capitalist country in Central America or elsewhere in the semicolonial world. Without easing the crisis in the countryside that results from capitalist domination of industry, trade, and agriculture, and without laying the nationalized foundation for steps toward a planned economy, no government efforts to reverse the crisis can be successful.

False analogy with Bolsheviks' New Economic Policy
35. To bolster his justification of the policy course of the Sandinista-led government, Tomás Borge in the March 1989 *Barricada* interview cited the example of "Lenin's New Economic Policy" in the Soviet Republic in the early 1920s. This analogy is fundamentally mistaken.

The NEP was a necessary retreat toward widening market relations between the towns and working peasants in the exchange of basic food products for light industrial commodities (consumer goods and light farm equipment and supplies). Its aim was to strengthen the worker-peasant alliance, which had been weakened during the previous period of imperialist military intervention and civil war.

Moreover, Lenin always insisted that the indispensable precondition for this retreat was the conquest of state ownership of industry, nationalization of the land, and the state monopoly of

216 SWP resolution (1989)

foreign trade. The NEP was implemented after, not before, these tasks were accomplished; that is, after the establishment of a workers state.[20]

36. In the interests of maintaining the social pact with capitalist manufacturers and landowners, the FSLN leadership is not only seeking to somehow freeze the class struggle but also to put political clarification of class realities on the back burner. FSLN leaders more and more often resort to language that obscures rather than clarifies conflicting class interests within Nicaragua. *Producers,* for example, has been transformed from a scientific term referring to exploited working people—those whose labor truly does produce for the benefit of society—to a term used by many government and Sandinista officials to include wealthy capitalist farmers and ranchers—those who exploit.

The social and political consequences of obscuring the truth about the causes of exploitation and oppression, and the road toward their elimination, are no more neutral than the workings of the capitalist market system itself. Political clarity, class consciousness, and organization and action on that basis are the only weapons the toilers have to advance their historic interests. The bourgeoisie, on the other hand, does not need such clarity; the very operations of its social system reproduce and intensify oppression and exploitation behind the backs of working people and capitalists alike.

No 'third road' between capitalism, communism

37. FSLN leaders also often assert that state property and a planned economy are incompatible with political liberties, or, as it is often put, that only the preservation of a "mixed economy" can guarantee "political pluralism." This argument, too, obscures the class truth.

The deepening of bourgeois-democratic rights is a progressive development that increases the space for the exploited to organize and practice politics. But such advances have a revolutionary dynamic and are sustainable only if linked to a deepening of workers democracy and control, strengthening the toilers in their struggle to do away with capitalist exploitation. Far from guaranteeing the maintenance and extension of political rights, the substitution of bourgeois parliamentary democracy and electoralism for concrete advances in workers' democracy opens the door to the restriction—if not destruction—of democratic freedoms that a restoration of capitalist political rule will inevitably bring.

To the degree that the FSLN leadership presents the forthcoming [1990] national election as a means in and of itself of bolstering the revolution, therefore, it is miseducating an entire generation of fighters. Moreover, the argument of the leadership of the FSLN and the government that the elections, by establishing the legitimacy of the FSLN government in the eyes of the world, can buy a breathing space from imperialist aggression is dangerously false and disorienting. As the example of revolutionary Cuba demonstrates, establishing international respect and political standing is not the same thing as garnering favorable bourgeois public opinion. It is only the former that strengthens the defense of a revolutionary government.

38. The leadership of the FSLN and the government is increasingly explicit in its rejection, as the way forward for Nicaragua, of the socialist road opened in the Americas by the Cuban revolution and advanced by its communist leadership. President Daniel Ortega and other Sandinista leaders have stated that the Nicaraguan government is modeling its policies instead on that of smaller imperialist powers, Sweden in particular.

The launching and deepening of the rectification process by the communist leadership in Cuba since 1986 marks the one political development in the region over the past half decade that builds on the revolutionary impulse of which the 1979 triumph in Nicaragua was a central part.[21] Cuban communists have acted on the understanding that the revolution can only advance by building a vanguard party that is increasingly proletarian in the composition of its membership and leadership. Instead of reaching out to link up with this deepening course toward socialism by the Cuban leadership, however, FSLN leaders have chosen an opposite path.

Communism, as the historic expression of the class course toward which all modern struggles of the working class lead, is increasingly rejected. FSLN leaders more and more often speak in terms of a specific Nicaraguan ideology that is supposedly neither capitalist nor communist, and will somehow, someday lead the country toward democratic socialism. "Democracy" in the abstract, shorn of any class content, is the watchword.

This supposed third road between capitalism and socialism is presented by many Sandinista leaders as applicable not only to Nicaragua but more generally to Latin America. Revolutionists from elsewhere in the Americas who look to the Nicaraguan revolution have been influenced to varying degrees by these anti-Marxist views, especially in the context of setbacks to revolutionary struggles in the region in the 1980s.

If the experience of the Nicaraguan revolution once again confirms anything, however, it is that there is no third road between capitalism and socialism. Any strategic orientation counterposed to mobilizing working people in a fight for socialism can lead only to the reinforcement of capitalist social relations with their devastating consequences for maintaining national sovereignty and extending economic development and social justice for the toilers.

Stalinism vs. communism

39. The perspectives expressed by FSLN leaders gain strength from their convergence with the policies of the perestroika stage of Stalinism, which attracts and lends momentum to all anti-Marxist forces within the working-class movement internationally.

The supporters of perestroika hold out the illusion that the world is becoming a more peaceful one as the result of the Gorbachev policies, which are helping to tame imperialism. This illusion finds support among those who are hoping that the imperialist aggressors will leave Nicaragua alone, that the world capitalist crisis will ease, and that large-scale aid and cooperation will be forthcoming from capitalist governments and financial institutions. This, they hope, will give Nicaragua a chance to develop along its own road.

Nicaragua's toilers need peace in order to be able to recover from the destruction of the war and begin to rebuild their country. But the world that is being brought into being by the bipartisan course of the imperialist government in Washington, and its efforts to negotiate "détente" with Gorbachev's perestroika policies, will not bring peace for anti-imperialist struggles or for workers and peasants fighting for tolerable living and working conditions.

In line with the Sandinistas' own increasing reliance on capitalist market mechanisms, Daniel Ortega has spoken in positive terms about recent changes in Soviet economic policy that make aid and trade with Cuba, Nicaragua, and other embattled Third World countries more conditional on profit considerations of individual Soviet enterprises, and thus less sure and reliable. "They're doing things more through business operations," Ortega said in a recent interview. "Before, the way things were done was fundamentally political; the political line was brought down and their companies implemented it. Now, with the business-style organization that they're promoting, new forms of cooperation that we couldn't see back then can be encouraged and explored, from company to company."

One of the foreign-policy and foreign-aid implications of perestroika is unambiguous: increasing pressure, direct and indirect, on revolutionary movements and governments to adjust their courses to place "regional conflicts" in the appropriate subordinate place and to settle them. But settlements do not mean peace with dignity, with honor, with independence; they mean peace on terms acceptable to imperialism.

40. Leading the toilers to establish, consolidate, and advance a workers state requires the construction of a communist party. The elimination of capitalist exploitation and the inauguration of a planned economy demand a deeper and broader class consciousness and firmness of the worker-peasant alliance than does the earlier step of toppling capitalist political rule. Such consciousness can be forged only with the existence of a communist vanguard leading the class struggle forward. At

the same time, it is only by leading the toilers in making this qualitative transformation from capitalism to the construction of socialism that a communist vanguard can become truly a mass, proletarian communist party.

Such leadership can never come from the ultraleft sects and Stalinist organizations in Nicaragua, whose antipeasant and anti-working-class strategic orientations have been and continue to be rejected by revolutionary-minded fighters. When Sandinistas say that they are more revolutionary, and even more communist, than the Communist Party of Nicaragua, the Nicaraguan Socialist Party, the Marxist-Leninist Party, and other groups claiming to be Marxist, they are speaking the truth.[22]

A communist vanguard of the Nicaraguan working class can be forged only within and among the revolutionary-minded who defend the FSLN, which has won and retains the right to lead the workers and peasants. No such communist vanguard has been forged. Without an advance in this process, the revolution has not been able to move forward to the historic steps necessary to prevent its retrogression. The increasingly explicit rejection by a number of FSLN leaders of Marxism, communism, and the road opened for all Latin America and the Caribbean by the Cuban socialist revolution poses the major obstacle to advancing the broad leadership capable of guiding Nicaragua's toilers to reverse the erosion of the foundations of the workers and farmers government.

Those FSLN members and supporters who are most committed to defending and advancing the class interests of the workers and peasants, and who have not been politically broken by the grind of the past decade, increasingly find themselves in opposition to the strategic course being charted, even if this opposition is not fully conscious or consistent. What is needed in Nicaragua today is an opposition to the current course that is utterly loyal to the revolution and to the FSLN, seeks to implement the Historic Program, defends the communist perspective, fights for Marxism, and points toward the example of the Cuban revolution. It would draw together in a struggle to defend the revolution the veterans of the revolutionary struggle who have not abandoned the road they set out on when they joined the FSLN as well as the class-struggle fighters of the younger generation.

Washington's bipartisan course

41. Like the Nicaraguan capitalists, the U.S. imperialists have no doubts that, although the Nicaraguan revolution today is not socialist, the workers and farmers government is the product of a true and profound revolution that has put political power in the hands of the working people. The U.S. rulers have no confidence in that government, and correctly so, despite the policies it is now implementing. This is because of the revolution itself and the class forces on which the government rests.

The bipartisan policy in Washington continues to be one of finding a way to replace the FSLN government, not merely to pressure it for more concessions. Negotiating probes by the U.S. rulers are accompanied by continuing covert support to murderous contra operations.

The Nicaraguan government's growing vulnerability does not satisfy the imperialists. It merely emboldens Washington to press harder toward its goal. The imperialists insistently demand greater concessions to Nicaragua's exploiting classes. Then, when the FSLN-led government is forced to take punitive measures against capitalists who despite these concessions challenge the social pact it is seeking to implement (such as the expropriation of three capitalist coffee growers in June 1989), Washington lashes out all the more harshly. This becomes another excuse for imperialist governments in Western Europe that do have economic relations with Nicaragua, as well as oil-exporting regimes in Latin America, to slow down on increasing grants and renegotiating loans and to demand even stiffer conditions for such assistance.

No matter how much the Sandinistas seek to mollify bourgeois world public opinion, such concessions will not cause the U.S. government and its allies to relent on pursuing their class interests. It is a trap not to recognize that fact.

Washington does not have, and cannot have, a stable strategy to advance its interests in Nicaragua and the rest of Central

America. Nor can it predict or control all the consequences of the forces it sets in motion. The U.S. rulers respond pragmatically to the evolution of the class struggle in Nicaragua, as throughout the world. Over the past two years, for example, the U.S. government has repeatedly misjudged its capacity to bring down the government in Panama through a combination of economic sanctions, military threats, and unrelenting propaganda. Washington remains capable of policy lurches that can lead to military adventures.[23]

42. The possibilities for large-scale action in the United States in defense of Nicaragua are more limited than they have been in past years. The end of the contra war has reduced, as an objective fact, the weight of Nicaragua as an issue in U.S. politics. Moreover, the political retreat of the FSLN and the Nicaraguan government in the face of enormous challenges has had an impact on the willingness of many of those who are partisans of that revolution to engage in action. This is reflected in the fact that possibilities for large-scale tours and work brigades to Nicaragua are fewer than they were in the past.

While necessarily affecting the weighting of priorities for communists in the United States, this does not alter the political axis of our work in relation to Nicaragua. We continue to take advantage of the opportunities that do exist for workers and farmers from the United States to visit Nicaragua, as well as opportunities to work with others to bring Nicaraguan revolutionaries to the United States. We continue to join with others to oppose Washington's attempt to use economic and political pressure, backed up by military threats, to impose a proimperialist regime on Nicaragua. This includes demanding an end to all U.S. aid to the contras and to the trade embargo, massive government aid to Nicaragua, and the unconditional normalization of relations with Nicaragua.

The broader changes and advances in U.S. politics and the class struggle—registered by the strike against Eastern Airlines, renewed labor struggles in the coalfields, the massive April 9 abortion rights demonstration in Washington, D.C., and greater receptivity to socialist publications—while modest, create better political conditions in which to build international working-class solidarity with fighting toilers the world over, from Central America to southern Africa.

Members of the Socialist Workers Party and Young Socialist Alliance, as well as the comrades who make up the party's active supporters, are partisans of and fellow fighters with the FSLN; our movement is its sister revolutionary organization. It is from this standpoint that we participate in defending and advancing the Nicaraguan revolution and workers and farmers government. And it is from this standpoint that we work with other political forces to draw workers and farmers into defending revolutionary Nicaragua against Washington and its allies.

Keeping revolutionary lessons in circulation

43. The circulation of the communist press to those throughout the world who are partisans of the Nicaraguan revolution is increasingly important. It is only in the pages of the *Militant* and *Perspectiva Mundial* that the story is being reported of the concrete unfolding of the class struggle in Nicaragua, often through the on-the-scene reporting team in the Managua Bureau.[24]

There needs to be an upgrading of the priority given to deepening the education of communist cadres about the experiences of workers and farmers governments not only in Nicaragua, but also in Cuba, Algeria, and Grenada. Education for Socialists publications and other Pathfinder titles (especially those by Joseph Hansen), as well as the *New International* magazine, are invaluable for this. We must introduce supporters of the Nicaraguan revolution to Pathfinder's books presenting the writings and speeches of Che Guevara, Fidel Castro, and other leaders of the Cuban revolution; the political legacy of the Communist International in Lenin's time; the works of U.S. communist leaders Farrell Dobbs and James P. Cannon; and the communist continuity on the fight for national liberation, women's emancipation, and the revolutionary transformation of the labor movement. This educational work is an essential component of the international efforts to defend the Nicaraguan workers and farmers government.

When supporters of the Nicaraguan revolution begin to understand the enormity of the consequences of the FSLN's current course, their first reaction is to step back and try to figure it out. Some become demoralized when their illusions are shattered and their hopes seem to become less realistic.

Our job is to pull them back from being disappointed, to pull them *into* the revolution as partisans of the toilers and of their world communist vanguard. We must help them recognize the stakes in defending the historic democratic and anti-imperialist gains of the Nicaraguan revolution, and the prospects it opened for the workers and farmers to march toward the conquest of the second workers state in the Americas. Only by helping them to understand the Nicaraguan revolution and its line of march from that standpoint can we help them to act, and lead others to act, in defense of the revolution. And only in this way can we contribute to the development of communist leadership, which is made more, not less, important by the world that is emerging in the closing decade of the twentieth century.

With this approach we can convince the best of the working people around the world who support the Nicaraguan revolution of the necessity of joining a proletarian party that fights for the communist future and of the correctness and historical urgency of the choice summed up by Fidel Castro as "socialism or death."

THE FRAME-UP OF
MARK CURTIS

A PACKINGHOUSE WORKER'S FIGHT FOR JUSTICE
by Margaret Jayko

Mark Curtis is serving a 25-year sentence in Iowa on frame-up rape and burglary charges. His real crime, in the authorities' eyes, is that he is part of a layer of young unionists active in the struggle to support the rights of immigrant workers, strengthen the unions, and campaign against U.S. government intervention from Cuba to the Mideast.

Curtis's fight for justice has won support around the world. This pamphlet details the facts and how you can help. 71 pp. $5.00

AVAILABLE FROM DISTRIBUTORS LISTED ON PAGE 2

JOIN THE FIGHT
to win
PAROLE FOR MARK CURTIS

Mark Curtis, a socialist and a unionist in the meatpacking industry, has spent more than five years in prison on frame-up charges. He has repeatedly been refused parole by the state of Iowa. To find out more about the frame-up, and about how you can help win Curtis's release, write for information to the Mark Curtis Defense Committee. Funds are needed to continue the fight.

CLIP AND MAIL TO THE MARK CURTIS DEFENSE COMMITTEE, BOX 1048, DES MOINES, IOWA 50311

❏ I would like information about the case and how I can help.

❏ Enclosed is my contribution of _____.

NAME _____ PHONE_____

ADDRESS _____

CITY_____ STATE _____ ZIP _____

COUNTRY _____ TITLE/ORGANIZATION _____

FROM
PATHFINDER

February 1965: The Final Speeches

BY MALCOLM X

Speeches from the last three weeks of Malcolm X's life, presenting the still accelerating evolution of his political views. A large part is material previously unavailable, with some never before in print. First volume in the new selected works of Malcolm X. 293 pp. $17.95

Peru's 'Shining Path'

BY MARTÍN KOPPEL

How can Shining Path's growth, and its mounting internal political crisis, be explained? Why are its perspectives so destructive to the working class in Peru and worldwide? What is the alternative for workers and peasants fighting to defend their interests against the landlords and factory owners? Booklet. 35 pp. $3.50

Letters from Prison

BY JAMES P. CANNON

Prison correspondence of a revolutionary workers' leader jailed during World War II. Discusses how to educate and organize a communist movement able to stand up to wartime repression and prepare for the big labor battles that were emerging during the closing years of the war. 362 pp. $21.95

The Jewish Question

A Marxist Interpretation

BY ABRAM LEON

What are the historical roots of modern anti-Semitism? How is it used by the capitalists in times of social crisis to mobilize reactionary forces against the labor movement and disorient working people in face of their exploiters? 270 pp. $17.95

PATHFINDER—See page 2 for distributors

A HISTORIC OPPORTUNITY IS BEING LOST

by Larry Seigle

T EN YEARS AGO THE WORKERS and peasants of Nicaragua, led by the Sandinista National Liberation Front, brought crashing down the U.S.-backed Somoza tyranny, one of the most hated and brutal dictatorships in the history of this hemisphere. In doing so they delivered a powerful blow to the Yankee empire, which the Sandinista hymn accurately labeled the enemy of humanity.

In achieving this historic victory, the toilers of Nicaragua fought their way onto the stage of world history. They reached out to fellow fighters everywhere. They reached out to the comrades of the Farabundo Martí National Liberation Front in El Salvador, who were struggling to extend the revolution in Central America. They reached into the Caribbean, to the workers and farmers government in Grenada headed by Maurice Bishop, which was embarking on a road parallel to the one on which Nicaragua was starting out. The working people of Nicaragua reached out to fighters for the independence of Puerto Rico, the U.S. Caribbean colony, in the conviction that by doing so they could help score another advance for liberty and further weaken U.S. imperialism.

They reached out to Cuba, whose example they were trying to emulate, whose volunteer fighters had already shed their blood on Nicaraguan soil, and whose generous internationalist aid for the reconstruction of the country was being loaded on planes

---

This report was presented August 8, 1989, to the International Active Workers and Socialist Educational Conference held in Oberlin, Ohio. Larry Seigle was the Managua Bureau director for the Militant *and* Perspectiva Mundial *from 1987 to 1990.*

and boats even before Somoza's "bunker" was finally captured.

They extended their ties beyond Latin America and the Caribbean as well. They reached out to southern Africa, to the African National Congress of South Africa and the South West Africa People's Organisation of Namibia, to link up with the fight against apartheid and help explain throughout Latin America and the Caribbean its world significance. They reached out to Thomas Sankara and the revolution in Burkina Faso.[1]

The Nicaraguan people also began forging contacts with workers and farmers in the imperialist countries. They not only demanded the solidarity that they had earned by their struggle and their victory over the Somoza dictatorship but also extended the hand of solidarity to anyone fighting against injustice and oppression. More than that, they began to see and to act on the common class interests that unite the toilers in the imperialist countries with those in the lands oppressed by imperialism. They reached out to organizations of revolutionists in North America, in Europe, and in the Pacific, helping in the process to pull us into the world as it is and as it is becoming. They helped those of us who live in the imperialist countries deepen our understanding of, and our participation in, the world revolution as we were advancing in becoming more proletarian and more communist.

The new government that the toilers brought to power in Nicaragua restored Nicaragua's sovereignty, which the Somoza dictatorship had sold to Washington. The FSLN government stood up and began saying no to the pressures, threats, blackmail, intimidation, and aggression from Washington and its allies. Nicaragua began to establish its own place in the world as a sovereign country with its own foreign policy, seeking aid from and giving aid to those it chose.

The revolutionary government began implementing far-reaching democratic reforms. It undertook a land reform, initiating the process of transforming class relations in the coun-

ENDNOTES FOR THIS ARTICLE BEGIN ON PAGE 321.

tryside. It codified the rights the toilers had conquered to speak, to assemble, to petition the government, and to organize without fear of being beaten up or shot by the tyranny's police. It took some first steps toward overturning the entrenched discrimination against women. And it began to search for the road, albeit with considerable difficulties that would have to be fought through, to uprooting discrimination against the indigenous peoples and the Black people of Nicaragua's Atlantic Coast.

The new government took the vital natural resources of the country out of the hands of imperialism. It began a series of far-reaching social programs, most notable among them a massive Literacy Crusade aimed at drawing into the modern world those who had been kept out by the illiteracy, the darkness, imposed by the Somoza dictatorship.

Workers and farmers government
But the revolutionary government, led by the FSLN, did something more than all of these things. The new government had been brought to power by a revolution that had succeeded in smashing the National Guard, the repressive arm of the old regime. It began constructing a new armed power of the toilers, a new police force, army, and volunteer militia.

The government and the FSLN responded to and helped lead workers' and peasants' mobilizations, land takeovers, and factory occupations. These actions, which often assumed mass proportions, demanded the expropriation of farms, factories, and other businesses of capitalists who were sabotaging production, taking their capital out of the country, and refusing to recognize the rights, including the right to organize unions, that the toilers believed had been won when the Somoza dictatorship was overthrown. In many cases these protests and direct actions resulted in government measures against the capitalists. The new government also took steps to guarantee the distribution of some basic food products at heavily subsidized prices to every resident of Nicaragua, to bring many areas of foreign trade under the control of the government, and to begin restricting the capitalists' ability to move capital out of the country.

In short, it began a course of action that infringed more and more on the sacred property rights and prerogatives of the exploiting classes. It was a workers and farmers government.

The draft resolution prepared for discussion by the National Committee of the Socialist Workers Party explains that the class foundations of such a workers and farmers government "are established by the revolutionary displacement of the bourgeoisie from political power, the assumption of that power by an administration based on the popular masses and that commands a new army, and the initiation of far-reaching changes in property relations."[2]

The establishment of this government meant that the opportunity existed for the workers and peasants of Nicaragua to use governmental power, the most powerful political weapon the toilers can have, to move forward to replace the capitalist foundations of the economy, and by doing so become the second people in the Americas to embark on the construction of socialism.

Now, ten years after the victory, the foundations of that workers and farmers government are being eroded as a result of the course being followed by the leadership of the FSLN and the government. Unless there is a fundamental reversal of the course—unless the anticapitalist direction and actions of the early years of the revolution are reasserted—the government will be restructured and consolidated on the basis of the capitalist property relations that exist.

The opportunity to extend the socialist revolution, the opportunity to join with Cuba in constructing socialism, is being lost. The policy decisions and events leading to this outcome do not lie ahead of us. They are not things we will see in the future; they lie behind us.

This is not what we want to hear. It is not what we and many others have fought to bring about. So we resist these conclusions. And we all have to work our way through one or more of the escape clauses, all of the easy ways out that we cling to in an effort to avoid facing the facts as they are. Some hope that one or another individual leader in the National Directorate of the

FSLN will come forward in the nick of time to prevent this outcome. Others wish for some group of class-struggle fighters in the farmworkers union or somewhere else, who can by sheer will and determination prevent this from taking place.

A historic opportunity is being lost, and it didn't have to be lost. We will mourn the loss of this opportunity for a moment as we absorb it. But then we will resume action. It is to be able to act politically, to continue defending the Nicaraguan revolution and advancing the worldwide fight against imperialism and for socialism, that we need a clear picture. We are participants in, not observers of, what is happening in Nicaragua. We need a clear understanding in order to become better fighters and to help others become better fighters.

We need this clarity to be able to pull back into action those defenders and partisans of the Nicaraguan revolution who are becoming demoralized and disoriented and to help pull them toward the fight for the socialist future as part of the world and part of the world revolution. We need this clarity to be able to speak effectively to class-struggle fighters in Nicaragua, in Latin America and the Caribbean, and throughout the world who are part of and aspire to become more a part of the forces fighting to rebuild a communist leadership of the workers movement on a world scale.

And we need this clarity in order to continue unchanged our decade-long fight to demand of Washington that it cease assaulting and affronting Nicaraguan sovereignty, and instead normalize relations, end all contra financing, and aid the Nicaraguan people in the reconstruction they have suffered so much to be able to carry forward.

Based on facts
As we work our way through the draft resolution we can see that some of the things that might seem at first glance to be the most controversial statements are not controversial at all, in Nicaragua or anywhere else.

There can be no challenge by any serious person to any of the facts on which the conclusions are based. This is true for the same reason that there has not been, nor could there be, any serious challenge to the facts about Nicaragua that have been reported in the *Militant* and in *Perspectiva Mundial*. The facts are reported objectively, not selected to bolster a line. Moreover, when we report the course being charted by the leadership of the FSLN and the government we focus not on "inside dope" but on the positions as argued and defended by the leadership in front of the toilers of Nicaragua.

Assertions in the draft resolution that might at first seem highly controversial—such as, that the leadership of the FSLN and the government has turned toward reliance on the capitalist market, and that it has retreated from the course of deepening inroads on the social rights and property rights of the exploiting classes—summarize the course that is being not only implemented but openly defended by the leadership itself. The same is true about the resolution's description of the shifting of the weight of the economic crisis onto the backs of the workers and peasants, who are left with little perspective of how to defend their class interests, and the cumulative result of this in the increasing divisions and demoralization of the toilers, who are being pushed out of real politics.

When the draft resolution states that the course being implemented is a reversal of the line of march presented in the FSLN's Historic Program, which was drafted by Carlos Fonseca in 1969, and that the example of the Cuban revolution is being increasingly rejected by the Nicaraguan leadership, it is simply reporting what is being done and what is being said by those who are doing it.

No one in Nicaragua who follows politics concretely will dispute the accuracy of these facts. Nor will they be challenged by any objective revolutionary-minded fighter who visits Nicaragua. (I do not include those who go to Nicaragua as though they were going to Mecca. Their beliefs are not based on facts, and you cannot argue with them anymore than you can argue about religion with a believer.)

It has taken those of us who have been assigned to the Managua Bureau of the *Militant* and *Perspectiva Mundial* a while to understand, living and working in Nicaragua, what is controversial and what is not controversial about what we publish. I, for one, kept anticipating—especially in the last year or two—that the coverage about Nicaragua in our press would provoke some challenge or disagreement from Nicaraguan comrades we work with there. What we report is read, and it's read by serious people and serious fighters. But there haven't been any challenges to the news we provide about Nicaragua.

Instead, we have learned, when *Perspectiva Mundial* and the *Militant* are controversial in Nicaragua—when they provoke strong reactions, when some people's eyes light up with pleasure and they reach out to grab a copy off the table and others get that stony, grim look that lets you know they've seen something they deeply dislike—is when Fidel Castro appears on the cover proclaiming that Cuba will never adopt capitalist methods, or that to be a revolutionary in today's world means more and more to be a communist. *That is* controversial. Some people, a lot of people, like it. But others think it is entirely the wrong message.

What is controversial about the *Militant* and *Perspectiva Mundial* is not what they accurately describe about what has happened in Nicaragua and the conclusions they point to about the outcome of what has transpired. Rather, what is controversial is the view that there is another road, another perspective. What is controversial, and deeply so, is the idea that beginning to build socialism is not impossible in Latin America and the Caribbean.

Need for proletarian communist party

At the heart of the draft resolution is the assertion of the need to build a proletarian communist party in Nicaragua—or, more precisely, its rejection of changing the perspective that was put forward by the Communist International in its founding years under Lenin's leadership and that has been a touchstone for revolutionary workers ever since. A Marxist party of the toilers is needed to unify and educate the working class and its allies. This is essential to enable the workers to lead forward the struggle to overturn capitalist property relations, beginning to transform themselves in the process into new women and new men capable of building socialism. The forging of such a party in Nicaragua would mark a historic advance for the world working-class movement in the fight to resolve the historic crisis of proletarian leadership.

Such a party is irreplaceable because the action that the toilers need to take in Nicaragua must be more than defensive action, more than united trade union action, and more than determined reaction to exploitation and oppression. It must be more than the action it took to overthrow the Somoza regime. It cannot be accomplished by a middle-class layer acting in the interests of, and on behalf of, the working class. It must be the conscious action of the working class, led by a vanguard of that class. It must be the action of workers and peasants who are becoming conscious of the reality of social relations and are ridding themselves of the fetishes and superstitions that mask these relations under capitalism. It must be the act of class-conscious women and men who see themselves as part of the modern world.

There has never been better human material with which to construct a communist party than the self-sacrificing and heroic fighters of the Sandinista National Liberation Front and the broad vanguard of the toilers, who have given so much for the revolution during the last decade. But this party has not been built. What's more, it has been pushed further and further away from coming into existence as a result of the systematic miseducation that creates prejudices against Marxism and communism, carried out by the leadership of the FSLN and the government. It is not only what has not been done, but the creation of additional obstacles to what must be done, that we have to see clearly.

There is no way to bypass this challenge and there are no shortcuts around it. The draft resolution points out that the only development that might open the possibility of once again placing the revolution on an anticapitalist course would be a major revolutionary victory in the world that directly affected Latin America and the Caribbean. Such a victory could inspire a broad vanguard of class-struggle fighters in Nicaragua to push forward. But this wouldn't solve the question of the need to build a communist party. It wouldn't offer a way around it. It would simply pose it again in a new, advantageous, and even sharper way. To move forward, such an upsurge by the toilers would have to interact with a qualitative break on the leadership level. A component of the established leadership would have to respond to this upsurge, embrace it, and then act to lead it forward to a higher plane. For this to happen there would have to be a break from the leadership consensus that has been established in the National Directorate of the FSLN around the current course. Such a political initiative from among the established and recognized revolutionary leaders would then inspire a further massive resurgence and open a new chapter in the history of the Nicaraguan revolution.

One of the final illusions some of us hold on to is the hope that some force from the outside can get things moving forward again. But it can't. It has to come from inside, even if it is substantially a response to developments outside. If the leadership doesn't exist to respond to such an upsurge from the toilers, to drive it forward and to generalize it, then it can end only in being dissipated no matter how much enthusiasm there may be. Without class-conscious leadership it's just enthusiasm. And like all enthusiasm, if it never gets beyond enthusiasm, it will dissipate.

There is no way around the problem of communist leadership. When Leon Trotsky and other Russian revolutionary fighters began to understand what was happening and what had happened in the Soviet Union following the death of Lenin—the consolidation of the rule of the relatively privileged bureaucracy headed by Stalin—some urged Trotsky to use his considerable authority among the troops and officers of the Red Army to act to remove Stalin and reverse the course of the party. But Trotsky rejected that course because he knew that the problem could not be solved except by solving the problem of the party. It couldn't be done around it. There is no way to move forward that does not confront the need for a conscious proletarian leadership organized through a communist party.

Test of theory
The draft resolution builds on earlier documents of the Social-

ist Workers Party regarding Nicaragua's revolution and the lessons of its workers and farmers government. The resolution adopted by the National Committee of the SWP in January 1980, just a few months after the overthrow of Somoza, is particularly worth studying.[3]

Rereading that resolution today is a test of how well the theoretical framework of the workers and farmers government has guided us in orienting ourselves to the decisive political tasks confronting the Nicaraguan workers and peasants. We can see that the course of events over the past ten years has confirmed, in a concrete test, the political value of the understanding of workers and farmers governments that our movement has conquered. This judgment is reinforced when the 1980 resolution is contrasted to the attempts various revolutionary-minded organizations made around the same time to provide an alternative theory of the Nicaraguan revolution.

There is very little that one would change today in that resolution. It confirms what we have learned and generalized from the course of the anticapitalist revolutions in our epoch. It is a striking confirmation of the value of this theoretical tool in aiding the working out of a political orientation. But there is one aspect of the 1980 resolution that should raise a question in our minds. The resolution did not anticipate that the Nicaraguan workers and farmers government could last ten years without either going forward to the establishment of a workers state or being driven back to the consolidation of a bourgeois government and state.

The 1980 resolution did not offer any timetable. In fact it argued against trying to impose preconceived timetables. But it is clear that the time span assumed in the resolution, within which the contradictions embodied in the workers and farmers government would be resolved one way or the other, was not a decade. Workers and farmers governments are unstable formations. None of the previous experiences with this type of government had lasted even half a decade.

What is the explanation for the workers and farmers government enduring for a decade in Nicaragua? The answer lies in

the single biggest objective political fact that has dominated the
Nicaraguan revolution through most of its existence since
1979: the imperialist-organized contra war. This is qualitatively
different than what confronted the workers and farmers governments in Cuba, Grenada, or Algeria.

Outside of Nicaragua it has sometimes been difficult to understand the magnitude of this war and what it has meant.
This is especially true for those who live in big countries, such
as the United States, and who have never lived through a major war. Whoever first used the term *low-intensity war* to describe the contra war was one of the greatest liars of the century. There was nothing "low intensity" about the contra war
in Nicaragua. The number of Nicaraguans killed in this war,
translated into figures proportional to the size of the population of the United States, is about two million. Two million
killed! That's nearly seven times the number of U.S. combat
deaths in World War II. Not to mention those wounded, dis-
abled, orphaned, or turned into war refugees. And not to
mention the massive destruction of the country's productive
resources.

Revolutionary patriotic war

This war lasted more than five years. It began in 1981, grew into
a full-scale mercenary war by 1983, and continued until the
contras were forced to sign a cease-fire agreement in early
1988. The mercenary war was countered by a revolutionary war
waged by Nicaragua's toilers led by the FSLN. This dominated
life and all politics in Nicaragua. This patriotic war, which succeeded in defeating Washington's mercenary army, was surely
one of the greatest revolutionary mobilizations in the history of
the Americas. It was, and continues to be, a source of pride and
self-confidence for Nicaragua's workers and peasants.

The FSLN and the government made winning the war the
most important single task they faced. And class-conscious
workers and peasants did so too. This, of course, does not mean
that all that was said and done by the government and the
FSLN in the name of winning the war was, or should have been,

supported by working people. The war didn't settle the question of the land reform. It didn't settle the question of the fight for women's rights, concretized in such issues as how to advance equal rights in hiring and on the job, how to combat violence against women, and whether abortion should be legalized. It didn't settle the question of whether to reverse the early reactionary policy of the FSLN against autonomy on the Atlantic Coast. It didn't settle the question of how workers could move toward establishing control over production.

Because of the overwhelming weight of the war and the sustained revolutionary mobilization that made winning the war possible, definitive judgments about the evolution of the relationship of class forces in the country had to be held in abeyance. The revolutionary mobilization held open possibilities that might otherwise have been foreclosed by the consequences of the FSLN leadership's retreat from the anticapitalist course that marked the first few years of the revolution.

Political demobilization of cadres

The approaching end of the war and the political alternatives this posed for the FSLN leadership marked a turning point in the revolution.

The extent of the cumulative negative effects on the toilers of the government and FSLN policies and explanations became evident only with the end of the war. It became clear when the momentum of the victory in the war was not turned toward driving forward along the line of march that had been summed up in the FSLN Historic Program. Thousands of young combat-proved soldiers had become educated and confident leaders as a result of what they went through and what they conquered. With the definitive defeat of the contras they were available for assignment, ready to be led and ready to lead others. They were ready to be led into the unions to deepen the fight for workers control and to begin the process of revitalizing the union structures, which had been badly eroded as the unions headed toward becoming organizations relying on a staff rather than on the power of a mobilized membership. They were ready to be organized to fight for deepening the integration of women in the work force, helping women break into jobs that had previously been closed to them, and defending those who had fought their way in from being driven back out of the work force by discriminatory layoffs. They were ready to step forward into leadership positions in the mass organizations, unions, peasant organizations, FSLN, and government itself. And they were ready to deepen their political education, to become communists or better communists than they already were.

But this was not what was organized. Just the opposite. The momentum of the victory in the revolutionary war has been turned into a political demobilization of the cadres who won the war. The young veterans of the revolutionary war have been kept largely idle in an army that has not been involved in a significant way in any social projects, even more than a year after the end of the war. Or they have been demobilized and dispersed in a routine way when their tours of duty expire, sent home with no orientation and no organization.

The perspective these army veterans have been given is symbolized by a sad, losing battle that some of them have been fighting with the Ministry of Transportation. It has refused to take action against the owner-operators of buses, who are refusing to honor the veteran's card that was supposed to guarantee a free bus ride. Honoring the cards would not be "profitable," the owners point out, and neither the government nor the FSLN does anything about it.

Cuban aid sold on market

Not long ago I had a conversation with a Cuban Communist who works in Nicaragua in the area of economic assistance. I asked him about some recent changes in the policy of the Nicaraguan government with regard to material aid that Cuba ships to the port of Puerto Cabezas, on the North Atlantic Coast. This new policy was reported in an article that Matilde Zimmermann wrote from Puerto Cabezas for the *Militant*.[4]

Every three months for a number of years now a Cuban ship

has arrived with food and other basic supplies needed to feed and clothe fifty thousand people, a third of the population of the North Atlantic region. The supplies are donated by Cuba. Under a new policy, the Nicaraguan government has been sell-ing these supplies on the free market. The only alternative to this would be to distribute the goods under a form of rationing, but this would be inconsistent with the policies the FSLN and the government are promoting. As a result of the new policy, the Cuban shipments often don't reach the toilers of the Atlan-tic Coast. Wealthier residents can buy what they want, of course, and merchants grab up the rest and resell it or truck it to Ma-nagua where they sell it at inflated prices.

I asked the Cuban comrade what he thought about this. He is someone who knows very well how much the Cuban people have to sacrifice to fill every ship that sails to Puerto Cabezas. He didn't say anything for a long time, but it was clear he found it troubling. Finally he gave a small shrug and said, "Well, it's their choice. There's nothing we can do."

The political retreat being directed by the FSLN leadership has become clearer since the end of the contra war. One of the expressions of this retreat is the growing emphasis on the uniqueness and originality of the Nicaraguan revolution. It is possible to get into many, mostly pointless, arguments about how unique a particular country and a particular revolution are. It is an argument that usually leads nowhere because it conceals what is really being discussed. When defenders of the current policies of the FSLN leadership argue their position by stressing how dif-ferent the Nicaraguan model is from any other model, the other model that they invariably have in mind is the Cuban one. That's what is involved. The issue behind the false debate is whether the Nicaraguan revolution should seek to follow the socialist path opened up in this hemisphere by the Cuban revolution. And it is a real issue because there are many revolutionary fighters, mem-bers or supporters of the FSLN, who have devoted their lives pre-cisely to bring Nicaragua along that path—not because they un-derestimate the uniqueness and originality of the Nicaraguan revolution or are trying to mimic another revolution, but because they believe that Fidel is correct when he says, "Socialism is and will continue to be the only hope, the only road for the peoples, the oppressed, the exploited, the plundered."[5]

Fonseca, Sandino, and the Cuban revolution

The draft resolution points out that one of the accomplishments of Carlos Fonseca, the central founder of the FSLN, was reknitting the revolutionary continuity of the new organization with Augusto César Sandino, who led a revolutionary anti-imperialist war in the late 1920s and early 1930s. Fonseca waged a struggle within the nucleus that would form the FSLN over the importance of this revolutionary continuity, and he continued until the end of his life to lead the effort to maintain and strengthen it.

But we should also be conscious of another side of this: it was the Cuban revolution that showed Carlos Fonseca the road to Sandino. It was under the impact of the Cuban revolution that Fonseca discovered the revolutionary continuity that tied the young FSLN to Sandino's struggle. That is a fact. It was through becoming a proletarian internationalist increasingly committed to the struggle to advance the world revolution, not simply a dedicated revolutionary patriot, that Fonseca was able to recover the links with the earlier struggles of the toilers of Nicaragua.

Carlos Fonseca found Sandino—the revolutionary leader, not the mystical cult figure—the same place he found Marxism: in Havana. Fonseca couldn't find Marxism in Nicaragua or anywhere else in Central America. There wasn't any; there had not been enough to maintain any continuity to Fonseca's day. The true lessons of what the Bolshevik revolution of 1917 had opened up for the world, including for the colonial and semicolonial countries, which were spread by the Communist International in the time of Lenin, never reached Central America in an organized way. When what was called Marxism and Communism finally arrived there, it wasn't Marxism at all, but its negation—Stalinism. It was Stalinism, masquerading as Marxism, that argued that there could be no perspective of fighting for socialism in Nicaragua or anywhere in Latin America or the Caribbean until some indefinite future time. Nor could the toilers strive to take the leadership of the struggle against domination by Yankee imperialism. Rather they had to confine themselves to supporting one or another section of the local bourgeoisie. Why? Because, the Stalinists argued, U.S. imperialism was too powerful, the proletariat was too small and weak, and the peasants could not be counted on to join with the workers in a revolutionary struggle.

But when the Cuban revolution triumphed in 1959, and in a little more than two years proudly declared its socialist character, suddenly a different perspective had opened up. Young, revolutionary-minded fighters from all over the Americas went to Cuba to learn and to participate. Some of them are in this hall today. Young people from North America went to Cuba, and a number of them came back and joined the Young Socialist Alliance and the Socialist Workers Party in the United States, or the Young Socialists and the League for Socialist Action [today the Communist League] in Canada. Comrades from Puerto Rico, who would form the Pro-Independence Movement, later to become the Puerto Rican Socialist Party, journeyed there. Youth from throughout the hemisphere rushed to see the new Cuba.

Among them was a small group of Nicaraguans headed by Carlos Fonseca. They didn't wait to be invited. They went there as soon as the revolution triumphed, along with every other revolutionary-minded person who had half a chance to do so, to be part of this new chapter in world history. Under the impact of the Cuban example and the Cuban revolution, Fonseca, Tomás Borge, and a handful of other members of this group of Nicaraguan youth began to find their way to revolutionary politics, working-class politics, to Marxism.

They threw out the old arguments of Stalinism, which they had been trained in. These arguments had become increasingly dissatisfying to them even before the victory of the Cuban revolution. But they didn't know what the alternative was, and they weren't even sure there was an alternative. Tomás Borge, who lived through this process, wrote about it in his biographical notes on Carlos Fonseca, published in English under the title *Carlos, the Dawn Is No Longer Beyond Our Reach.* The victory of the Cuban revolution, Borge wrote,

> more than just giving us joy, was the parting of innumerable curtains, a flash of light that shone beyond the naive and boring dogmas of those times. The Cuban revolution sent a shiver of terror through Latin America's ruling classes and was a violent assault on the suddenly dismal relics with which we had begun adorning our altars.[6]

The little Stalinist icons that these comrades had been told to worship were suddenly exposed as relics from a dismal era, the era between the ascendancy of Stalinism and the victory of the Cuban revolution.

It was this revolutionary perspective that led Fonseca to restore to its proper place the class content of the Sandino-led national liberation war, summed up in Sandino's conclusion that "only the workers and the peasants will go all the way." It was this perspective that led Fonseca to fight to rescue from the darkness of the historical cover-up, maintained by the Somoza dictatorship and the Stalinists alike, the lessons of the earlier struggle.

Sandino's peasant army

Fonseca explained what Sandino's peasant army, fighting a rural guerrilla war against the U.S. marines and their local allies, was able to achieve, and what it was an anticipation of. He also explained the limits history put on what Sandino's struggle could accomplish at that stage of social development in Nicaragua, with a very weak and politically inexperienced working class. That the army led by Sandino was almost totally peasant in composition, Fonseca said, was at one and the same time both "the glory and the tragedy of that revolutionary movement."[7] It was the glory of a peasant movement striving to reach out for allies in a revolutionary anti-imperialist war. But it was also the tragedy of a working class that was too small and too inexperienced, with no communist leadership, and unable to join the struggle and lead it forward.

It was necessary, Fonseca and his comrades concluded, to raise a Sandinista army again. But the new struggle could not have the same goals as those proclaimed by Sandino's army thirty-five years earlier. Since Sandino's time class relations in Nicaragua had been transformed. The spread of capitalist agriculture had led to widespread expropriation of the peasantry and rapid differentiation of classes in the countryside. The domination of the capitalist market had also given birth to a hereditary working class.

The working class had been forged from the peasants whose land had been seized by capitalist producers of coffee, cotton, cattle, and sugar; and from the urban artisans pauperized by the development of industrial production of commodities such as textiles and clothing. The expansion of capitalist production brought vast wealth to a few. For the big majority it brought the horrors of landlessness, homelessness, unemployment, social dislocation, impoverishment, poisoning by herbicides and pesticides used for the new export crops, and the deforestation and ensuing soil erosion and vulnerability to drought that the new techniques of production brought to Nicaragua. With it all came a deeper economic dependence on the U.S. market, a tighter political grip by imperialism, and the cultural subjugation—the Coca-Colaization—of Nicaragua.

By the 1960s the newly created hereditary working class was still small, even by comparison to most other countries of Latin America. But its existence was a decisive fact for the struggle. Its historic interests lay in the fight for the abolition of capitalist property relations. It was this working class that could take the lead in the struggle, forging a close alliance with the peasants and giving the new revolutionary movement its character and its program. To the struggle for national sovereignty had to be added the struggle to resolve acute social problems that had been created by the rapid spread of capitalist agriculture and agricultural processing industries throughout much of Nicaragua.

"The strategic approach of the FSLN," Fonseca said, "is to combine the struggle for national liberation with the struggle for socialism—a struggle that has problems, and where socialist revolutions have not always lived up to their promise and their program, but which history has shown nonetheless is the road forward for the world's working people."

Rationalizations for political retreat

This is the perspective, this is the continuity and the conquest, being rejected today as the leaders of the FSLN seek to justify and rationalize the political retreat they are leading. This political retreat even affects terminology, something revolutionists have learned must be treated seriously. For example, many of us are familiar with the term "patriotic producers," which is widely used by FSLN and government officials to refer to those capitalist farmers who support the FSLN government or at least are not involved in antigovernment political activity. But these capitalist farmers, like capitalists anywhere, don't produce; they grow wealthy off the labor of those who do. They are able to do so because they own capital, which can command the labor power of those who own nothing. And, like others of their class throughout the Third World, they will sacrifice the sovereignty of their country to imperialism before they will risk being expropriated by the toilers. In other words, taken as a class, these "patriotic producers" are neither patriotic nor producers. The term is no good.

Along with the corruption of scientific class terminology, fundamental conquests of Marxism are being discarded by leaders of the FSLN, including those who in the past had understood their importance. The draft resolution cites as one example an argument offered by Tomás Borge to provide some theoretical backing for the government's current "free market" policies. In an interview with the FSLN daily, *Barricada,* in March 1989, Borge said:

> From the beginning, the theories of scientific socialism discarded the idea of associating commodity relations

with capitalism alone, as if they were alien to socialism. We could go back to the New Economic Policy, Lenin's NEP, and other historical events that show that monetary commodity relations are objective relations. The key is to use them in a conscious way and to prevent them from operating blindly. Capitalism uses market mechanisms to promote the reproduction of its own system and its ruling groups, just as socialism uses them to achieve its own ends. Our society, which is not capitalist, which aspires to be a socialist society, cannot put itself outside these general economic laws.[8]

But commodity relations are not ahistorical "objective relations" or "general economic laws." As the draft resolution points out, the market "is not a fact of nature but a social relationship that arises with class society and becomes generalized with the worldwide spread of capitalist domination and exploitation."

Market laws not neutral

The laws of the market are not neutral. The working class cannot take them, as though they were laws of physics and engineering to be used in constructing a tower, and put them at the service of building socialism. This view, that the mechanisms that capitalist development generalizes and extends are universal laws that can and must be used to advance toward socialism after a victorious popular revolution, is not new. It has its post-1917 origins in the ideological justifications by the victorious social caste in the Soviet Union in the 1930s, which claimed to be building socialism while driving the working class away from any control over decisions about the priorities and administration of the course of the Soviet economy and society. Near the end of his life, Stalin codified this ideological rationalization in an article entitled "The Law of Value under Socialism."[9] Such views have been repackaged by many ever since, right down to the middle-class technocrats who surround Gorbachev today. They are the central assumption behind all variants of the post-

Lenin Soviet model of planning and economic management.

This is the course that the Leninist opposition fought so hard against following Lenin's death and that Che Guevara combated in the early years of the Cuban revolution. Without growing communist consciousness, organization, and control by the working class, Che explained, there can be no progress toward building socialism. "The pipe dream that socialism can be achieved with the dull instruments left to us by capitalism," Che said, ". . . can lead into a blind alley. And you wind up there after having traveled a long distance with many crossroads, and it is hard to figure out just where you took the wrong turn. Meanwhile, the economic foundation that has been laid has done its work of undermining the development of consciousness. To build communism it is necessary, simultaneous with the new material foundations, to build the new man."[10]

The women and men engaged in building socialism, Guevara explained, can advance that goal only by struggling to limit the domination of capitalist market mechanisms. That can be accomplished only by fighting to advance workers' control, by bringing the toilers more and more directly into deciding and carrying out economic and social priorities, and by building a communist party among the vanguard of the working people.

These are the communist views that Fidel Castro and other Cuban communists, as an integral part of the rectification process, are fighting to make part of the debate and discussion on the way forward for humanity today. That's why it's important for us to study and help promote some important tools that are now broadly available. Among these are: *Che Guevara and the Cuban Revolution,* which includes, among other things, Che's article "Planning and Consciousness in the Transition to Socialism: On the Budgetary Finance System"; the Pathfinder pamphlets *Socialism and Man in Cuba* and *'Cuba Will Never Adopt Capitalist Methods';* and two recently published books, *In Defense of Socialism* by Fidel Castro, and *Che Guevara: Economics and Politics in the Transition to Socialism* by Carlos Tablada.[11]

Another example of the FSLN leadership's flight from Marxism, from working-class politics, appeared in a recent interview with Luis Carrión, a member of the National Directorate of the FSLN and the minister of the economy. This was one of a series of interviews done in connection with the tenth anniversary of the revolution. "Over the past ten years," Carrión was asked, "the government has shown inconsistency in its attempts to satisfy popular demands at the same time as taking into account the desires of the agro-bourgeoisie. Why is this?"

His answer: "Big producers always want more; they're never satisfied." True. "And the workers always demand a fair share, proportional to their contribution." False. The historic goal of the working-class movement is not to get a "fair share" under capitalism, but to end the system of wage-slavery. The entire product is their "contribution."

Carrión's answer goes on: "Our role is to maneuver between these contradictions, guaranteeing that a share of the country's wealth is distributed among the poorest sectors and also that big private producers have profits."

The interviewer then asks Carrión about the current government policy known in Nicaragua as *concertación,* that is, seeking a social pact, an agreement among all classes. Question: "Is the stage of *concertación* a qualitatively new one?" Answer:

> We're making an effort to bring together all the sectors of the nation, including the private sector, in order to deal with the economic crisis. This could lead to a qualitatively new style of government in the economic aspect, a style that would assure that the points of view and interests of all sectors are taken into account when it comes to formulating economic policy. But that can only be consolidated if the private sector adopts a constructive stance.

Question: "Does this mean a planned economy with private sector participation?" The questioner misses the point about a planned economy, which can only be based on nationalized property. Talk about planning a capitalist economy is nonsense. Carrión tries to explain this in his answer: "At this point we no longer talk of a planned economy. . . . A planned economy becomes less and less possible to the extent that the policy we have been following grants more and more weight to market forces in the functioning of the economy."

Next question: "In the last year and a half drastic economic measures have been implemented. Were other options discussed?" Carrión's answer:

> The options open were few. Only two were considered: the one being applied and that of a war economy, going back to the experience of past years but with more rigor—price controls, rationing of foodstuffs, planned distribution of products. From the point of view of domestic policy and military defense, the war economy option was attractive because it would have meant an egalitarian distribution of resources and would have been received well by the poorest. . . . After analyzing it all, we concluded that it couldn't be done for economic and political reasons and that it would have resulted in a worse crisis. Perhaps there would have been a momentary positive political impact, but it would have aggravated the economic situation and also caused international isolation.

Negative impact on class struggle

That is the perspective that is being offered. These are the rationalizations for what is being given up. And every day these justifications for the retreat are posing additional obstacles to the struggle of workers and peasants in Nicaragua. And this gets translated into day-to-day politics.

A few months ago the *Militant* ran a story on a union struggle going on at a capitalist farm in Matagalpa Province. The owner of the farm is considered a "patriotic producer." His son had been a member of the FSLN, killed in the struggle against Somoza. This capitalist farmer is a supporter, or at least not an opponent, of the government. But he has maintained one stubborn position: he won't allow a union to be organized on his farm. Every time there has been an attempt to set up a union he has fired the organizers and hired new workers. This has happened several times since 1979.

It happened again this year, but this time the union organizers who were fired refused to leave the farm. They just stayed there. They were armed, too. They were demanding that the government either order the boss to give them their jobs back or nationalize the farm and turn it into a collective or a state farm. And they began trying to get support for their fight from the Rural Workers Association (ATC) and others. This is one of many battles, isolated and not widely publicized, that are now taking place on capitalist farms as the employers, sensing a weakening of the working-class movement and drawing strength from the government's *concertación* policy, are on an offensive to weaken and break unions, drive down wages, and impose worse working and living conditions. This is posing a sharp challenge to the labor movement as a whole and to the ATC in particular.

After we had visited the farm and talked to the workers we went to the office of the ATC in Matagalpa and met with the regional president of the union. This comrade is a class-struggle fighter who has been through many battles, like most of the leaders of the ATC. And he is a revolutionary. But it soon became clear that the struggle the farmworkers were waging on this farm was not a source of inspiration for him but a headache. Militant union action under way, workers trying to fight their way into the ATC to strengthen the union and strengthen the position of farmworkers throughout the country—this was a source of worry and concern for him. He was responding in this instance like the class-collaborationist union leaders we all know so well.

'Geopolitical framework'

After a long conversation, he finally said, "Look, I know the workers are right. I know that. If I were in their shoes I would be doing exactly what they are doing. But we can't look at things just from the standpoint of this one struggle on this one farm." We have to start, he said, from the world picture, what he called the "geopolitical framework." The FSLN and the government, he said, can't afford any action that might set back the attempt to reach an agreement with the "patriotic producers," or that might provoke U.S. imperialism to take stronger action against Nicaragua. "We need peace," he said. "We need to buy some time under peaceful conditions to allow us to get the economy back on its feet."

And, referring to a discussion we had been having earlier about the Cuban revolution, he added, "We can't follow the Cuban model no matter how much we would like to, no matter what our desires." The government of the Soviet Union, he said, has made it clear that it will not aid Nicaragua as it has aided Cuba, and the European imperialists "are putting more and more pressure on us to give greater space to the private sector in return for the little bit of aid we can get. Within this broader framework, confiscating this little farm just doesn't make sense."

Many of us have heard one or another variation on these "geopolitical" arguments. They disorient and confuse even revolutionary-minded workers who are trying to find a way to defend the revolution's conquests. One can see how they are an obstacle to defending the class interests of the workers and farmers. But is there some truth to these arguments? The answer is no. They are false, dangerously false. These "geopolitical" arguments are false on their own terms, and they are false because of what they leave out.

There is no prospect for long-term capitalist recovery and economic growth, not just in Nicaragua but elsewhere in Latin America and the Caribbean. There is not going to be a repetition of the growth in the region that came as a by-product of the long imperialist boom of the decades after the Second World War. Just the opposite is the case. Even during the upswing in the capitalist business cycle through most of the 1980s the accumulating pressures have produced eight years of debt crisis and a massive, accelerating outflow of capital from the region.

In how many countries of Latin America and the Caribbean, even where the U.S. imperialists and the "patriotic producers" have a government of their choice, has there been economic growth and development in the past decade? Where will there be in the 1990s? And keep in mind, more of the same is the *best* that supporters of capitalism can hope for. The reality is likely to be much worse, when we consider the inevitable consequences for the entire hemisphere when the imperialist economies enter a downturn in their business cycle—not to mention the devastation that will be wrought by the major capitalist crisis that is looming in the 1990s.

And there won't be peace either, unless Gorbachev is right and Castro is wrong. If imperialism has become more peaceful, if capitalism offers the prospect of growth and world harmony, the Cuban communist leadership is wrong. Then capitalism, not socialism, would be the road forward in Latin America and everywhere else. But that is not the case.

Prospects for international aid

And what about Nicaragua's prospects for international economic aid? It is true that the Soviet government has not sent the aid that Nicaragua needs. The Gorbachev regime is using economic pressure to back up its "advice" to the Nicaraguan leadership to seek an accommodation with Washington. But that's not a new attitude.

How did the Cuban revolution win the aid from Moscow that it has gotten, aid that has made it possible to survive? Do you think Fidel Castro went to Moscow in 1960 and said, "Comrades, we're considering our options. We have only two, and one of them is to make a socialist revolution. We want to know, if we make that choice, how much aid can we count on from the Soviet Communist Party?" Who knows what the answer might have been? But that isn't what happened. The Cuban workers and peasants began building socialism, earning authority and respect among revolutionary-minded fighters throughout the world. They stood up to imperialism, to the blackmail and aggression— as the Nicaraguans did in defeating the contras—and in the course of that fight they won the aid they received from the Soviet Union and other workers states. The Cuban revolutionaries have fought for and won every barrel of oil, every machine, and every gun that they've gotten.

Is Nicaragua in a worse position to fight for and win such aid than Cuba was thirty years ago? No. Nicaragua is in a better position than Cuba ever was to wage a moral and political fight for aid—and not just from the workers states but from the capitalist world as well. The Nicaraguan revolution is in a better position than Cuba ever was to appeal, for example, to working people and anti-imperialists in countries such as Mexico and Venezuela and Ecuador to join in a campaign to get some oil from nearby. Nicaragua is much less isolated than Cuba was. The relationship of forces between imperialism and the semicolonial countries in the hemisphere has changed. Nicaragua would never have to go through the almost complete political, economic, and diplomatic isolation that the imperialists were able to impose on Cuba for more than twenty years. And we should never forget one very important fact. The Nicaraguans have an ally that the Cubans didn't have: they have Cuba.

Decisive actors: the toilers
So the "geopolitical" argument is false on its own terms. But even more importantly it leaves out the decisive actors. It totally ignores the Nicaraguan toilers—the producers, the real patriotic producers. It leaves out the potential productive efforts, energy, creativity, and originality that can be unleashed if the workers and farmers are led and educated and organized to take things into their own hands, to shake off the death grip of the technocrats and the free marketeers and the geopolitical analysts, and to begin developing the forces of production, to begin economic planning on the basis of the nationalization of basic industry.

Does anybody think that the Nicaraguan comrades—the ones we've all worked with and fought alongside of, the ones who overthrew Somoza, the ones who led a victorious war against the mercenary invaders—won't be ready to organize volunteer work brigades in Nicaragua? To build houses, schools, and child-care centers. To build roads and bridges in order to open farmland to be worked and developed. They can do all that and still have enough dedicated comrades left over to send internationalist brigades to other countries as they deepen their revolution. Is there any doubt that this people—which has shown the world its capacity for struggle and for sacrifice, its abilities, and its leadership capacities—can accomplish all this and more?

In Camagüey, Cuba, on July 26 [1989], Fidel Castro summed up what the Cuban revolution has accomplished in Camagüey, and in particular what it has accomplished in the three years since the rectification process got under way. He turned to the invited guests on the platform—who included, sitting right next to the podium, Jaime Wheelock, Nicaragua's minister of agriculture and a member of the FSLN National Directorate. The revolution has turned Camagüey, Fidel said, "into a development model for the Third World and, first of all, a model for food production and social development." Look what we have done since we rescued and revived volunteer labor, Fidel was saying, since we got the party and youth organizations in Camagüey into this, leading by example. Look what the producers have built!

Cuba *is* the model. Not Sweden. Not the perestroika stage of the crisis of Stalinist-governed workers states. The socialist road opened for all the Americas by the Cuban revolution is the road forward for us all—including Nicaragua. But this perspective—the extension of the socialist revolution to Nicaragua, which Carlos Fonseca fought for and won others to in 1961, which the FSLN popularized and championed during nearly twenty years of struggle against the Somoza dictatorship, and which guided the FSLN and the toilers in pressing forward the anticapitalist measures taken in the early years of the revolution—this perspective is what has been given up.

Democratic and anti-imperialist conquests
This does not mean that the anti-imperialist and revolutionary-democratic perspective and conquests of the Sandinista people's revolution, with which the anticapitalist measures were intertwined, have been lost. They remain and they can remain for some time, although they will inevitably be weakened.

The land reform won't be reversed. The old landlords won't come back. If the peasants fight hard enough there could even be some further advances in land distribution. But as long as capitalism exists, as long as the land is not nationalized, as long as wholesale food trade and distribution is in the hands of capitalists, class differentiation will work its way back into the countryside, even where the peasants have benefited from the land reform and capitalist holdings have been taken over. Some peasants will be driven off the land. Even if their farms are not foreclosed by the bank—and there aren't any foreclosures now in Nicaragua—they can get so heavily in debt and the prices they have to pay for inputs can be so high in relation to the prices they can anticipate for their crops that they see no choice but to give up their farms. They will become part of the landless semiproletarian and proletarian layers again.

The land will begin to be reconcentrated into the hands of new capitalist farmers. Some of these will develop from the collective farms themselves, especially those with good land and advanced production techniques. They'll plant more and expand their hiring of labor. They will start lending money at higher and higher rates to poor peasants and start renting plots to those with no land. The old relationships will reassert themselves.

Similarly, the gains made in the struggle for autonomy on the Atlantic Coast won't necessarily be reversed. Even a bourgeois republic can make concessions, sometimes far-reaching concessions, to deep-going revolutionary-democratic struggles. Over time, of course, even if the form of autonomy remains, the content will be more and more eroded.

Nor does the end of the workers and farmers government in Nicaragua automatically mean the end of the anti-imperialist stance and actions of the government. Bourgeois regimes, especially when they come out of deep-going popular revolutions, can have some sharp conflicts with imperialism.

The regime in Algeria that followed the overthrow of the workers and farmers government headed by Ahmed Ben Bella continued to take anti-imperialist positions that brought it into conflict with Paris and Washington. The Coard gang in Gre-

nada—the Stalinist murderers who overthrew the workers and
farmers government—claimed to be even more "anti-imperialist" than Bishop, whom they falsely derided as a social demo-
crat. Their posturing may seem like a small point in light of
what happened a week later when the U.S. marines invaded,
taking advantage of the counterrevolution the Coard gang had
carried out. But it tells us an important fact nonetheless about
the character of governments that can emerge when workers
and farmers governments are replaced.

The anticapitalist actions that workers and farmers governments carry out are intertwined with their democratic and anti-
imperialist actions, but these two are not the same thing. The
loss of the first doesn't require the immediate loss of the second. We will not understand what is happening in Nicaragua
and to the FSLN if we don't see this. The comrades in the National Directorate of the FSLN have rejected the socialist road
for Nicaragua. But it's wrong to assume they do not remain
firm in their anti-imperialist commitment and determination.
President Ortega still stands up to Washington, exposes the
U.S. maneuvers, and defends Nicaraguan sovereignty. Borge remains committed to autonomy for the Atlantic Coast.

That's not what has changed. Revolutionary fighters who
don't advance to become communists, or who don't become
communist enough to remain communist under the kind of intense pressure and challenges that Nicaragua has faced, don't
turn into counterrevolutionaries. That's not the way it works.
Many remain ready to fight, even to die, for the revolution as
they understand it. But they become obstacles to the development of a communist leadership, without which the revolution
cannot move forward and without which it will be pushed backward.

Change in government
What is the most likely government to replace what until now
has been the FSLN-led workers and farmers government? The
answer is, another FSLN-led government. It can be largely,
though not completely, the same individuals. You should stop

looking for the Coard. Stop looking for the coup. Stop looking for the split in the leadership. The course is unanimous. It's 9-0. Every one of the members of the National Directorate has publicly endorsed the current course. There's not going to be a split in the cabinet or in the National Directorate over replacing the workers and farmers government with a restructured capitalist government.

A new government will be elected in February 1990. Daniel Ortega will be president. Sergio Ramírez will be vice president. The cabinet will be overwhelmingly members of the FSLN. Some non-FSLN members may be brought into the government in some capacity. That is clearly the desire of the FSLN leadership, but it is impossible to make predictions because we can't know what the course of the opposition and the Bush administration will be.

Just a few days ago, on August 4, the FSLN government signed a broad agreement with the opposition bloc. It is the first such agreement since July 1979. We don't know all the terms of the agreement. We have only the U.S. press reports, and we don't know what private commitments may have been involved. We do know that the accord includes further changes in the election procedures, suspension of the draft until after the elections, and a decision by all the parties to call on the summit meeting of the Central American presidents this past weekend to implement the decision to disband the contras. And yesterday at the summit meeting that decision was adopted, registering a big blow to Bush and a big victory for Nicaragua and all of us who fight for its sovereignty and peace.[12]

But from the standpoint of the evolution on the governmental level inside Nicaragua, we should note that for the first time in a decade the members of the capitalist-led opposition bloc, including the petty-bourgeois radicals who are part of this alliance, are speaking favorably about an agreement reached with the FSLN government. The Associated Press reported from Managua August 4, "Opposition leaders told reporters they were generally satisfied with today's agreement, even though it was not all they wanted." According to the AP, Duilio Baltodano of the National Action Party called the accord, "a triumph of patriotism." And Eli Altamirano, leader of the so-called Communist Party of Nicaragua and a member of the procapitalist opposition bloc known as UNO, said the accord is "a great achievement even though there are a lot of things . . . to be resolved."

This is new. It reflects a further evolution of the political framework inside Nicaragua.

Will there be resistance in the future to the consolidation of capitalist political rule? Will there be renewed attempts by the workers and the peasants to push forward? Yes. And that will pose again the challenge of the party, the challenge of forging a communist vanguard. It will pose anew the challenge of leading the transformation that took place in Cuba following the overthrow of Batista. The central leadership of the July 26 Movement, a revolutionary petty-bourgeois organization that had led the armed mass struggle against the Batista dictatorship, set out to build a communist, working-class party that would be capable of leading the toilers in the next step in history. This was done, among other things, by systematic Marxist and socialist education of the working class. This education was so successful that when Fidel Castro explained in December 1961 that the new party being built in Cuba would be a Marxist and a Leninist party, hundreds of thousands of workers and farmers stood with him because they understood it and they believed in it. And when he said, "I am a Marxist-Leninist, and I will be a Marxist-Leninist to the end of my life," he was speaking not just for a small handful but for an entire vanguard of the working class.[13]

The construction of this kind of vanguard of the Nicaraguan working class will be based among the cadres and supporters of the FSLN, among those who are loyal to the FSLN, which has won and retains the right to lead the workers and peasants. It will be forged by those comrades who are determined to find the road to the implementation of the Historic Program of the FSLN. By those who want to continue to fight to bring Nicaragua into the vanguard of the world revolution, not see it pushed back. By those who want to bring the toilers into real politics, not see them forced out by becoming "voters" instead of cadres. By those who want to defend the communist perspective and want to extend the victory of the Cuban revolution.

Immediate responsibilities

Finally, we have two immediate responsibilities in our own countries in relation to Nicaragua. The political retreat by the Nicaraguan leadership is having negative consequences on many supporters of the Nicaraguan revolution. For some of the activists in the solidarity movement, with whom we have stood shoulder to shoulder in action to defend the Nicaraguan revolution against the imperialist onslaught, it has led to some deeper thinking about the challenges facing the revolution. For others it has led to disillusionment and even demoralization.

Our responsibility is to work to minimize those who respond by turning away from Nicaragua, away from politics, and away from what they started toward when they were inspired by the advances of the Nicaraguan revolution to become political and to become fighters. We will carry out this responsibility in the only way it can be done: by pulling them toward seeing themselves as part of the world revolution, as partisans of the toilers who are pushing forward to create a new world. That means, as we have been discussing throughout this conference, winning them to be supporters and active defenders of the Cuban revolution. The point is not to seek to replace Nicaragua with Cuba as a country more worthy of their interest or support—that's not the choice—but rather to help draw them into the world through Cuba, a living socialist revolution led by a communist party.

For a long time you could fight your way into the world through Nicaragua. You could become part of the world revolution through Nicaragua. Many did, and some became communists as a result. More than a few of us here today followed that path. But that is one of the things that is less and less possible now. That road is being blocked off as a consequence of the political retreat. The leadership in Nicaragua is not oriented to the world revolution. It is oriented to the capitalist world, even to the smaller imperialist countries.

But you *can* enter the world through becoming a partisan of the Cuban revolution. Now more than ever in the history of the revolution, action in defense of Cuba is a bridge into the world revolution. You can reenter the fight to defend Nicaragua and its workers and peasants through Cuba, through understanding the perspective that Cuba represents. You can see the place of the Nicaraguan revolution. You can see what has been accomplished and appreciate it, even as you understand what has been lost.

By winning to the fight to defend Cuba those with whom we have worked in solidarity with the Nicaraguan revolution, we can draw them into what is not only a source of inspiration but also a source of real education. And as they become inspired, as they learn how to fight to defend Cuba, to defend Nicaragua, they will learn to be part of the world revolution.

We also have a second responsibility. There has never been a moment when defenders of the Nicaraguan revolution, and revolutionary fighters throughout the world, have had a greater need for timely, accurate information on the unfolding of the class struggle in Nicaragua. This is a moment when there is a premium on providing the facts so that class-struggle fighters can draw the lessons from what is happening. It is a moment when in order to act and encourage others to act in defense of the revolution the objective picture is an urgent necessity. It is a moment when sugarcoating is poison and when the truth is a powerful weapon for every fighter.

It is for these reasons that we will continue the work we began ten years ago. We will keep on getting out the truth about the Nicaraguan revolution through the pages of the *Militant* and *Perspectiva Mundial.* And we will keep on making available in Nicaragua communist periodicals, as well as the books and pamphlets that reflect the ideas of those fighters who never turned back and who must be emulated by those revolutionary workers who are on the road to becoming communists.

The
RUSSIAN REVOLUTION

Collected Works of V.I. Lenin

Writings of the central leader of the Bolshevik Party, the October 1917 Russian revolution, the young Soviet republic, and the early Communist International. Available in set only, 45 vols. plus 2-vol. index. $500.00

Two Tactics of Social-Democracy in the Democratic Revolution
by V.I. Lenin

Written in 1905, this pamphlet explains the strategy that enabled an alliance of workers and peasants to overturn the monarchy, landlordism, and capitalist rule in Russia twelve years later. 160 pp. $5.95

Alliance of the Working Class and the Peasantry
by V.I. Lenin

From the early years of the Marxist movement in Russia, Lenin fought to forge an alliance between the working class and the toiling peasantry. Such an alliance was needed to make possible working-class leadership of the democratic revolution and, on that basis, the opening of the socialist revolution. 447 pp. $17.95

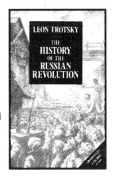

The History of the Russian Revolution
by Leon Trotsky

The social, economic, and political dynamics of the first victorious socialist revolution, as told by one of its principal leaders. Unique in modern literature. Unabridged edition, 3 vols. in one. 1,358 pp. $35.95

'The workers and farmers government is the most powerful instrument the working class can wield as it moves along its line of march toward establishing a workers state'—JACK BARNES

For a Workers and Farmers Government in the United States

BY JACK BARNES

Reviewing lessons from the Russian revolution through Nicaragua and Grenada, this report advances a working-class strategy for such a government in the United States and worldwide. $8^{1}/_{2}$ x 11 format. $7.00

The Workers and Farmers Government

BY JOSEPH HANSEN

Hansen discusses how experiences in revolutions in Yugoslavia, China, and Cuba following World War II, enriched communists' theoretical understanding of how revolutionary governments of the toilers can open the road to the expropriation of the capitalist class and the establishment of workers states. $8^{1}/_{2}$ x 11 format. $7.00

Class, Party, and State and the Eastern European Revolution

BY JOSEPH HANSEN, TOM KERRY, AND OTHERS

The social transformations that overturned capitalist property relations and bourgeois rule in Eastern Europe following World War II. $8^{1}/_{2}$ x 11 format. $7.00

Workers and Farmers Governments since the Second World War

BY BOB CHESTER, WITH A PREFACE BY JOSEPH HANSEN

Articles on the governments that came to power in the revolutions in Yugoslavia, China, Cuba, and Algeria. Such workers and farmers regimes, writes Hansen in his preface, are examples of "the first form of government that can be expected to appear as the result of a successful anticapitalist revolution." $8^{1}/_{2}$ x 11 format. $6.00

THE WORKERS AND FARMERS GOVERNMENT: A POWERFUL ANTICAPITALIST WEAPON FOR WORKING PEOPLE

by Larry Seigle

T HE PURPOSE OF THIS POINT on the agenda is to continue the discussion on the draft resolution on Nicaragua.[1] This discussion began at last month's meeting of the National Committee, in which a number of comrades from other countries took part. Here at Oberlin, during the international conference and during the convention of the Young Socialist Alliance,[2] we have had a chance to have many informal discussions with comrades from all over the world.

We had a report on the draft resolution a few days ago at the conference, and we don't need a similar one to kick off the discussion today. Instead, I will introduce this round of discussion by touching on two additional aspects of the resolution that it would be useful to talk out in more detail.

The first of these concerns how this discussion on Nicaragua helps to enrich our theoretical understanding of workers and farmers governments. The second point is the practical political adjustment we have been making and will continue to make

---

This report was adopted at a meeting of the National Committee of the Socialist Workers Party held immediately following the August 1989 International Active Workers and Socialist Educational Conference in Oberlin, Ohio.

ENDNOTES FOR THIS ARTICLE BEGIN ON PAGE 322.

in relation to solidarity work with Nicaragua. I am most familiar with the situation facing our movement here in the United States, but much of what we face confronts groups in other countries as well.

One of our solid accomplishments over the past year is the political preparation of the movement for this draft resolution. The best measure of this success is that the facts cited and the conclusions drawn by the draft resolution and the report on it at the international conference did not come as a surprise, but instead helped comrades understand what they knew was taking place. It advanced our collective thinking. The leadership work that has gone into making this possible includes the coverage in our press, trips to Nicaragua, and the party summer educational classes on the workers and farmers government leading up to the conference. All of these have been essential to preparing for what we were able to achieve at the conference.

We should note in particular that through following the news coverage in the *Militant,* comrades throughout the world have had access to all the essential facts from which the resolution draws its major conclusions. This shared pool of information is irreplaceable in a discussion that leads to greater political homogeneity in our movement.

We have seen the importance of this confirmed in a negative way as well. Comrades from other organizations who have not followed our coverage or other sources of accurate information about Nicaragua had much greater difficulty with the general assessment contained in the draft resolution. They simply have not had access to the information that our conclusions rest on. Often their judgments are based on things they remember from five or six years ago, from earlier stages of the revolution. Even when memories are accurate—and they seldom are—they are patchy and selective, missing the sweep of the last eleven years as a dialectical totality.

A second accomplishment of this international leadership, over a considerably longer period of time, is our collective work on the theory of workers and farmers governments and our ability to take the SWP's communist continuity on this and make it our own, enriching it in the process. This has been essential to orienting ourselves programmatically and politically and to understanding the trajectory of the Nicaraguan revolution and seeing it in its world context, not as an exception but as an example.

Alternative analyses of Nicaraguan revolution

In thinking this through it is helpful to look again at the two major alternative analyses of the Nicaraguan revolution that have been offered by those who consider themselves Marxists.

One of these is that the revolution in 1979 brought into existence a workers state, the dictatorship of the proletariat. This analysis severs the class character of the state from the property relations the state defends and on which it rests. It discerns the class character of the state in other places: in the political stance of the government, and in whether the government came to power through an armed struggle in which the masses played a decisive role. One of the consequences of this analysis is rapid abandonment of a materialist approach to the workers states. The criteria of nationalized basic industry, monopoly of foreign trade, and a planned economy on that basis are scrapped.

This revision of Marxism leads those who embrace it to "discover" workers states where the dominant property relations are capitalist, as in Nicaragua. And, because it replaces property relations with political criteria as the foundation of a workers state, this view leads in the direction of concluding that there is less and less reason to defend the Soviet Union and other workers states ruled by Stalinist bureaucracies, where the working class has been politically demobilized and effectively disenfranchised.

The assessment that Nicaraguan working people established the dictatorship of the proletariat in 1979 also constitutes a political barrier to understanding the central political challenge facing the Nicaraguan workers and peasants: how to advance toward ending the domination of capitalist property relations. If the dictatorship of the proletariat has already been established in Nicaragua, then the question of capitalist control of the commanding heights of the economy is a nonissue. This analysis points away from the decisive political task.

It points instead toward something else. "Democracy" becomes the main political question in Nicaragua. But it is democracy severed—like the character of the state—from any class criteria. Those who follow this way of thinking find themselves concentrating on how to refine what are in fact forms of bourgeois democracy that exist today in Nicaragua, rather than fighting to make the qualitative leap to a higher form of democracy, proletarian democracy, through advancing the struggle for the toilers to take the economy into their own hands.

The second alternative analysis is that the FSLN government is a radical bourgeois government, a left-leaning and anti-imperialist bourgeois regime not qualitatively different from many others. The corruptions of theory required to make this hold together are as great as in the case of the first alternative. What credit it gives the bourgeoisie! What potential for historic advances it restores to the capitalist ruling classes in the semicolonial countries! And what nonsense it makes out of the course of the Nicaraguan bourgeoisie in relation to the government that was established following the overthrow of Somoza!

Those who followed this analysis, if they were consistent in doing so, called on the workers and peasants to overthrow the FSLN government from July 1979 on. They defended the Nicaraguan government against U.S. imperialism's assaults but argued that the government was an obstacle to the workers and peasants. Those who held such a position were outside the revolution, obviously, and unable to understand the course of events in Nicaragua. They were blind to the advance and missed the retreat; it has all looked the same to them.

I mention these alternative views to emphasize how important to our political orientation the theoretical tool of the workers and farmers government has been. The draft resolution is based on the concrete richness of the experience of this revolution, one that we know very well because of the work that we've done, because we are and have been part of this revolution in a thousand ways. There haven't been all that many experiences with workers and farmers governments in our epoch from which to generalize. Drawing the lessons from each one—in the only way it can be done, from inside its line of march as a partisan and participant—should be of central concern to every communist.

Correcting an error about Algeria

Let's look at one particular aspect of what we are incorporating into our understanding of the dynamics of a workers and farmers government. Reviewing our analysis of the Algerian workers and farmers government, Joe Hansen pointed out that looking back on it we could see one mistake we had made. Joe wrote:

> It is a correct assessment that when the Ben Bella regime did not carry things forward to establishment of a workers state, a process of deterioration set in. (This is where a correction is to be made in our previous analysis.) Right after the June 19 [1965] coup, we called that event the turning point, although we had already noted the stagnation that had set in under Ben Bella and had called attention to the danger it represented. In retrospect, it is clear that the *turn* in direction came earlier than June 19; it came with the period of stagnation.[3]

This "turn in direction" by the Ben Bella leadership, Joe wrote, included concessions to the more right-wing forces, a movement away from mass mobilizations, and the assumption by Ben Bella of more and more personal powers. "The deterioration became more and more marked until the Ben Bella regime lost its 'socialist option,' a fact registered qualitatively by the June 19 coup," he added.

At the time of the coup led by Boumédienne we thought we were seeing the turning point. But looking back later it became clear that the turn in policy direction of the leadership had already occurred. We had seen the stagnation, and we had noted the dangers that it represented. Our error was in not seeing the necessary outcome of this process of deterioration if it was not reversed. These are the lessons we are now drawing on in relation to Nicaragua. We are learning from previous experiences.

This relates to one of the political questions that comrades have raised about the draft resolution, a question that gets expressed in various ways: What is ahead of and what is behind us? Is what lies ahead going to be cold, or not so cold, or hot? Does the final replacement of the workers and farmers government have to be violent? Will we miss it when it happens?

Answering these questions requires disentangling several distinct pieces of the process. We start from the point, stated clearly in the draft resolution, that the course of action embarked on by a workers and farmers government heads in an anticapitalist direction. This political course consists of concrete steps that encroach on the property rights and social rights of the capitalist class and its allies. This is based on material foundations: mass organizations with leaderships, mass mobilizations, armed bodies of men and women, and other institutionalized expressions of the relationship of classes to each other and to the government. Each of the major steps taken by a workers and farmers government, in turn, affects that relationship of forces.

The anticapitalist course of action is reflected in the choice of individuals who make up the government. When a bourgeois government gives way to a workers and farmers government, there are always changes made in the faces in the cabinet or other executive bodies. There doesn't have to be a 100 percent change—there rarely has been. But the personnel changes are visible and important. We saw this in Cuba, for example, with the changes in key ministry-level positions that accompanied the qualitative step of the coming into being of a workers and farmers government. We'll come back to this point later, because a similar thing happens in reverse when a retreat reaches a qualitative turning point.

Turn in policy direction
If there is no proletarian leadership to lead a broad vanguard of the toilers in advancing the anticapitalist course of the workers and farmers government and moving toward the transfor-

mation of property relations, it will be pushed backward. The foundations of the workers and farmers government will start to be eroded. The institutions on which it rests will be weakened. The mass mobilizations will decline. The organizations of the toilers will begin to be gutted of their popular, democratic content and combat potential. And the leadership that exists will be pushed away from a convergence with modern world communism and its continuity.

"Stagnation," as Joe called it, is what the draft resolution documents. It is what has been taking place in Nicaragua. There has been a turn in direction. It isn't a 180-degree turn, for two reasons. First, because it wasn't a straight line to begin with when the revolution was moving forward; there were contradictions and hesitations. Second, because following the turn in direction not everything moves backward along exactly the same path or at the same rate. The land that has been expropriated is not necessarily going to be turned back to the former owners; nationalized industries aren't all being returned to private hands. Fundamental questions like these are settled in class struggle.

But the turn in policy direction is more than simply hesitations or pauses, which go on all the time under the pressures that bear down on a workers and farmers government. This is why we always see this after it happens, and correctly so. Even if we're pointing to tendencies and moves that weaken the revolution as we go along, it's only after new policies become established, defended, and therefore reinforced that we can say a new course has been definitively established, a turn in direction has taken place.

This is what became unambiguously clear in Nicaragua after the war ended. It was not unambiguously clear during the war or even in its immediate aftermath. This is where the September 1987 memorandum of the Political Committee, "The New Situation in Nicaragua," fits in.[4] We could see that the contras had been defeated. We could see what was opening up and the choices being posed. The memorandum correctly pointed to what had been accomplished and what had to be done. It underscored the momentum coming out of the successful revolutionary mobilization to fight the war and what that made possible. The memorandum outlined a political orientation, not a set of predictions. That was correct.

A 'cold' change?

A turn in policy direction by a workers and farmers government doesn't settle everything. Why? Because the policy direction can be reversed again, back toward its original anticapitalist direction. That is what the draft resolution says is not precluded in Nicaragua, however unlikely it may be. That is what was not ruled out prior to the Boumédienne coup in Algeria. The question is not settled until there is another qualitative change, another qualitative turning point, beyond which the direction of the government can no longer be reversed, beyond which it no longer has the content of a workers and farmers government. That is what has not yet happened in Nicaragua— at least it is premature to say so definitively.

How cold or hot does the coming change have to be? There was a sentence in the earlier draft of the resolution, which the National Committee discussed in July, that said something along the lines of, "It won't be completely cold, but it doesn't have to be very hot either." As you can see, it wasn't much help in answering the question, so it was dropped.

In the overturn of the workers and farmers government in Algeria there was not a great deal of violence. There was a coup, but there wasn't a lot of fighting, and there weren't many executions. Ben Bella himself was simply placed under house arrest.

We remember the violence in Grenada [in October 1983] because of the horror of what happened with the assassination of Bishop and the other leaders who were fighting to bring the workers and farmers government back to power. But this was because Bishop organized a fight, even if it was a very short-lived one, against the Stalinist gang that had taken over. Bishop refused to go along with the Coardites' majority rule in the Central Committee and in the narrow membership of the New

Jewel Movement itself, a majority that did not represent the line of march of the toilers. Bishop wouldn't go along with the "collective leadership" the Coard faction tried to impose; he wouldn't go along with house arrest. Because Bishop launched a fight, a mass fight, there was finally the violence. Had he been less of a communist, had he buckled to the threats and the pressure, there would not have been much violence. There would have been no leadership to organize the resistance.[5]

If we turn now to Nicaragua, it is clear in light of these experiences that the replacement of the workers and farmers government does not have to be accompanied by much violence. It's not likely to be very violent because there is not likely to be organized, fighting resistance to the change. That's the meaning of the unanimous agreement within the National Directorate to the present course. Nobody in the top leadership of the FSLN has to get arrested, even put under house arrest.

But if it doesn't have to be very violent, it does have to be a sharp political change, one that is expressed to one degree or another in a change in government personnel. It will be visible, and its meaning will not be lost on the politically advanced working people of Nicaragua. Will we miss it? No, not only will we not miss it, it cannot be missed by the vanguard workers and peasants in Nicaragua.

In order not to miss its significance we have to see the evolution of the FSLN and the government, and in particular the earlier turn in policy direction. This is not automatic. Joe pointed out in his article on the Algerian workers and farmers government that at the time of the Boumédienne coup there was not agreement among our comrades that it signaled a qualitative turning point.

The comrades closest to the situation—the comrades working in Algeria and many of the comrades in France—denied that the coup registered a qualitative change. They argued that the new Boumédienne regime was pursuing a course not much different from what had in fact been the direction followed for some time under Ben Bella.

Their position was wrong. But what is important to see is that they were led to that conclusion because they had internalized and already discounted the results of the stagnation and retreat under Ben Bella. By failing to understand the importance of the turn in policy direction that led to the erosion of the foundations of the workers and farmers government they also missed the qualitative point marked by the coup. This led many of these comrades to minimize the earlier accomplishments and gains of the workers and farmers government. They took the weakened and eroded workers and farmers government that paved the way for the coup and superimposed it back on the workers and farmers government that had been moving forward earlier.

To see how this worked, think of what conclusions would be drawn by someone who looked at the Nicaraguan workers and farmers government in August 1989 and assumed that it wasn't qualitatively different from what existed in 1980 or 1981. They would conclude that the workers and farmers government is not such a powerful anticapitalist weapon in the hands of the toilers, not such an important conquest. After all, look what it has led to. However, it is not the workers and farmers government that has led to the current situation and its coming resolution but the erosion of the foundations of that government, the retreat of its leadership.

Evolution of Ortega's place within the leadership

What can we say about the likely form of a change in the class character of the government in Nicaragua? For one thing, President Daniel Ortega doesn't have to replaced. He is not likely to be. We should pay attention to an important side of the political evolution of the FSLN government. In the first few years, Ortega was one of nine members of the National Directorate. There was a division of labor: Ortega was the coordinator of the Junta of the Government of National Reconstruction; Tomás Borge was the head of the Ministry of the Interior; Humberto Ortega the head of the army, and so on.

Over time, this changed. Ortega, though still one of the nine, became more equal than the others. His voice became much more authoritative than the other eight on all questions of policy. More recently there has been another evolution, one that is accelerating. When Ortega speaks now it is more and more not as a member of the National Directorate or any governmental body, not as a representative of the toilers through their vanguard organization, but as the president of "all the people." This has been an important evolution.

The FSLN leadership would like to put together something different coming out of the elections set for February: Ortega as chief executive of a newly elected government, Sergio Ramírez as vice president, and some type of "national unity" government that would include—as part of the cabinet or in some other capacity—representatives of some bourgeois opposition forces. We can't predict the forms because they will depend not only on what the FSLN wants to do but on what the various opposition formations do, which in turn will depend to a considerable degree on what the Bush administration does.

Regardless of the form such a development might take, it will be a sharp political change. There will be reaction against it from the working-class vanguard, who will see it as a qualitative turning point. Bourgeois forces will see it that way, too. This doesn't have to be unanimous; they won't all react in the same way at the same time. But it will be seen that way by a substantial component of the capitalist political opposition.

Adjustments in solidarity work

The second point I want to take up is an aspect of our practical work. There is a sharp shift required in what, for lack of a better term, we call Nicaragua solidarity work. It is a shift that the SWP and YSA have largely already made. We are devoting less time and less leadership resources to activities in connection with Nicaragua solidarity. This has been a necessary response to the growing limits on what can fruitfully be done. It is not only that we have upgraded work around Cuba and put it in its proper political place or that we have a better understanding of the weight of solidarity with the struggles in southern Africa. We are also making an adjustment to objective facts about Nic-

274   Larry Seigle (1989)

aragua solidarity work and the character of the organizations that are doing it.

This is worth looking at from a couple of points of view. We can start with what seems obvious. We have limited resources, limited cadres, and even more important, we have limited leadership resources to organize these cadres. Therefore we set priorities. In the area of what we call solidarity work, broadly defined, we have a double criteria.

First, we try to orient as best as we can toward those struggles where the biggest blows can be dealt to imperialism. We try to pick the front line of the advance of world revolution to concentrate on. We zero in on it, become part of it to the degree that we are able to. From this standpoint, there has been an objective change. With the end of the contra war the weight of Nicaragua in U.S. politics, and in the politics of other countries, has declined. That is a fact having nothing directly to do with us or our analysis.

At the same time, with the political retreat of the FSLN leadership there has been a further evolution that has broader political implications. The direction is not toward the establishment of a workers state but away from it. The direction is not toward a modern proletarian party but toward a petty-bourgeois front with a growing importance placed on its electoral policy. This reduces Nicaragua's weight in world politics. Like every other political force, we have been adjusting to that.

The second criteria that we use in determining our priorities in solidarity work is our judgment about where we can do party-building work most successfully. Sometimes we don't like to say that because our enemies often accuse us of trying to "take advantage" of some struggles to build our own organization. Of course communists take advantage of the openings presented by the class struggle to build communist organizations. How else would they be built? How else have they ever been built?

But the accusations of our opponents are not only false, they are slanderous in their implications. What we *don't* do is to counterpose building a communist organization to helping organize and lead on their own terms demonstrations or organizations or coalitions whose goals we support. We don't abuse those organizations. We don't seek to substitute communist aims for their aims. We don't manipulate them for our purposes. And we organize ourselves so that we don't hinder the work of those coalitions or groups that don't agree with our priorities.

'Managua trail'

This is where we have to continue making an adjustment. There has been a change in the political character of the individuals and groups involved in Nicaragua solidarity work. It is different today than it was five years ago. How could it be otherwise in light of all that has changed? The discussion yesterday at the YSA convention on this point was very helpful. Many comrades who spoke during the discussion on Nicaragua explained that they had first come toward the communist movement through solidarity work with Nicaragua and through traveling the "Managua trail"—a term we have used to refer to those who visit or spend time working in Nicaragua because they are attracted to and want to work to defend the revolution.

These comrades explained that they were first attracted to the YSA and the party because of our activity in the solidarity movement. But almost all of them added that there has been a political evolution in the groups that are engaged in solidarity work. There has been a change in the people who are attracted to the Nicaraguan government and the FSLN, what it is that they are attracted toward, and what they learn and internalize from it.

The trekkers on the Managua trail were never homogeneous. This reflected the reality of the Nicaraguan revolution and the FSLN. It was always different than the "Havana trail," which—while not homogeneous either, as we well know—nevertheless, because of the socialist nature of the Cuban revolution and the communist character of its leadership, has drawn young people interested in the Cuban revolution toward Marxism. Revolutionary-minded people who are attracted to Cuba are also more attracted to a communist organization.

Those on the Managua trail have always been much more diverse. Some people were attracted to the revolutionary action, to the workers and farmers, and to the anticapitalist course of the revolution. Those are the ones we had a chance to win to communism, and we have won a good number of them. But others were drawn to different aspects of the Nicaraguan revolution. Some were attracted to what was less communist and less working-class about the FSLN than the Cuban Communist Party. This was often presented as what was supposedly new and original about the Nicaraguan revolution: less dogmatic, less rigid, less "square." Some liked the Nicaraguan revolution because they thought it was more Christian. Some middle-class radicals were particularly attracted to the proposition that we could get rid of stale Marxist concepts such as *working class* and *petty bourgeoisie*— and especially the distinction between the two—and not just in Nicaragua.

Although the composition of the activists in the solidarity movement has always been diverse, there has also been a marked change over the last couple of years. The layer of those attracted to the anticapitalist advances of the revolution and to the struggles of the workers and peasants in Nicaragua has increasingly dried up. Young people are less likely to be politicized as a result of traveling the Managua trail than at any time since 1979. They are less likely to be attracted to a communist perspective by their experience because they are less likely to encounter such a perspective in Nicaragua. Fewer are attracted to Carlos Fonseca and more are attracted to the middle-class, anticommunist perspective outlined, for example, in the book *Fire in the Americas,* by Orlando Núñez and Roger Burbach—a book that reflects the thinking of significant layers in the leadership of the FSLN.

Avoiding factional wrangles

In light of these objective changes, we are making a double adjustment. First, we are helping comrades who are carrying organizational responsibility, institutional responsibility, in various solidarity committees and organizations to extricate themselves from such positions. We have to do this in a way that is responsible to all involved, including to those people with whom we loyally collaborate and will continue to loyally collaborate. We must take this step because our comrades cannot lead the Nicaragua solidarity work as it exists now. We cannot lead it given the character of its participants and its political direction, which generally incorporates the priorities and direction advocated by the FSLN leadership.

If we try to lead it one of two things happens. One is that comrades get very good at it and in the process their axis shifts away from communist politics. To lead this movement today they have to get comfortable with its current trajectory, which is counterposed to a working-class course of action. They have to internalize it.

The second alternative is that we get into a lot of wrangles and factional fights that not only cannot be won, but worse, damage our political relations with people with whom we can and should maintain fraternal relations of integrity and trust. If we don't find a way to avoid these quarrels, we will damage the work of the party and solidarity simultaneously.

There is no point in arguing with fellow activists about the need for a working-class perspective and what is wrong with the present direction of the solidarity movement unless they are attracted in a different direction and being pulled in a different direction by what is happening in Nicaragua itself. What's the point? We are not in the business of trying to save souls. All you get is a destructive wrangle.

This involves facing up to something that not all of us have faced yet. The conclusions about Nicaragua contained in the draft resolution may be absolutely correct, absolutely logical, and absolutely necessary, but this doesn't make them at all convincing to someone who isn't part of or attracted toward the working-class movement.

What's more, the analysis in this resolution will be totally uninteresting to most people active in the solidarity movement. Most of them would find it just as boring as you would find a book about the internal problems of the Rainbow Coalition. You are only interested in that if you are part of it or if it is converging with the class line of march you're on. Why

else would you be interested? Some people will find what
we're talking about today just as boring. We're not trying to
proselytize them. We have to recognize the limits to the power
of the word.

This is something we've gone through with groups involved
in solidarity with El Salvador work. We have learned that it is
not only useless but politically counterproductive to walk into a
meeting of the Committee in Solidarity with the People of El
Salvador (CISPES), for example, and get into an argument
about why projections of an imminent insurrection in El Salvador are false and damaging. We don't change the minds of anyone there. And, what's worse, regardless of our intentions, we
can make ourselves vulnerable to accusations that we are trying
to obstruct what they are convinced needs to be done.

Enthusiastic collaboration
It is much better instead to concentrate on those activities they
initiate that are not diversionary to the working-class movement and are useful politically in fighting against U.S. imperialist intervention in El Salvador and Central America. We lend
support to those activities and help promote them. At the same
time we say what we think about El Salvador in our press. We
say what we think when we speak publicly. We say it to anyone
who is interested in our point of view. We don't have to say it in
the form of polemics against CISPES. And we don't go around
vainly trying to persuade those who look to one of the components of the FMLN for their political line that they should instead look to us for their political line.

We participate in demonstrations and other actions demanding an end to U.S. intervention in El Salvador and are part of
political tours to El Salvador, even helping take responsibility
for them under exceptional circumstances. We organize Militant Labor Forums on El Salvador, including with different
points of view on these questions.

We are enthusiastic participants in solidarity actions as long
as others don't demand that a condition of participating in actions they initiate is that we have to agree with their views on El

Salvador and agree to say what they say about it. Any group that imposes those conditions is an obstacle to united action in solidarity with El Salvador or any other struggle. We are loyal collaborators in action around concrete initiatives. We find things we can agree with to work on. We don't go in to try to change their priorities to make them conform to ours.

Finally, we do what we can with all of these solidarity groups and coalitions, whether around Nicaragua or any other struggle, to draw them into actions in defense of the Cuban revolution. We encourage them to recognize the place of Cuba in the world and the importance of international solidarity with it. We urge them to participate along with others in broadly sponsored events around Cuba. We encourage them to learn about Cuba. And in the course of doing this we meet those who respond politically to the example of the Cuban revolution and those who are interested in a communist and working-class perspective.

SUMMARY OF DISCUSSION

T HE DISCUSSION HAS BEEN a wide-ranging one. I will focus on three or four of the points that ought to be clarified further. The draft resolution explains that the Socialist Workers Party and Young Socialist Alliance are sister organizations of the FSLN. This is not an expression of sentiment. It is a way of summing up a decisive component of the line of the resolution. As "partisans of and fellow fighters with the FSLN," the resolution says, "we participate in defending and advancing the Nicaraguan revolution and workers and farmers government. And it is from this standpoint that we work with other political forces to draw workers and farmers into defending revolutionary Nicaragua against Washington and its allies."

Is this accurate? One of the comrades posed this question in the discussion. Isn't there a contradiction between reaffirming that political orientation and seeing clearly the increasing rejection by the FSLN leadership of the only course that can advance the interests of the workers and peasants? How can we oppose the course being implemented by the National Directorate and continue to regard the FSLN as our sister organization?

Together with class-conscious workers and peasants in Nicaragua, we recognize that the FSLN is the organization that has won and retains the right to lead working people. This is not a question of theory or abstract preference but a concrete political fact. Those fighters who made the revolution and who have fought to lead it forward to the best of their abilities in the face of all the obstacles and pressures they have confronted are members and supporters of the FSLN today.

They do not look to any other organization. The draft resolution points out that the various opposition groupings that present themselves as socialist or Marxist do not and cannot offer a working-class alternative. They branded themselves forever as enemies of the interests of the toilers during the war, when they stood aside from—and many of them actively opposed—the revolutionary anti-imperialist mobilization against the contra forces. That is one good reason why there are no revolutionary forces in Nicaragua today other than those who are part of and loyal to the FSLN.

Is it possible to have a "sister organization" that is leading the toilers in the wrong direction? It wouldn't be the first time in the history of the international workers movement in this century. Let's take an example we are familiar with. The Soviet Communist Party—and I am not drawing a general analogy between the Stalinized Soviet party and the FSLN—remained the locus of all proletarian politics for some time after its leadership not only abandoned the Bolshevik program but opened war on it and on the cadres who were fighting to continue to implement it. Bolshevik-Leninists throughout the world regarded the Soviet Communist Party for nearly a decade following Lenin's death as their sister organization despite its accelerating betrayal of the program of Lenin. This did not remain true indefinitely, however. By 1933 a qualitative turning point had been passed.[6]

The political situation in Nicaragua can change. The FSLN's relationship to the revolutionary workers of Nicaragua can change qualitatively. But today the reality is that a communist vanguard of the Nicaraguan working class can be built only by being based among those revolutionary-minded fighters who defend the FSLN and who remain loyal to it.

Convergence of communist forces

This is closely connected to another aspect of the discussion today. A couple of comrades expressed the opinion that the resolution makes a necessary correction in an earlier overestimation of the FSLN leadership. One comrade suggested we were wrong to say the FSLN was part of a communist convergence on a world scale. What's more, she added, we made the same mistake with regard to Sinn Féin and other groups—erroneously viewing them all as part of a nonexistent international convergence of communist forces.

This is not the point of view expressed in the draft resolution. The resolution documents the *change in direction* of the FSLN and the Nicaraguan government. It has not been a straight line, which we couldn't see before but we can see looking back on it. The FSLN leadership has changed course. We *were* converging. *Now* we are diverging. Both are true.

There is now a growing divergence between the FSLN leadership and communist politics. This does not mean, however, that if you look back with all the benefit of hindsight you can discern that the convergence was merely an illusion. You can't read the class struggle backward. You can't look at the world and say that every political force has always been headed toward where it is now. It's not true. That substitutes the retrospective word for the deed with a vengeance. It is a fallacy to think that if you could have pinpointed the flaws in the FSLN leadership's theoretical foundation, if you could have put your finger on the weakness of their analysis, you could have predicted the future and warned everybody.

Leon Trotsky fought during the last part of his life against those who tried to explain what happened in the Soviet Union by finding the flaw in Lenin, the flaw in the Bolshevik Party, the flaw in the tactics of the communist opposition that continued and advanced Lenin's unfinished fight, or the flaw in Marxism itself that would "explain" why it all was destined to wind up in the consolidation of the Stalinist counterrevolution. Trotsky insisted that the victory of Stalinism wasn't inevitable. It wasn't foreordained. It couldn't have been predicted—and those who did "predict" it forgot that their "prediction" was itself a deed, one that placed them outside the struggle where the outcome was being determined, thereby weakening the fight.

There was a convergence with the FSLN. However, there was never a historic convergence with Sinn Féin. No resolution or report adopted by the Socialist Workers Party ever suggested that there was. Perhaps some comrades had a different evaluation at an earlier stage, but if so they were wrong, as we all would now agree. Sinn Féin was not moving toward becoming part of the resolution of the crisis of communist leadership on a world scale. Nor were other organizations that were occasionally proposed as candidates for this convergence, such as the Communist Party of the Philippines, the Communist Party of the Dominican Republic, or, earlier, the Black Panther Party, the Chinese Communist Party, and some others. Some comrades began looking for—hoping for, more accurately—a development toward communism by these groups, but the hope never lasted very long because there was no objective basis for it.

To say now there never was a convergence with the FSLN would lead in the direction of unraveling everything we have conquered and enriched our program with in the last decade. We were converging with the FSLN. Then there was a change in direction by the leadership in Managua. That change is what we are focusing in on. If we lose that, we lose the point of this resolution.

Place of FSLN Historic Program

This is related to the FSLN's Historic Program. One of the comrades suggested in the discussion that you can find substantial threads of continuity from weaknesses in the FSLN's Historic Program to the policy direction being implemented by the

FSLN National Directorate today. It is true, of course, as the comrade pointed out, that the Historic Program is not a communist program. It does not present itself as a communist program. It is a revolutionary-democratic and anti-imperialist program with far-reaching social content. And it was drafted by revolutionists who were fighting to find a road toward building a communist leadership among the vanguard of Nicaragua's workers and peasants.

The policy course of the FSLN National Directorate today is not in continuity with the Historic Program. There is a discontinuity. The comrade tried to substantiate his point by reading part of a sentence from the section of the Historic Program entitled "The Agrarian Revolution," saying this showed some of the roots of the current policy toward the so-called patriotic producers. This is the part he read: "It [the revolution] will protect the patriotic landowners who collaborate with the guerrilla struggle. . . ."

We should note, by the way, that it says "landowners," not "producers." I don't think the term *patriotic producers* appears anywhere in this program or in any of the other FSLN documents of this time. But, more important, listen to the whole passage: "It will protect patriotic landowners who collaborate with the guerrilla struggle. They will be paid for their holdings that exceed the limits established by the revolutionary government." That is, the new government would put an upper limit on landholdings. What the limit would be is not specified. That was to be determined in struggle—although the program does pledge to "expropriate and eliminate the big landlords, both capitalist and feudal" and to "turn land over to the peasants free of charge, in accordance with the principle that land should belong to those who work it."[7]

Anything over the upper limit would be taken away. The difference between those big landowners who helped the guerrillas and those who opposed them would be that those who aided them would get compensation for their land. This is a sensible revolutionary stance, isn't it? Nothing in this pledge points in the direction of the current policy toward capitalist

284   *Larry Seigle (1989)*

farmers in Nicaragua. If this one provision were carried out, if a maximum limit on landholding were established and implemented, if the "capitalist and feudal estates" were turned over to the peasants "in accordance with the principle that the land should belong to those who work it"—that would be a giant step forward, wouldn't it?

THE FIGHT TO IMPLEMENT the Historic Program in Nicaragua, as the draft resolution points out, will be part of any revolutionary opposition to the current course of the FSLN leadership and the government. We can make more use of this program and its companion piece "Nicaragua: Zero Hour," both written by Carlos Fonseca in 1969, and both included in the Pathfinder volume *Sandinistas Speak*. I share the opinion of the comrade who said that this book is politically stronger than the other book—the bigger, more expensive one—*Nicaragua: The Sandinista People's Revolution*. The smaller book holds up better because it has more fundamental programmatic material in it, and it has more by Carlos Fonseca in it. We should promote both books together, because only by seeing the place of the Historic Program and articles such as "Nicaragua: Zero Hour" can the revolutionary continuity of the FSLN be understood.

I admit to being somewhat biased in favor of Fonseca's writings. Maybe it is a result of being assigned to the Managua Bureau, living and working in Nicaragua. If you read Fonseca's work—some of which Pathfinder is going to publish in English—and you compare it to Lenin, or Marx, or some other communist leaders you will find flaws and weaknesses. It reflects what the FSLN was and what it wasn't while Fonseca was alive, including the limits of its working-class composition and base in the labor movement. You will see the difficulties Fonseca ran up against as he struggled to understand and come to grips with Stalinism, in Nicaragua and internationally. You will find a certain shrill tone in a bit of it, where the rhetoric of frustration gets up a little steam.

But if you compare Fonseca's writings to what is being offered in Nicaragua today to justify the course of the FSLN leadership, if you compare them to the worldwide anticommunist and anti–Cuban revolution chorus of perestroika-ites, if you compare them to the flight from working-class politics that is dominant among groups claiming to be Marxist today throughout Latin America and the rest of the world—then Fonseca's writings are great stuff. They are powerful, clear, inspiring, timely, and educational works by a working-class and communist leader of great stature and personal courage. We will all learn from them and others will too.

I may also be somewhat biased in favor of Fonseca's works because they are so hard to get hold of, even in Nicaragua. The Fonseca writings—with the exception of the Historic Program—are largely unavailable in Nicaragua. They have been out of print for several years, and there is no sign they are going to be reprinted. This is a political question, not a matter of scarce resources. A lot of books have been published in Nicaragua in the last couple of years. There are thick historical novels by Vice President Sergio Ramírez, new editions of books by Nicaraguan bourgeois historians long out of print, and—my favorite of the past year—a novel by Gioconda Belli, a prominent FSLN writer, about a young bourgeois woman in Managua in the 1970s who becomes inhabited by the spirit of an Indian mediated through an orange tree, joins the FSLN, and is killed in action. But Fonseca's works remain out of print.

A comrade made the prediction in the discussion that the FSLN is going to replace the Historic Program with a new document. There was some published speculation in Nicaragua along those lines in the past year, and it certainly seemed possible. But my own view is that it is less likely now. Why? Because a new program is not needed to advance the course being followed. The FSLN has its candidates and its election campaign. The FSLN leaders are defining their program by what they are doing. The Historic Program can have its permanent place in the libraries—even as a little pamphlet for those interested in the history of the Nicaraguan revolution.

There is no need to replace or revise it. It is less and less a living document.

Form of government that 'rapidly appears'
One sentence in the draft resolution is worth coming back to for a closer look. A workers and farmers government, it says, is "the form of government that can be expected to rapidly appear as the result of a successful anticapitalist revolution." The word "rapidly" here is new.

In his 1978 introductory note to Robert Chester's compilation *Workers and Farmers Governments since the Second World War*, Joe Hansen wrote that a workers and farmers government "is the first form of government that can be expected to appear as the result of a successful anticapitalist revolution."[8] But it is not necessarily the first. In Cuba the emergence of the workers and farmers government came after a brief period of a radical bourgeois coalition government. In Nicaragua a somewhat similar development took place, but in such a different form and on such a compressed timetable that we often forget about it and collapse the actual course of events into a shorthand formula by saying the workers and farmers government came to power on July 19, 1979. That oversimplifies what happened.

What did happen is worth reviewing. In the two months leading up to July 19 deep-going popular insurrections took place in the main cities in Nicaragua, coordinated with an FSLN military offensive. There were general strikes and armed uprisings in the cities, land occupations and other mobilizations in the countryside. During these two months, the FSLN leadership was convinced that the provisional revolutionary government they would participate in after the collapse of the Somoza dictatorship would initially be a coalition regime, with bourgeois forces holding the majority. They believed that this was dictated by the relationship of forces.

In fact, such a government was actually formed, albeit only on paper, in Costa Rica on July 9, 1979. An agreement was reached between the FSLN and some of the bourgeois opposition forces to establish such a regime to replace the Somoza dictatorship. This government was to be made up of a five-member junta and a Council of State in which the bourgeois forces held a decisive majority. The Council of State was to have veto power, by two-thirds vote, over the junta's decisions and to share all legislative powers with the junta. There was also agreement to incorporate some National Guard units into the new army.

But the relationship of forces that this agreement expressed was altered by the direct intervention of the toilers before the bourgeois coalition government came into being. Somoza fled on July 17, leaving behind a stand-in, Francisco Urcuyo, who had promised to turn over power to the new junta. But the Yankee stooge refused to live up to the bargain—a severe miscalculation—and he blew up the whole deal in the process. This provoked the final massive insurrection by the toilers and the FSLN's military push on Managua, led by guerrilla cadres and internationalist volunteers. The National Guard shattered, tens of thousands of weapons were captured and distributed to working people, and the FSLN columns entered the city.

The new governing power was qualitatively different from the bourgeois coalition government outlined in the July 9 Costa Rica accord. The changed relationship of forces opened the possibility for the FSLN to follow another course, and within a matter of weeks it became clear that it was taking it. In the first weeks after July 19 it was still assumed that the bourgeois-dominated Council of State would quickly be installed. But the target date of September 15 came and went without its convocation. Toward the end of October the junta announced that the convening of the council was being put off until May 1980. In the intervening months the council was to be completely restructured, stripping the bourgeois forces of their majority and giving the organizations of the toilers the dominant position. Executive power was in the hands of the FSLN-dominated junta and the nine-member National Directorate of the FSLN.

Thus we can see that the workers and farmers government did

not take definitive shape immediately after the fall of Somoza, but it did emerge rapidly.

Lessons of the New Economic Policy

A number of comrades spoke about various aspects of the political lessons of the Bolsheviks' New Economic Policy and their relevance to the Nicaraguan revolution. I want to address only one of the questions raised. Were we disarmed politically, one comrade asked, by drawing an analogy between the NEP and the course of the FSLN government in the early years of the revolution?

I don't know all the analogies comrades around the world used. Let's concede that it is possible, even likely, that things were said on this subject that were wrong. But that doesn't get us very far. If you look back at the resolutions dealing with Nicaragua adopted by the Socialist Workers Party and the various articles in *New International,* which constitute the continuity of our international movement on the Nicaraguan revolution— you won't find anything we would write substantially different today. Here is one example from the SWP resolution of January 1980:

> In Nicaragua, the outcome of this fundamental contradiction between the class character of the workers and peasants government and the capitalist state still hangs in the balance. The designation of Nicaragua today as a workers and peasants government in no way implies that a workers state will automatically be the outcome of the process under way. The big class conflicts that will settle that question still lie ahead.
>
> As the workers and peasants press forward to win their demands, the imperialists and Nicaraguan bourgeoisie will strike blows. They will have to be met with counterblows. Each new encroachment against capitalist property and prerogatives will meet stiffening resistance by the reaction. Open breaks will occur within the government and all other Nicaraguan institutions.

A workers and peasants government is by its very nature an unstable and transitory formation: It must either
move forward to the establishment of a workers state, or—
failing to decisively break the economic power of the
bourgeoisie—*fall back* and open the way to a reassertion
of capitalist political power and reinforcement of the
bourgeois state. How this unstable situation will be resolved in Nicaragua depends in large part on how well
the FSLN responds to the initiatives of the masses and
succeeds in educating, organizing, and mobilizing them.
They will have to defeat the counterrevolutionary
threats. And they must be prepared to face the eventuality of direct U.S. military intervention aimed at preventing the triumph of a second workers state in the
Western Hemisphere.[9]

Precisely correct.

Of course, the NEP has been invoked in Nicaragua to justify
all kinds of policies that have nothing to do with the NEP, nothing to do with Lenin, and nothing to do with communism.
This, I should add, is a stage that is being quickly left behind as
the FSLN leadership less and less often tries to rationalize its
course by quoting Lenin. But you still run into it sometimes,
and a year or two ago it was very widespread. The argument is
simple: the NEP was the original experiment with a "mixed
economy"; the FSLN is doing today what the Bolshevik Party
under Lenin finally came to in 1921.

As the draft resolution explains, this is fundamentally false.
The NEP was a necessary retreat. It could be done without en-
dangering the dictatorship of the proletariat because there was
state ownership of basic industry, nationalized land, and a state
monopoly of foreign trade, as well as a tested communist leadership of a very high caliber leading an explicitly socialist revolution and deeply committed to subordinating its fortunes to
advancing the revolution internationally. But the Nicaraguan
toilers have not yet established the dictatorship of the proletariat nor has a communist leadership been forged.

290 Larry Seigle (1989)

The political lessons Lenin drew from the Bolsheviks' experience both before and during the NEP, however, are relevant to Nicaragua. This is where we have drawn some limited analogies, focusing on two closely related points.

First, no preconceived timetable for nationalizations can be imposed from outside the development of the class struggle in Nicaragua. There were those who tried to impose such a schema. They accused the FSLN of betraying the revolution because it didn't meet some schedule for expropriation of capitalist holdings. We rejected that approach then, and we reject it now. The problems the toilers face today do not stem from the fact that the FSLN government did not go faster than it did toward expropriating capitalist property in 1979 or in 1980 or in 1981. The problem is that the FSLN government is no longer traveling on the road it was traveling in 1979, 1980, and 1981. It is no longer preparing the Nicaraguan toilers to move toward a socialist revolution. It is going in the opposite direction.

Price of administrative measures

Second, attempts to resolve problems by resorting to administrative measures, instead of finding ways to strengthen the consciousness and organization of the toilers and the alliance of the workers and peasants, weaken the revolution and the workers and farmers government. This was one of the main points Lenin hammered away at in explaining the necessity for the NEP retreat.[10]

Our point is the same as Maurice Bishop's: you can't make a revolution the way you make a cup of instant coffee.[11] We understand even better now what Bishop was fighting against when he insisted on this point. We understand even better the stakes involved. The Coardites were the instant-coffee advocates. That's who Maurice was talking about—the Stalinist gang that congealed in the New Jewel Movement and bad-mouthed Bishop because he opposed the use of administrative measures that undermined rather than strengthened the confidence and consciousness of the toilers.

We reject the Coard road. It's not the road to a workers state, by the way, even an imperfect one—unless you think that Pol Pot created a most imperfect but most firm workers state in Cambodia, as some who consider themselves Marxists have argued, incredible as that sounds. The Coard policy wouldn't have led to a workers state in Grenada either, even if the U.S. troops hadn't been sent in.

In this connection, the resolution underlines an important political fact: the punitive expropriations of certain capitalist holdings that have been carried out recently by the FSLN government do not represent a reversal of direction. This is worth thinking about because we probably have not seen the last of these expropriation decrees. The government uses these expropriations, and the threat of decreeing more, in its attempts to convince the capitalists to go along with the social-pact policy. The workers don't figure into the plan at all. They are seen largely as passive observers. The government ministers say to the capitalists: "If you want class struggle, we'll give you class struggle. But if you want to cooperate, we'll give you back your farms." This cynical invocation of "class struggle" as a threat or bargaining chip is no different from what some union bureaucrats in this country do at times as they pursue ultraleft tactics in the midst of a strike they are leading to defeat through their class-collaborationist course.

We saw this at the big San Antonio sugar complex in Nicaragua, which was expropriated last year. It was one of the biggest nationalizations carried out by the revolution since 1979, but it didn't mark an advance. What happened there? There was a protracted political battle in the union, which supporters of the FSLN and the government lost. Opposition unions were dominant politically, and the supporters of the FSLN were on the retreat and being pushed back further. As a result there was no effective fight against the decapitalization of the mill and the vast sugar plantation surrounding it. In fact, the pro–bourgeois opposition union leaders were part of the whole corrupt deal.

It was a critical situation for the workers, and for the country as a whole, because the whole complex was in danger of being shut down. Instead of charting a course to mobilize the strength of the workers, in which a nationalization decree might have been a big help, the government resorted to a purely administrative act. The workers there woke up one morning—literally—to find that a new administration appointed by the government had replaced the private managers. That was all that had changed. The workers were no more part of running that operation than they had been before, and there was no projection that this would or should change.

Some revolutionary-minded workers responded to this punitive expropriation very favorably anyway, just as some supported the recent punitive expropriations of some capitalist coffee farms. They see these as a blow against the capitalist class, and they hope they will be followed by other moves. But this enthusiasm can't last because these administrative measures don't lead to any real change. They are simply one aspect of the general policy of political retreat from the historic goals and perspectives of the revolution.

We would not alter any of the things we have said about the danger of using government power in an administrative way, rather than using that power to politically advance the organization and political self-confidence of the toilers, to draw them each day toward greater control over productive activity—and in the process begin changing themselves, as Che explained so well. In fact, heavy-handed administrative methods were more widespread in Nicaragua and did even more damage politically than we knew at the time. This is certainly the case in relation to the Atlantic Coast, where the real extent of the disastrous policies implemented by the FSLN government against the Indian and Black populations has only become clear relatively recently and is still not completely known.

A parallel problem caused difficulties in relation to the small peasants. For a number of years the Ministry of Agrarian Development and Reform followed a policy of compelling peasants seeking land to form collective farms as a condition for grants of land. The policy was to use this leverage to try to prevent peasants getting land under the agrarian reform from becoming individual farmers. Individual farmers were seen as unreliable allies, at best. The land policy relied on coercion, not on voluntary cooperation by peasants who *wanted* to form cooperatives or collectives because they were convinced they would be better off.

Does land distribution strengthen capitalism?

A similar political approach by many in the government, including in the agrarian reform ministry, justified the slow pace of land distribution in the countryside by arguing that transforming proletarian and semiproletarian layers in rural areas into property owners by giving them plots of land would represent a step backward, weakening the working class and actually leading to an expansion of capitalism in the countryside. It is no accident that government policy, justified by this ultraleft "theory," coincided with pressure from capitalist farmers who were desperately trying to hang on to their supply of cheap farm labor, especially seasonal hands, which depended on maintaining a large layer of landless peasants. More land distribution would have cut into the profits of these capitalist farmers, who already were having considerable trouble with farmworkers organizing into unions and fighting for better wages and improved conditions.

Distributing land to the peasants does not have to lead to a strengthening of capitalism. That is false, from more than one point of view. First, as the experience in Nicaragua showed, *not* distributing land rapidly enough, and not distributing it on terms freely chosen by the peasants, undermined support for the revolution and actually contributed to giving the contra forces an opening to organize among some layers of peasants. It was this danger, as the draft resolution notes, that forced the FSLN government to modify its land reform policy, speeding up the pace of land distribution and easing the coercive pressure on peasants to agree to work the land in collective farms.

There is an even more general point: Capital accumulation by independent commodity producers is constantly fostered by the continued existence of the bourgeoisie and its domination of manufacturing and commerce. As long as capitalist relations remain dominant in Nicaragua, capitalism will be continuously bred and re-bred in agriculture. Class divisions will be regenerated in the countryside, and the worker-farmer alliance undermined and eventually shattered. It is the maintenance of capitalism—not the distribution of land to landless peasants—that leads to this outcome. It can be avoided only by taking steps to move forward to the expropriation of the capitalist class, which can open the door to eliminating this source of class conflict between workers and peasants.

This is not what is happening in Nicaragua today, however. What we are seeing is another confirmation that a genuine agrarian reform cannot be reduced to distribution of land. As long as the system of rents and mortgages isn't eliminated and as long as capitalist relations dominate, all the old problems will reappear. We can see this in what is happening to small peasants today in Nicaragua, including those who have been given land under the agrarian reform. Those with the worst land are being driven under. This is true whether the land is worked individually, as a cooperative, or as a collective farm. Many can't make a go of it. They can't get a guaranteed price for their products. They can't plan. They can't stay out of debt. They can't sell their products at a price that will allow them to buy what they need to survive, to farm. They fail. This does not take place through bank foreclosures, which have not taken place, but it takes place just the same.

A small number of peasants, however, do very well. They move up into the ranks of capitalist farmers. This can occur on a collective farm, that is, on a producers' cooperative, too, if it has good land with technically advanced methods and equipment. Some partners buy out the others. They start hiring a little labor. They have to. They become capitalist enterprises in all but name, and they take their place beside other capitalist farms owned by "patriotic producers." A reconcentration of land begins, and there is a new rise in landlessness. This will be accompanied by the maintenance and growth of renting of land, moneylending, sharecropping, and other forms of exploitation.

The distribution of land alone is not the solution. It doesn't do it. The expropriation of the exploiting class is necessary to open up the possibility of voluntary collaboration by workers and small peasants in the development of agriculture along noncapitalist lines and the construction of socialism.

The struggle for a proletarian party

LEON TROTSKY   JAMES P. CANNON

In Defense of Marxism
THE SOCIAL AND POLITICAL CONTRADICTIONS OF THE SOVIET UNION
by Leon Trotsky
Why only a party that fights to bring growing numbers of workers into its ranks and leadership can chart a revolutionary course. In response to rising pressures of bourgeois public opinion on the middle classes in the buildup toward World War II, Trotsky explains why workers must oppose imperialist assaults on the degenerated Soviet workers state, and defends the materialist foundations of scientific socialism. 280 pp., $18.95

The Struggle for a Proletarian Party
by James P. Cannon
The political and organizational principles of Marxism, presented in a debate that unfolded as Washington prepared to drag U.S. working people into the slaughter of World War II. A companion volume to *In Defense of Marxism.* 302 pp., $19.95

Background to "The Struggle for a Proletarian Party"
by Leon Trotsky and James P. Cannon   45 pp, 8¹/2 x 11, $6.00

The Structure and Organizational Principles of the Party
by Farrell Dobbs   37 pp., 8¹/2 x 11 format, $6.00

AVAILABLE FROM PATHFINDER. SEE PAGE 2 FOR DISTRIBUTORS

Join the
PATHFINDER
READERS CLUB

Pathfinder is the leading international publisher of books and pamphlets by revolutionary fighters whose struggles against capitalism, racism, and all forms of exploitation and oppression point the way forward for humanity.

Over 250 titles by Karl Marx, Frederick Engels, V.I. Lenin, Leon Trotsky, Rosa Luxemburg, Ernesto Che Guevara, Fidel Castro, Malcolm X, Farrell Dobbs, James P. Cannon, Joseph Hansen, George Novack, Evelyn Reed, Nelson Mandela, Thomas Sankara, Maurice Bishop, Carlos Fonseca, and others.

For a US$10 annual fee, Readers Club members receive a 15 percent discount on all Pathfinder books and pamphlets at any Pathfinder bookstore around the world. You get even higher discounts on special selected titles.

TO JOIN anywhere in the world, contact the Pathfinder bookstore nearest you, or send US$10 to Pathfinder, 410 West Street, New York, NY 10014.

NOTES

In This Issue

1. Castro's speeches of July 19, 1980, and July 26, 1980, can be found in *Fidel Castro Speeches: Cuba's Internationalist Foreign Policy 1975-80* (New York: Pathfinder, 1981) pp. 310-15 and 316-338.

2. In Elizabeth Stone, ed., *Women and the Cuban Revolution* (New York: Pathfinder, 1981), p. 129.

3. Mary-Alice Waters, *Proletarian Leadership in Power: What We Can Learn from Lenin, Castro, and the FSLN* (New York: Pathfinder, 1980), p. 15.

In 1984 Waters authored a feature article for the third issue of *New International*, which concluded with a section on Nicaragua placing that revolution in the historic framework of the fight by the working class for political power since the beginning of the scientific communist movement in the middle of the last century. That article, "Communism and the Fight for a Popular Revolutionary Government: 1848 to Today," is one of several that have appeared in issues of *New International* drawing on the experiences of the workers and peasants of Nicaragua to enrich the theoretical tools and programmatic heritage of the international working-class movement. Among other such articles are "Their Trotsky and Ours: Communist Continuity Today" by Jack Barnes in *New International*, no. 1 (fall 1983); " 'A Nose for Power': Preparing the Nicaraguan Revolution" by Tomás Borge, translated for *New International*, no. 3 (spring-summer 1983); and "The Fight for a Workers and Farmers Government in the United States" by Jack Barnes in *New International*, no. 4 (spring 1985).

4. For the Castro interview with Mervyn M. Dymally and Jeffrey M. Elliot, see *Fidel Castro: Nothing Can Stop the Course of History*, (New York: Pathfinder, 1986), p. 158. See also *Maurice Bishop Speaks: The Grenada Revolution and Its Overthrow, 1979-1983* (New York: Pathfinder, 1983).

5. Carlos Fonseca, "Nicaragua: Zero Hour" in Tomás Borge,

298 Notes for pages 16-19

Carlos Fonseca, Daniel Ortega, et al, *Sandinistas Speak* (New York: Pathfinder, 1982); also to appear in a new translation in *Carlos Fonseca Speaks* (New York: Pathfinder, 1994).

6. In face of preparations by the Democratic Party administration of President John F. Kennedy to invade Cuba to drown in blood the socialist revolution there, the Cuban government in 1962 signed a mutual defense agreement with the Soviet government that included the deployment of Soviet nuclear-tipped missiles in Cuba. In October of that year, Washington announced publicly that its intelligence flights over Cuba had detected the missiles and that it had imposed a naval blockade ringing the island. Within a few days, in face of this confrontation between nuclear-armed powers, Moscow came to agreement with Washington on withdrawal of the missiles; Soviet premier Nikita Khrushchev did not consult beforehand with the Cuban government on this decision or the terms of the withdrawal, nor even inform Havana of the agreement prior to its public announcement.

In an October 1992 interview with NBC television interviewer Maria Shriver on the thirtieth anniversary of these events, Castro said that if Cuban revolutionists had known in 1962 what they knew now about the political orientation of the Soviet leadership, they would not have accepted the deployment of the missiles on Cuban soil. He explained his view that Cuba had paid an unacceptable political price for agreeing to the missiles under the conditions demanded by Moscow. He said that the Cuban government had strongly opposed Moscow's insistence that the military agreement between Cuba and the Soviet Union be kept secret. Cuban leaders had argued that the pact should be made public, presenting the U.S. government's invasion plans as the reason for the missile deployment. Cuban revolutionists accepted the missiles only when it became clear to them that Moscow would never agree to this public pact. They did so, Castro said, in the mistaken belief that this was in the best interests of defending the world struggle for socialism.

But in accepting deployment under these conditions of secrecy, Castro told the interviewer, the Cuban revolution lost some of the moral and political high ground it had achieved among workers and farmers in the Americas and elsewhere in the world. Cuba had an unqualified sovereign right to enter into a mutual defense agreement against foreign aggression with any government it chose, he said. But the secrecy undercut the clarity of its political goals in the eyes of hundreds of millions the world over. Moreover, he said, the whole course pressed on Cuba by the Soviet government turned out, under these conditions, to be sheer adventurism that led the world to the brink of nuclear war. See Fidel Castro, *Misiles en el Caribe* (Havana: Editora Política), available from Pathfinder.

7. The interview was conducted by the Mexican daily *El Sol de México* and reprinted in the Cuban press, including the May 5, 1993, issue of *Granma International.*

8. *New York Review of Books,* March 3, 1994.

9. See "Washington's Fifty-Year Domestic Contra Operation" by Larry Seigle in *New International,* no. 6 (1987).

10. For a more detailed description of the U.S. slaughter in Iraq and its political lessons, see "The Opening Guns of World War III" by Jack Barnes in *New International,* no. 7 (1991).

11. Shortly before Angola's independence from Portuguese colonial rule on November 11, 1975, the country's new government was attacked by invading South African troops. Apartheid's forces were allied with the rightist National Union for the Total Independence of Angola (UNITA), which was funded by Washington. Cuban volunteers responded to the Angolan government's appeal for international aid in repelling the aggression. The South African troops were pushed back, but renewed incursions and armed counterrevolutionary actions by UNITA continued over the next dozen years. In early 1988 Cuban, Angolan, and Namibian forces dealt a decisive military defeat to South Africa's troops, who were driving to capture the town of Cuito Cuanavale in southeastern Angola. That stand, combined with a determined campaign by Cuban and Angolan forces to reinforce the defense of southern Angola, led to an accord signed in December 1988 in which Pretoria agreed to withdraw its troops from Angola and to begin negotiations that culminated in granting independence to Namibia in March 1990.

12. For further reading on the communist approach to the fight for national liberation, and the Stalinists' counterrevolutionary reversal of it, see "Their Trotsky and Ours: Communist Continuity Today" by Jack Barnes and "Communism and the Fight for a Popular Revolutionary Government: 1848 to Today" by Mary-Alice Waters in *New International,* nos. 1 and 3; the theses and report by

V.I. Lenin on the national and colonial question in *Workers of the World and Oppressed Peoples, Unite! Proceedings and Documents of the Second Congress, 1920,* which outline the programmatic foundations of the communist approach; and *The Transitional Program for Socialist Revolution, The Third International after Lenin,* and *Leon Trotsky on China,* by communist leader Leon Trotsky. For the experience in Cuba, see *Dynamics of the Cuban Revolution: A Marxist Appreciation* by Joseph Hansen.

13. The speech can be found in the pamphlet by Fidel Castro entitled *Cuba Will Never Adopt Capitalist Methods* (New York: Pathfinder, 1988).

14. For more on the 1919 revolutions in Hungary and Bavaria and the lessons from their defeats drawn by the Communist International in Lenin's time, see Farrell Dobbs, *Revolutionary Continuity: Birth of the Communist Movement, 1918-1922* (New York: Pathfinder, 1983). For more on the experience of other workers and farmers governments in this century, see in particular Joseph Hansen *The Workers and Farmers Government* and Jack Barnes *The Workers and Farmers Government in the United States,* both published by Pathfinder.

15. Some 150 former FSLN soldiers, calling themselves the Workers and Peasants Revolutionary Front, had seized control of the northern town of Estelí, demanding implementation of government pledges to provide land, credit, and housing to demobilized troops. These actions won little popular support, given their character as an isolated armed adventure that included outright robberies of stores. Army commander Humberto Ortega ordered in troops to reassert control in Estelí, killing up to sixty of the rebels.

16. Chamorro made the announcement with Humberto Ortega sitting alongside her at the armed forces celebration. No retirement date has been set, however.

17. Karl Marx, "The Civil War in France," in Marx and Engels, *Collected Works,* vol. 22 (Moscow: Progress Publishers, 1986), pp. 335, 339.

18. Karl Marx, "Theses on Feuerbach," in Marx and Engels, *Collected Works,* vol. 5 (Moscow: Progress Publishers, 1976), p. 8.

19. *The Second Declaration of Havana* (New York: Pathfinder, 1962), p. 21.

1979: The Revolutionary Character of the Sandinista National Liberation Front

by Jack Barnes

1. At the time this report was given the Socialist Workers Party was a fraternal affiliate of the Fourth International. For three decades differences within the Fourth International over the SWP's proletarian traditions were numerous, but from 1979 on the course and character of the SWP markedly diverged from that of the leadership bodies of the Fourth International. This accelerating divergence centered on different political assessments of the revolutionary victories in Grenada and Nicaragua, and the character of the workers and farmers governments established through those victories; the historical importance and weight of the communist leadership in Cuba and its political trajectory; the importance of defending the gains of the 1979 Iranian revolution from imperialist attack; and the necessity for communist forces the world over to decisively turn toward building parties that are proletarian in composition and leadership as well as program and perspectives. A parallel process occurred with communist organizations in a number of other countries.

At the end of the 1980s the SWP and the Communist Leagues in Australia, Britain, Canada, Iceland, New Zealand, and Sweden each decided to terminate their affiliation, whether fraternal or statutory, to the Fourth International. Through their political work, internationalist collaboration, and place within communist continuity and tradition, these parties had for some time already been communist organizations that no longer considered themselves Trotskyist and were separate from the world Trotskyist movement and its various competing parties and international groupings.

2. The Bolshevik Faction, of which Argentine Trotskyist Nahuel Moreno (1924-1987) was the central public figure, split from the United Secretariat immediately before the World Congress of the Fourth International in November 1979. In the summer of 1979 Moreno's supporters from a number of countries organized the

Simón Bolívar Brigade, an armed contingent that entered Nicaragua in July 1979 after Somoza's fall. Usurping the name and banner of the FSLN, the brigade refused to function under the command of the Sandinistas and carried out provocative actions that set back the revolutionary struggle, especially in the Atlantic Coast city of Bluefields.

The Organizing Committee for the Reconstruction of the Fourth International, whose central figure is Pierre Lambert of the Internationalist Communist Organization of France, was formed in 1972. This international current grew out of forces that refused to participate in a 1963 reunification of the Fourth International, which had been split since the early 1950s. The OCRFI denied that a socialist revolution had occurred in Cuba and took a sectarian stance toward the unfolding class struggle in Nicaragua.

3. The non-Nicaraguan members of the Simón Bolívar Brigade were expelled from the country by the new Sandinista-led government.

4. On November 4, 1979, students occupied the U.S. embassy in Tehran—dubbed the "spy den"—as an expression of popular determination to defend the Iranian revolution, which had successfully ousted the U.S.-backed monarchy of the shah in February of that year. Massive mobilizations took place in support of the embassy occupation in Iranian cities and villages. The students occupied the embassy for more than a year. The action was in response to the U.S. government's invitation to the deposed shah to come to the United States earlier that fall. Many working people and youth in Iran saw the invitation as a major new step toward organizing a counterrevolution. Twenty-six years earlier, when popular mobilizations forced the shah to flee the country, the CIA had organized a coup through the U.S. embassy to return his brutal regime to power.

5. The original junta consisted of Daniel Ortega, Moisés Hassán, and Sergio Ramírez of the FSLN, and capitalist figures Violeta Chamorro and Alfonso Robelo. Chamorro and Robelo resigned in April 1980. The National Directorate of the FSLN replaced them in May 1980 with Arturo Cruz, then president of the Central Bank, and Rafael Córdova Rivas, a liberal lawyer. Chamorro is the widow of Pedro Joaquín Chamorro, the editor of the liberal opposition daily *La Prensa*, who was assassinated by Somoza in January 1978. She was elected president of Nicaragua in February 1990. Robelo is a millionaire businessman who became a leader of a wing of the armed contra

forces based in Costa Rica. He returned to Nicaragua in 1989.

6. See "Nicaragua: How the Workers and Farmers Government Came to Power" on pp. 77-116 of this issue.

7. The workers and farmers government's initial thrust was toward guaranteeing supplies of basic foodstuffs for working people at affordable prices. ENABAS, the National Basic Foods Corporation, was established for this purpose in September 1979. It tried a variety of means in the initial years, including setting price ceilings on basic items, subsidizing prices to keep staples affordable, supplying workplace commissaries, supplying retail store owners with commodities at wholesale prices (the *expendios populares*), and establishing state-owned retail stores (the *tiendas populares*). In 1982 ration cards were also introduced. Initially, ENABAS hoped to control 40 percent of the total market, which the government expected would give it a great deal of leverage in dealing with capitalist speculators and hoarders and thus help stabilize prices. In 1980 ENABAS succeeded in buying only 12 percent of the production in beans and corn. It did manage to supply some 40 percent of most basic foods sold, primarily through importing.

By the mid-1980s, however, the FSLN leadership was retreating from the earlier policies that sought to provide every Nicaraguan with basic commodities at subsidized prices. Government control over exports was also weakened. This retreat was part of the FSLN course of moving away from mobilizing working people to extend workers control over capitalist production and distribution.

8. In an August 30, 1979, speech, Democratic senator Frank Church announced his "discovery" that Soviet combat troops were stationed in Cuba. On October 1 President Carter announced moves that included a mock amphibious assault at the U.S. Naval Station at Guantánamo, Cuba, creation of a Caribbean Joint Task Force based in Key West, Florida, and an increase in spy flights aimed at Cuba. Within the U.S. government there was talk of imposing a complete naval blockade. These actions came in the wake of the revolutionary victories in Grenada and Nicaragua.

U.S. government threats against Cuba had escalated in November 1978 with claims by the Carter administration that MIG-23 fighters received by Cuba from the Soviet Union might be capable of launching nuclear weapons. U.S. spy flights over Cuba were increased, naval maneuvers off the Cuban coast took place, and in August 1979 family reunification visits to Cuba were suspended.

In response to the escalation of imperialist threats and provocations, the Cuban government organized two Marches of the Fighting People: one on April 19, 1980, of one million people in Havana, the other on May 17 of five million in numerous cities throughout Cuba. The intervening May Day rally in Havana mobilized 1.5 million. In September 1980 Cuban president Fidel Castro announced that a Territorial Troop Militia would be formed. Organized in early 1981, the militia comprised 1.5 million Cuban workers, farmers, students, and housewives as of January 1990.

9. On October 15, 1979, a group of Salvadoran army officers ousted dictator Carlos Humberto Romero in a military coup. This move was designed to check the swiftly developing revolutionary upsurge in El Salvador in the wake of the Nicaraguan victory. While most revolutionary forces opposed the new regime, the Salvadoran Communist Party offered its support, as did several other opposition organizations.

10. Joseph Hansen, "The Character of the New Cuban Government" (1960), published in *Dynamics of the Cuban Revolution* (New York: Pathfinder, 1978), p. 68.

11. The FLN, or National Liberation Front, of Algeria helped lead a coalition of diverse forces in the nearly eight-year war of independence from France beginning in 1954. Independence was won in 1962. The FLN itself was very heterogeneous, with a leadership that included both a radical petty-bourgeois component led by Ahmed Ben Bella and a bourgeois component led by Mohammed Khider, Ferhat Abbas, and others. A workers and farmers government led by Ben Bella came to power soon after independence and mobilized the masses of the toilers in their own interests initially. The revolutionary government retreated from this anticapitalist course, however, and was finally overthrown in a coup in June 1965.

The July 26 Movement in Cuba was founded in 1955 by veterans of the 1953 attack on the Moncada garrison in Santiago de Cuba, led by Fidel Castro, young activists from the left wing of the bourgeois Orthodox Party, and others fighting to overthrow the dictatorship of Fulgencio Batista. With the revolutionary victory over Batista on January 1, 1959, the left wing of the July 26 Movement, led by Fidel Castro, Ernesto Che Guevara, and others, and relying on mass mobilizations, moved to implement policies in the interests of the workers and farmers, including the first stage of a radical land reform. In the process the bourgeois forces were ousted from the coalition government, and by the fall of 1959 a workers and farmers government had come to power. As the prosocialist direction and actions of the left wing in the July 26 Movement, the Rebel Army, and the government led by Castro became more and more evident over the next twelve months, various procapitalist forces came into conflict with the workers and farmers regime. These forces were defeated and a workers state came into being by late 1960, as working people were mobilized to expropriate both Cuban and imperialist-owned industrial and commercial enterprises.

For more on the character and trajectory of the Ben Bella and Castro leaderships, see Jack Barnes, *For a Workers and Farmers Government in the United States* (New York: Pathfinder, 1985); Joseph Hansen, *The Workers and Farmers Government* (New York: Pathfinder, 1974); and Joseph Hansen, *Dynamics of the Cuban Revolution* (New York: Pathfinder, 1978).

12. "Dual power" is the term Bolshevik leader V.I. Lenin used to describe the political and military balance of class forces that existed in Russia in the period just after the February 1917 revolution that toppled the regime of the tsar, which was replaced with a bourgeois-dominated Provisional Government. "The highly remarkable feature of our revolution is that it has brought about a *dual power,*" Lenin wrote in early April 1917. "What is this dual power? Alongside the Provisional Government, the government of the *bourgeoisie, another government* has arisen, so far weak and incipient, but undoubtedly a government that actually exists and is growing—the Soviet of Workers and Soldiers Deputies. . . .

"The bourgeoisie stands for the undivided power of the bourgeoisie.

"The class-conscious workers stand for the undivided power of the Soviets of Workers, Agricultural Laborers, Peasants, and Soldiers Deputies—for undivided power made possible not by adventurist acts, but by *clarifying* proletarian minds, by *emancipating* them from the influence of the bourgeoisie.

"The petty bourgeoisie—'Social-Democrats,' Socialist Revolutionaries, etc., etc.,—vacillate and, thereby, *hinder* the clarification and emancipation.

"That is the actual, the *class* alignment of forces that determines our tasks." See "The Dual Power," in Lenin, *Collected Works*, vol. 24, pp. 38-41.

13. In April 1961, 1,500 Cuban-born mercenaries organized by the U.S. government invaded Cuba at the Bay of Pigs. The invaders immediately met a determined response by thousands of militia members and regular troops. After seventy-two hours the last invaders surrendered at Playa Girón (Girón Beach), which is the name Cubans use for the battle. Nicaraguan revolutionaries then living in Cuba participated in the military defense of the island. One, Carlos Ulloa, was killed in action.

14. A selection of writings by Carlos Fonseca will be available in the forthcoming Pathfinder collection *Carlos Fonseca Speaks.*

15. Joseph Hansen, preface to Ernesto Che Guevara, *Che Guevara Speaks* (New York: Pathfinder, 1967), p. 6.

Nicaragua: How the Workers and Farmers Government Came to Power

1. The original junta consisted of FSLN partisans Moisés Hassán and Sergio Ramírez, FSLN leader Daniel Ortega, and capitalist figures Violeta Chamorro and Alfonso Robelo. Chamorro and Robelo resigned in April 1980.

2. See "Statute on the Rights of Nicaraguans," in *The Nicaraguan Revolution* (New York: Pathfinder, 1979), pp. 43-55.

3. Edén Pastora, who led an FSLN commando team in the 1978 capture of Somoza's National Palace, was vice-minister of defense until he left Nicaragua in 1981. The following year he broke with the revolution and formed a counterrevolutionary armed force that was based out of Costa Rica.

4. This figure was based on estimates provided by the revolutionary government at the time. In fact, when accurate statistics were subsequently compiled on the amount of land actually confiscated, the figure was just over 20 percent.

5. For information on ENABAS, see note 7 on p. 303.

6. See note 8 on pp. 303-4.

7. By early 1983 the new government had built some 8,000 new houses and given out 18,000 lots for families to build their own houses. Despite initial steps in 1983 toward a radical housing reform that would have converted tens of thousands of rental homes

into the tenants' property, the leadership retreated from this perspective under the pressures of the contra war, economic crisis, and the consequent deepening class polarization in Nicaragua.

8. Quoted in *The Transitional Program for Socialist Revolution* (New York: Pathfinder, 1977), p. 134. The Transitional Program was one of the founding documents of the Socialist Workers Party. Written by Leon Trotsky, a central leader of the October 1917 Bolshevik-led revolution in Russia, and adopted by the SWP in 1938, it was later adopted as part of the program of the Fourth International, the world communist organization the SWP helped initiate and politically lead.

9. Quoted from the "Theses on Tactics" of the Fourth Congress of the Communist International held in 1922; see Joseph Hansen, *The Workers and Farmers Government* (New York: Pathfinder, 1974), pp. 39-40.

10. A discussion of further lessons to be drawn by revolutionists from the defeat of the workers and farmers government in Algeria can be found in the article, "The Workers and Farmers Government: A Powerful Anticapitalist Weapon for Working People" by Larry Seigle, published on pp. 263-95 in this issue.

11. Augusto César Sandino rejected the betrayal of Nicaragua's national sovereignty the year after the 1926 civil war, in which he had fought as a general. In response to the occupation of Nicaragua by U.S. marines, he led an army of workers and peasants in a six-year guerrilla struggle. The marines were forced out, but Sandino was murdered on February 21, 1934, on the orders of the U.S.-installed head of the National Guard, Anastasio Somoza García.

12. Carlos Fonseca Amador discusses the political origins of the Sandinista National Liberation Front in the article "Nicaragua: Zero Hour" and other writings to be published in the forthcoming Pathfinder collection *Carlos Fonseca Speaks: Building Nicaragua's Sandinista National Liberation Front, 1960-1976.* "Nicaragua: Zero Hour" is also available in *Sandinistas Speak: Speeches, Writings, and Interviews with Leaders of Nicaragua's Revolution* (New York: Pathfinder, 1982).

13. See note 4 on p. 302.

14. *Fidel Castro Speeches: Cuba's Internationalist Foreign Policy 1975-80* (New York: Pathfinder, 1981), p. 268.

15. In the 1970s Cuba was giving massive internationalist material and military support to defend newly independent Angola's sovereignty in the face of a U.S.-supported South African invasion, and to

stop a U.S.-backed invasion of Ethiopia. The Cuban revolution had been giving assistance to liberation movements in Africa since the early 1960s, aiding struggles in Mozambique, Angola, Guinea-Bissau, South Africa, Algeria, the Congo, Cameroon, Sierra Leone, and Guinea.

16. At the massive July 26 celebration in Holguín, Cuba, one week after the victory of the insurrection over Somoza, Cuban president Fidel Castro challenged the governments of the entire world to a contest to see who could provide the most aid to revolutionary Nicaragua to begin rebuilding from the devastation inherited from imperialist domination. His speech, on the twenty-sixth anniversary of the opening of the Cuban revolution with the attack on the Moncada garrison on July 26, 1953, was devoted entirely to the revolution in Nicaragua. The rally had as its guests of honor twenty-six young Sandinista commanders who had led various fronts in the offensive that toppled Somoza. The text of the speech is found in Fidel Castro, "The Triumph of Nicaraguan Independence," *Fidel Castro Speeches: Cuba's Internationalist Foreign Policy, 1975-80* (New York: Pathfinder, 1981), pp. 293-309.

17. The Frente Obrero (Workers Front) was the main target of the campaign against ultraleftism. It was the trade union arm of the MAP (People's Action Movement), a centrist group of Maoist origin that earlier had split from the FSLN. The MAP had an armed wing during the insurrection called the Milicias Populares Antisomocistas (MILPAS—Anti-Somoza People's Militias).

18. For more on the SWP's relationship to the Fourth International, see note 1 on p. 301.

19. For further on the origins and evolution of the Bolshevik Faction, see note 2 on pp. 301-2.

The Socialist Workers Organization (OST) was a sectarian Trotskyist grouping in Costa Rica. It held that the FSLN was the main obstacle to the advance of the workers and farmers of Nicaragua. Its central leader was Fausto Amador, a one-time member of the FSLN who had broken with it in 1969. The Revolutionary Socialist Group (GRS) was a small band of his followers in Nicaragua that existed for only a brief period of time. Amador remained an opponent of the Sandinistas after they led the successful overthrow of Somoza, did not return to Nicaragua to participate in the revolution, and moved steadily to the bourgeois right, openly aligning himself politically with armed counterrevolutionary forces. In

1987 Amador participated in a Central America Symposium with open counterrevolutionaries held in Washington, D.C.

The Revolutionary Marxist League (LMR) was another sectarian Trotskyist group in Nicaragua. Formed in the 1970s, it ceased to exist by the mid-1980s.

20. In the October 1962 "Cuban missile crisis," as it was called in the U.S. media, President John F. Kennedy demanded removal of Soviet nuclear missiles installed in Cuba following the signing of a mutual defense agreement between the Soviet and Cuban governments. Washington ordered a total naval blockade of Cuba, stepped up its prior course toward an invasion of the island, and placed U.S. armed forces on nuclear alert.

Thirty years later, in an October 1992 NBC television interview, Castro said that if Cuban revolutionists had known in 1962 what they know today about the political orientation of the Soviet leadership, they would not have accepted the deployment of the missiles. He said the Cuban government had opposed Moscow's insistence that the military agreement be kept secret. Cuban leaders proposed that any missile deployment be made public, with the explanation that the U.S. government was preparing to invade Cuba. When it became clear that Soviet officials would not agree to a public pact, Castro said, Cuban leaders accepted the missiles in the mistaken belief that this was in the best interests of the world struggle for socialism.

The rapid armed mobilization of working people in Cuba to defend their revolution convinced Washington that U.S. forces would take very heavy casualties in an invasion, risking destabilizing political consequences at home and throughout Latin America. The Kennedy administration sought an accommodation with Moscow; on October 28, with no consultation with the Cuban government, Soviet premier Nikita Khrushchev ordered the withdrawal of the missiles.

"Had we known that Khrushchev was preparing to withdraw the missiles, we would not have been opposed," Castro told a conference of U.S., Russian, and Cuban academics and political figures held in Havana in January 1992. "There had to be a solution. But U.S. verbal guarantees [that Washington would not invade Cuba] were not enough. Nikita should have traded the missiles for guarantees satisfactory to Cuba."

The Coming Showdown in the Caribbean

1. Since the early years of the revolution, the U.S. government has used emigration as a weapon against Cuba. The Cuban government has always maintained that anyone wishing to leave was free to do so; Washington on the other hand has imposed severe restrictions, seeking to keep political pressure on Cuba.

On April 1, 1980, six Cubans crashed a bus through the gates of the Peruvian embassy in Havana, killing a Cuban guard. When the Peruvian government refused to hand over the killers, Cuba responded by removing its guards around the embassy. Within days ten thousand Cubans wanting to emigrate had crammed into the compound.

In the face of increasingly shrill U.S. propaganda, Cuba turned the tables on Washington by allowing privately owned U.S. ships to pick up anyone wishing to leave at the port of Mariel. Despite a warning against ship owners, Washington was unable to stop the flotilla. By late September, when the sealift was ended, some 125,000 Cubans had reached the United States.

The contrast between Cuba's willingness to open its doors and U.S. reluctance to accept those it had encouraged to leave was a defeat for Washington and a victory for the revolution, as was the mobilization of millions of Cuban working people in support of the revolution during these events.

2. Castro's May 1, 1980, speech to a rally of 1.5 million in Havana's Plaza of the Revolution, is contained in *Fidel Castro Speeches: Cuba's Internationalist Foreign Policy 1975-80* (New York: Pathfinder, 1981), pp. 271-90.

3. On May 17, 1980, an all-white jury in Tampa, Florida, acquitted four Miami police officers who had been charged in the beating death five months earlier of Arthur McDuffie, an insurance executive who was Black. The verdict sparked a rebellion in Miami's Black community that was brutally suppressed by thousands of police and National Guard troops. In the course of three days, 16 were killed, 300 wounded, and over 1,200 arrested.

4. In the wake of the victories of the Nicaraguan and Grenada

revolutions, Washington waged a concerted campaign to topple the government of Jamaican prime minister Michael Manley in 1980. The U.S. rulers were concerned about the Manley government's relations with Cuba, Nicaragua, and Grenada and its refusal to simply accept all International Monetary Fund demands to impose deep-going austerity measures. Washington's efforts included an attempt to squeeze the country economically, a campaign of media lies, and the formation of gangs of armed thugs and rightist hit squads, resulting in the death of nearly 900 persons.

As a result of these efforts, and the failure of the Manley regime to provide a perspective of struggle for Jamaica's working people, Manley was defeated in the November 1980 elections and replaced by the openly proimperialist Edward Seaga.

The Historic Program of the FSLN
by Carlos Fonseca

1. *Zambo* is a Latin American term referring to persons of mixed Black and Indian ancestry, or sometimes simply to any Latin American who is Black. In Nicaragua the word largely dropped out of use in the 1980s with the revolution's advances in overcoming centuries of discrimination against Blacks and Indians in that country's Atlantic Coast region.

War and Revolution in Central America and the Caribbean: The Center of World Politics

1. In 1978 the Socialist Workers Party responded to opportunities that had opened up for communists to carry out centralized political work and build the party in the industrial working class and industrial unions. Due to the combined effects of the McCarthyite witch-hunt of the early 1950s and a quarter century of relative capitalist economic expansion following World War II, the party had to retreat temporarily from organizing its cadres to carry

out the party's program in a centralized way in the industrial unions. The changes wrought by the 1974-75 worldwide capitalist recession, the first since the Great Depression of the 1930s, and the effects on the attitudes of workers of the conquests of the civil rights battles, anti–Vietnam War movement, and women's rights fights signaled new openings to bring the social composition and organized activity of the party into harmony with its proletarian program and foundations.

At the time this report was given the SWP had organized groups, or fractions, of party members in nine industrial unions.

For a discussion of the place of political work in the trade unions in building a communist party, see Jack Barnes, *The Changing Face of U.S. Politics: Working-Class Politics and the Trade Unions* (New York: Pathfinder, 1994).

2. In presidential elections held November 4, 1984, nearly 80 percent of the eligible voters participated, giving the FSLN a 67 percent majority. Daniel Ortega and Sergio Ramírez were elected president and vice president. While the main bourgeois opposition forces declined to participate in the elections, three capitalist parties were listed on the ballot, receiving 29 percent of the vote.

3. *Escoria,* meaning "scum" in Spanish, was a popularly used expression in Cuba in the early 1980s for Cubans who turned their backs on the revolution, enticed by hopes for personal enrichment in the imperialist United States.

4. On February 4, 1962, nearly a million Cubans massed in Havana to protest the U.S.-inspired decision to exclude Cuba from the Organization of American States. Cuba's reply, presented by Fidel Castro, was a manifesto known as the Second Declaration of Havana. See *The Second Declaration of Havana* (New York: Pathfinder, 1962), p. 19.

5. Extensive material by Lenin on the New Economic Policy is found in volumes 32 and 33 of his *Collected Works.* For a contribution to the discussion surrounding the place of the NEP in communist strategy today, see Jack Barnes, "For a Workers and Farmers Government in the United States" (New York: Pathfinder, 1985); Jack Barnes, "The Fight for a Workers and Farmers Government in the United States," in *New International,* no. 4 (spring 1985); and Steve Clark and Jack Barnes, "The Politics of Economics: Che Guevara and Marxist Continuity," in *New International,* no. 8 (1991).

6. The show trial of Bernard Coard and his backers, marked by

blatant irregularities, began in April 1986. Fourteen defendants, including Coard, were sentenced to death. In August 1991 their sentences were commuted to life imprisonment by Grenadian prime minister Nicholas Brathwaite.

For a fuller assessment of the achievements and overthrow of the Grenada revolution, see "The Second Assassination of Maurice Bishop" by Steve Clark in *New International,* no. 6 (1987).

7. The entire interview was printed in the Cuban magazine *Bohemia;* major excerpts are published in English in in *War and Crisis in the Americas: Fidel Castro Speeches, 1984-85* (New York: Pathfinder, 1985), pp. 1-19.

The 1987 Peace Accords:
A New Situation in Nicaragua

1. Signed by the presidents of Nicaragua, Honduras, Costa Rica, El Salvador, and Guatemala on August 7, 1987, in Guatemala City, the accords stipulated that by November 7, 1987, each of the five governments establish a cease-fire with "irregular" military forces fighting in their country, extend full amnesty to those who had taken up arms, and lift all restrictions on civil liberties entailed in the state of emergency instituted in 1982 in response to the contra war. The Nicaraguan government moved immediately to implement the accords.

2. In December 1984 the FSLN reversed its initial opposition to autonomy for the peoples of the Atlantic Coast and began to champion this demand, leading to adoption of the Autonomy Law in 1987. For a description of this process see "Defend Revolutionary Nicaragua: The Eroding Foundations of the Workers and Farmers Government" on pp. 185-224 of this issue.

3. War communism was the course adopted by the young Soviet republic to ensure its survival during the capitalist- and landlord-instigated civil war and imperialist intervention of 1918-20. The axis of this policy was the compulsory requisitioning of peasants' grain to supply the Red Army and the working class in the cities. The war-caused slaughter of workers and the massive physical destruction resulted in a precipitous decline of industrial produc-

314   Notes for pages 178-180

tion, which meant that few manufactured consumer goods could be supplied to the peasants in exchange for their crops and livestock.

As the civil war ended, many peasants who had accepted requisitioning as a necessary evil to block the return of the landlords became increasingly hostile to the policy, in some cases going into open revolt. In order to reknit the worker-peasant alliance, on which the Soviet republic was based, the Communist Party leadership abandoned war communism in 1921 and instituted the New Economic Policy (NEP), which opened up private trade in the countryside, permitting peasants to sell their produce on the market after supplying a set amount to the government to meet basic food needs.

4. In late 1986 a series of disclosures came out about secret U.S. funding of the Nicaraguan contra forces funneled through illegal arms sales to Iran, allegedly in exchange for U.S. hostages in Lebanon. The resulting scandal became known variously as Iran-Contra, Contragate, and other terms. For a discussion of the significance of these revelations, see "In This Issue" at the front of the magazine.

5. On September 21, 1987, a U.S. military helicopter in the Persian Gulf attacked an Iranian ship without warning, killing five. The attack was conducted by U.S. forces deployed to support the Iraqi regime in its war against Iran that began in 1980. The Iran-Iraq war ended in 1988.

On September 17, 1987, FBI agents kidnapped a Lebanese national in the Mediterranean Sea. The prisoner, abducted illegally in international waters, was brought to the United States on charges of air hijacking.

6. In July 1987 federal judge Robert Bork was nominated by President Ronald Reagan to fill a vacancy on the U.S. Supreme Court. Because of his right-wing views on abortion rights and other democratic rights, affirmative action, and other issues, openly stated in congressional hearings, the nomination sparked widespread public opposition. Bork's nomination went down to defeat in October when it was rejected by the Senate Judiciary Committee.

Defend Revolutionary Nicaragua: The Eroding Foundations of the Workers and Farmers Government

1. Further information on the centrality of the worker-peasant alliance in the fight to establish a workers and farmers government can be found in Jack Barnes, *For a Workers and Farmers Government in the United States* (New York: Pathfinder, 1985); Barnes, "The Fight for a Workers and Farmers Government in the United States," in *New International*, no. 4 (spring 1985); Mary-Alice Waters, "Communism and the Fight for a Popular Revolutionary Government: 1848 to Today," in *New International*, no. 3 (spring-summer 1984); and Barnes, "Their Trotsky and Ours: Communist Continuity Today," in *New International*, no. 1 (fall 1983).

2. Ahmed Ben Bella, a central leader of the left wing of the National Liberation Front (FLN) of Algeria, was deposed in a coup led by then–minister of defense and vice president Houari Boumédienne on June 19, 1965, and imprisoned until 1980.

Maurice Bishop, the founder and central leader of the New Jewel Movement of Grenada, and prime minister in the People's Revolutionary Government, was ousted and murdered in October 1983 by forces loyal to a Stalinist faction led by Bernard Coard. A U.S. military invasion followed on October 25.

3. A discussion of further lessons to be drawn by revolutionists from the defeat of the workers and farmers government in Algeria can be found in the article, "The Workers and Farmers Government: A Powerful Anticapitalist Weapon for Working People" by Larry Seigle, on pp. 263-95 of this issue.

4. The Historic Program, drafted by FSLN founder Carlos Fonseca in 1969, can be found on pp. 129-40 of this issue.

5. For discussion of the experience of the working-class movement in this century in the transition from a workers and farmers government to the consolidation of a workers state, see Jack Barnes, *For a Workers and Farmers Government in the United States* (New York: Pathfinder, 1985).

6. Fidel Castro reaffirmed the commitment of Cuban communists to this view in his February 1994 closing speech to the Fourth Latin American and Caribbean Conference for Solidarity, Sovereignty, Self-Determination, and the Life of Our Peoples, held in Havana. "Capitalism," he said, "a system that is currently at the zenith of its power and of its political, economic, and military might, and which can offer humanity nothing. . . . Capitalism is a system of injustice, of unequal distribution, of exploitation of man by man. . . ."

7. This resolution can be found in its entirety on pp. 77-116 of this issue.

8. See note 8 on pp. 303-4.

9. See English-language excerpts of the 1986 interview by Tomás Borge with Rodolfo Matarollo entitled "Tomás Borge on the Origins of Marxism in Nicaragua," in the *Militant,* November 14, 1986.

10. For more on the rents and mortgages system see Doug Jenness, "The Crisis Facing Working Farmers," in *New International,* no. 4 (spring 1985), especially pp. 110-13 and 123-27.

11. See Larry Seigle, "Nicaragua: Sugar Harvest Under Way at Recently Nationalized Mill," in the *Militant,* December 23, 1988. For background to the situation at the San Antonio Sugar Mill, see Harvey McArthur and Larry Seigle, "Sandinista Union Launches Campaign to Win Over Workers at Big Sugar Mill," in the *Militant,* August 26, 1988.

12. See, for example, the debate and discussion on the national and colonial questions at the Second Congress of the Communist International, in sessions 4 and 5 and appendix 2 of *Workers of the World and Oppressed Peoples, Unite! Proceedings and Documents of the Second Congress, 1920* (New York: Pathfinder, 1991); and at the Comintern-sponsored congress of nationally oppressed peoples a few months later, recorded in *To See the Dawn: Baku 1920—First Congress of the Peoples of the East* (New York: Pathfinder, 1993).

13. See note 1 on page 313.

14. In January 1992 an accord was signed between the Farabundo Martí National Liberation Front (FMLN) and the Salvadoran government. It brought to an end the country's eleven-year civil war in which over 75,000 had died—the vast majority at the hands of the Salvadoran government and its death squads. The agreement registered the inability of the Salvadoran government and Washington to break the resistance of the country's working

people, despite a decade of severe repression. At the same time, the FMLN had not been able to lay the foundations for a victorious insurrection against the landlord-capitalist regime.

Stipulated in the 1990 agreement was the dismantling of the FMLN's military apparatus and the reintegration of FMLN members into legal political activity. At the same time the government agreed to reduce the size of its armed forces by more than half; to remove officers guilty of human rights violations; and to dissolve the Treasury Police, National Guard, and National Police, creating a new police force open to FMLN members.

By 1990 the FMLN leadership had retreated from its original stated objective of fighting to take power out of the hands of El Salvador's exploiting classes and use it to advance the interests of the workers and peasants. Joaquín Villalobos, a central FMLN commander, explained this evolution. "In El Salvador there is a need to cut off the extremes," he stated in 1991. "In our case that means the thinking of dogmatic Stalinism and traditional, classic Communism. At the other extreme is the orthodox right wing, which in El Salvador is something from the Stone Age." Villalobos said he would like to model El Salvador on Germany, Japan, or Costa Rica.

In 1993 revelations came out implicating the U.S. government in the worst massacres of Salvadoran workers and peasants that took place in the 1980s. At the same time there has been a renewal of death squad assassinations of former FMLN figures. In first-round elections held in March 1994, the right-wing Arena party won close to 50 percent of the vote, with the candidates supported by the FMLN running second with over a quarter of the votes. The FMLN-backed candidates pointed to numerous instances of vote fraud, a charge that some major big-business dailies in the United States have largely corroborated. Second-round elections were scheduled for April 1994.

15. U.S. troops invaded Grenada October 25-26, 1983. The invasion by a force that eventually numbered more than seven thousand began six days after the murder of Prime Minister Maurice Bishop on October 19.

In April 1965 more than twenty thousand U.S. troops invaded the Dominican Republic to crush a popular rebellion. Thousands of Dominicans were killed. The country was occupied and Joaquín Balaguer became president through fraudulent elections in June 1966. The last U.S. troops left in September 1966.

16. Michael Manley became prime minister of Jamaica with the victory of the People's National Party in February 1989 parliamentary elections. Manley, seeking close relations with the U.S. government, pledged to honor payments on the country's massive foreign debt and instituted severe austerity measures. Manley's PNP had governed the country from 1972 to 1980, instituting some social reforms and establishing relations with Cuba. It was driven from power by a bloody campaign of hooliganism instigated by Washington.

Peronist party leader Carlos Saúl Menem took office in July 1989 and reinstituted interest payments on Argentina's foreign debt, which had been suspended in April 1988 by the previous government. Menem has carried out sweeping austerity measures, reprivatizing huge sections of industry and public services, increasing taxes, laying off large numbers of workers, and devaluing the Argentine austral.

17. The Anti-Imperialist Organizations of the Caribbean and Central America, founded in Havana in 1984, comprised groups from more than twenty English-, Spanish-, French-, Dutch-, and Creole-speaking countries. For the record of its meetings and political accomplishments, see Don Rojas ed., *One People, One Destiny: The Caribbean and Central America Today* (New York: Pathfinder, 1988).

18. Interview with Tomás Borge by Carlos F. Chamorro in *Barricada,* March 7, 1989. English-language excerpts can be found in *Barricada International,* March 25, 1989.

19. For more on the effects of the market in reproducing capitalist social relations in a society on the road from capitalism to socialism, see *New International,* no. 8 (1991), "Che Guevara, Cuba, and the Road to Socialism." Readers can also refer to *Che Guevara and the Cuban Revolution: Writings and Speeches of Ernesto Che Guevara* (New York: Pathfinder, 1987); along with Carlos Tablada, *Che Guevara: Economics and Politics in the Transition to Socialism* (New York: Pathfinder, 1990). For an appraisal of these matters in the 1930s, following the consolidation of a privileged bureaucratic caste in the Soviet Union under Stalin, see Leon Trotsky, *The Revolution Betrayed* (New York: Pathfinder, 1972).

20. See note 3 on pp. 313-14.

21. The rectification process was initiated by the Communist Party of Cuba in 1986 to reverse the mounting negative consequences of the economic planning and management course the Cuban leadership had adopted in the early 1970s modeled on that

of the Soviet Stalinist regime. By the early 1980s this course had resulted in accelerating political demobilization and demoralization of working people in Cuba. In face of this growing political disorientation, Cuban communists began to reach back toward the course that had been argued for by Ernesto Che Guevara during the early 1960s and that had begun to be implemented in limited ways in those years.

By the close of the 1980s, however, the Cuban revolution confronted big political pressures from the defeats of revolutionary workers and farmers governments in Nicaragua and Grenada and their impact in pushing back revolutionary struggles elsewhere in Central America and the Caribbean. At the beginning of the 1990s, Cuba was also jolted by the collapse of its aid and beneficial terms of trade with the countries of Eastern Europe and the Soviet Union, from which it obtained some 85 percent of its imports. The ensuing shortages and economic dislocation undercut the momentum of rectification by bringing to an end many of the measures at its heart, such as the volunteer construction minibrigades and contingents.

In face of these conditions, the Cuban leadership has been forced to retreat from aspects of rectification, while fighting under the slogan "Socialism or death!" to maintain a revolutionary way forward for Cuban working people. For further information, see Mary-Alice Waters, *Che Guevara and the Fight for Socialism Today: Cuba Confronts the World Crisis of the '90s* (New York: Pathfinder, 1992); "Cuba's Rectification Process: Two Speeches by Fidel Castro," including the introduction "Cuba: A Historic Moment," by Mary-Alice Waters, in *New International*, no. 6 (1987); Fidel Castro, *In Defense of Socialism: Four Speeches on the Thirtieth Anniversary of the Cuban Revolution* (New York: Pathfinder, 1989); and *New International*, no. 8 (1991), entitled "Che Guevara, Cuba, and the Road to Socialism."

22. During the U.S.-sponsored contra war against Nicaragua, these Stalinist organizations refused to rally their forces to defense of the revolution and Nicaragua's national sovereignty. While aligning themselves ever more openly with bourgeois opponents of the revolution, these parties claimed demagogically that the workers and farmers government was in fact a bourgeois or petty-bourgeois government that should be overturned by the working class.

The Nicaraguan Socialist Party (PSN), founded in the 1940s, was the traditional Stalinist party in Nicaragua. Many revolutionary-minded youth passed through the PSN in the 1950s. In the 1960s and 1970s, they rejected it to join the FSLN. The PSN, seeking to undermine the workers and farmers government that replaced Somoza, took advantage of its control of the construction workers union SCAAS to carry out provocative job actions aimed at discrediting the government. In the late 1980s, in response to the growing crisis of Stalinist regimes in the Soviet Union and Eastern Europe, the PSN declared itself social democratic. It joined the Washington-orchestrated National Opposition Union (UNO) electoral coalition in 1990. President Violeta Chamorro appointed PSN leaders to several high posts in the land reform and education ministries upon taking office.

The Communist Party of Nicaragua (PCN) arose from a 1960s split in the PSN. Following the 1979 triumph the PCN increasingly found common cause with bourgeois opponents of the FSLN and revolutionary government. By the time of Nicaragua's 1990 presidential elections, the PCN had joined UNO. It functions in a bloc with the most right-wing elements in UNO such as Vice President Virgilio Godoy.

The Marxist-Leninist Party, better known as the People's Action Movement–Marxist-Leninist (MAP-ML), originated from a 1971-72 split in the FSLN. It held Maoist positions for a period and later concluded that both China and the Soviet Union were state-capitalist societies. Unlike the PSN and PCN, the MAP did not join the UNO coalition in the 1990 elections. It ran its own slate.

23. Washington finally decided that only through direct military intervention in Panama could its aims be accomplished. On December 20, 1989, Guillermo Endara was declared president at Fort Clayton in the canal zone, and shortly after, U.S. troops began a massive assault on Panamanian military bases and working-class neighborhoods. U.S. forces quickly reached 26,000, including the 12,000 stationed there prior to December 20. Having installed the client regime, they cracked down on popular organizations and on the political space for struggles for national sovereignty and social justice. In the process, Washington undermined the Panama Canal treaties, ensured the continued use of thirteen U.S. military bases in the country, and strengthened U.S. domination in the region. Thousands of Panamanian civilians were killed, wounded, or left homeless as a result of the U.S. bombing raids and shelling in the capital city. See Cindy Jaquith, Don Rojas, Nils Castro, and Fidel

Castro, *Panama: The Truth about the U.S. Invasion* (New York: Pathfinder, 1990).

24. The *Militant* and *Perspectiva Mundial* established a reporting bureau in Managua shortly after the July 19, 1979, victory. Following ten and a half years in continuous operation, the bureau was closed by the *Militant* in December 1990.

A Historic Opportunity Is Being Lost
by Larry Seigle

1. See *Thomas Sankara Speaks: The Burkina Faso Revolution: 1983-87* (New York: Pathfinder, 1988), especially pages 145-48 and 198-200.

2. See the resolution "Defend Revolutionary Nicaragua: The Eroding Foundations of the Workers and Farmers Government" on pp. 185-224 of this issue.

3. See "Nicaragua: How the Workers and Farmers Government Came to Power" on pp. 77-116 of this issue.

4. See "Atlantic Coast Residents Discuss How to Control Food Prices," in the *Militant,* May 12, 1989.

5. Fidel Castro, December 5, 1988, "As Long as the Empire Exists We Will Never Lower Our Guard," in *In Defense of Socialism: Four Speeches on the Thirtieth Anniversary of the Cuban Revolution* (New York: Pathfinder, 1989), p. 30.

6. Translated from the Spanish. See Tomás Borge, *Carlos, el amanecer ya no es una tentación* (Havana: Casa de las Américas, 1980), p. 27. An English-language translation can be found in the July 11, 1980, *Militant,* and in Borge, *Carlos, the Dawn Is No Longer Beyond Our Reach* (Vancouver: New Star Books, 1984).

7. Carlos Fonseca, "Nicaragua: Zero Hour," in *Sandinistas Speak* (New York: Pathfinder, 1982), p. 30. It will also be available in the forthcoming Pathfinder collection *Carlos Fonseca Speaks.*

8. Translated from an interview with Tomás Borge by Carlos F. Chamorro, entitled "Concertación es discutir la desconfianza histórica," in *Barricada,* March 7, 1989. English-language excerpts can be found in "Overcoming Years of Distrust: The Challenge of Concertation," in *Barricada International,* March 25, 1989.

9. See J.V. Stalin, "The Law of Value under Socialism," in *Economic Problems of Socialism in the U.S.S.R.* (Peking: Foreign Languages Press, 1972), pp. 18-24.

10. Ernesto Che Guevara, "Socialism and Man in Cuba," in *Che Guevara and the Cuban Revolution: Writings and Speeches of Ernesto Che Guevara* (New York: Pathfinder, 1987), p. 250. It can also be obtained in pamphlet form in Fidel Castro and Ernesto Che Guevara, *Socialism and Man in Cuba* (New York: Pathfinder, 1989).

11. See note 21 on pp. 318-19.

12. A meeting of the presidents of Nicaragua, Honduras, El Salvador, Costa Rica, and Guatemala August 4-7, 1989, in Tela, Honduras, decided to implement a February 1989 plan to demobilize the contras by December 1989.

13. This December 1961 speech is reprinted in the 1992 edition of *Selected Speeches of Fidel Castro* (New York: Pathfinder, 1992). Given on December 2, 1961, it was part of the broad political discussion to unify all Cuban revolutionaries in a single, communist party. This process culminated in the founding of the Communist Party of Cuba in October 1965.

The Workers and Farmers Government: A Powerful Anticapitalist Weapon for Working People

by Larry Seigle

1. See "Defend Revolutionary Nicaragua: The Eroding Foundations of the Workers and Farmers Government" on pp. 185-224 of this issue.

2. The Young Socialist Alliance—an independent youth organization in political solidarity with the Socialist Workers Party—voted in April 1992 to dissolve as a separate organization as the best way at that time to reach out to and involve in political activity other young people who were being attracted to the socialist presidential campaign of SWP candidates James Warren and Estelle DeBates. Over the next year, a number of former YSA members who had not previously been members of the SWP joined the party, as did

other young people who were collaborating as part of the socialist movement in the election campaign and in various social protest actions in defense of the Cuban revolution, against cop brutality, in support of abortion rights, and in solidarity with striking workers. By early 1994 young members of the SWP were working with other youth in independent young socialists groups that had been formed in New York, Minneapolis–St. Paul, and several other cities; these groups have formed an alliance of young socialists groups to coordinate their efforts on a national scale.

3. Joseph Hansen, "The Algerian Revolution and the Character of the Ben Bella Regime," in *The Workers and Farmers Government* (New York: Pathfinder, 1974), p. 18.

4. Printed on pp. 175-81 of this issue.

5. For a detailed account of the counterrevolutionary coup that overthrew the Bishop-led workers and farmers government in Grenada, see Steve Clark, "The Second Assassination of Maurice Bishop," in *New International*, no. 6 (1987).

6. The "qualitative turning point" refers to the response of the increasingly Stalinized Communist International (Comintern) and German Communist Party to the rise and triumph of fascism in Germany. The coming to power of Adolf Hitler and the Nazi party in 1933 was made possible in large part by the policies of the Comintern leadership, which were applied by the Communist Party of Germany. From 1929 to 1933, these policies were marked by efforts to block unity in action against the rising fascist danger between the millions of workers who supported the Communist Party and those millions who backed the Social Democratic Party, which the Stalin-led Comintern characterized as "social fascists."

This defeat in Germany was the worst suffered by the working class in the twentieth century. With it came the crushing of bourgeois-democratic institutions and the rights to organize trade union and political activity that the workers movement had fought to establish and defend in Germany for nearly a century; the violent destruction of the unions and the mass Socialist and Communist parties in Germany; and the subsequent interimperialist slaughter of World War II and genocidal concentration camps that exterminated millions of Jews, Gypsies, and others. The fact that in the days and months that followed the Nazis' triumph in 1933, the Comintern sought to cover up its responsibility for the catastrophe—and that no party affiliated to the Comintern protested the

324 Notes for pages 280-290

policy, or even asked for it to be reviewed and discussed—signaled that the ten-year effort of communists fighting to reform the Communist parties and Comintern now had to be replaced by the effort to forge new parties and a new International.

For more on these events, see Leon Trotsky, *The Struggle against Fascism in Germany* (New York: Pathfinder, 1971).

7. See "The Historic Program of the FSLN" on pp. 129-40 of this issue.

8. Reprinted in Jack Barnes, *For a Workers and Farmers Government in the United States* (New York: Pathfinder, 1985), p. 34.

9. This resolution can be found in its entirety on pp. 77-116 of this issue.

10. See note 3 on pp. 313-14.

11. *Maurice Bishop Speaks* (New York: Pathfinder, 1983), p. 112.

New International
A MAGAZINE OF MARXIST POLITICS AND THEORY

No. 4

The Fight for a Workers and Farmers Government in the United States

BY JACK BARNES

The shared exploitation of workers and working farmers by banking, industrial, and commercial capital lays the basis for their alliance in a revolutionary fight for a government of the producers. Also includes "The Crisis Facing Working Farmers" by Doug Jenness and "Land Reform and Farm Cooperatives in Cuba." $9.00

No. 3

Communism and the Fight for a Popular Revolutionary Government: 1848 to Today

BY MARY-ALICE WATERS

Traces the continuity in the fight by the working-class movement over 150 years to wrest political power from the small minority of wealthy property owners, whose class rule, Waters says, is inseparably linked to the "misery, hunger, and disease of the great majority of humanity." Also includes " 'A Nose for Power': Preparing the Nicaraguan Revolution" by Tomás Borge. $8.00